"And I, in My Turn, Will Pass It On"

Knowledge Transmission among the Kayapó

SIL International
Publications in Language Use and Education

Publication 2

Publications in Language Use and Education is a serial publication of SIL International. The series began as a venue for works covering a broad range of topics in sociolinguistics and has been expanded to include topics in education, including mother-tongue literacy, multilingual education, and nonformal education. While most volumes are authored by members of SIL, suitable works by others will also form part of the series.

Series Editors

Gloria E. Kindell
Graduate Institute
of Applied Linguistics

Stephen L. Walter
Graduate Institute
of Applied Linguistics

Volume Editors

Mary Ruth Wise
Rhonda Hartell Jones

Production Staff

Bonnie Brown, Managing Editor
Karoline Fisher, Compositor
Kirby O'Brien and Hazel Shorey, Graphic Artists
Bàti Kayapó, Cover Artist

"And I, in My Turn, Will Pass It On"

Knowledge Transmission among the Kayapó

Isabel I. Murphy

SIL International
Dallas, Texas

© 2004 by SIL International
Library of Congress Catalog No: 2004-100209
ISBN: 1-55671-155-7
ISSN: 1545-0074

Printed in the United States of America

All rights reserve

All rights reserved. No part of this publication may be reproduced, stored in a retrieval system, or transmitted in any form or by any means—electronic, mechanical, photocopy, recording, or otherwise—without the express permission of the SIL International. However, short passages, generally understood to be within the limits of fair use, may be quoted without written permission.

Copies of this and other publications of SIL International may be obtained from

International Academic Bookstore
SIL International
7500 W. Camp Wisdom Road
Dallas, TX 75236-5699

Voice: 972-708-7404
Fax: 972-708-7363
E-mail: academic_books@sil.org
Internet: http://www.ethnologue.com

Dedication

In memoriam, and with loving appreciation to my fathers *(ibãm):* Roy and Raymond Murphy and Eudaldo Lima; and my grandfather *(ba ingêt)* Thomas Murphy, whose memories inspire my every endeavor.

Contents

List of Tables xi

List of Figures xi

Preface xiii

1 Introduction 1
   The people and their environment 2
   Underlying theoretical issues 5
      Learner as object or learner as subject 6
      Influence of spatial categories upon knowledge transmission . 7
      Ritual as education 9
   Research procedures 13
      Data gathering and analysis 15
      Research questions 16

2 Spatial Categories and Knowledge Transmission 21
   Background and setting 22
   Time and gender as spatial markers 27
   Spatial map as social map 28
      Village 31
      House 33
      Backyard 36
      Rough clearing 36
      Garden 37
      Rainforest 38
   Summary 40

3 Kayapó Ways of Knowing 43
Categories of Kayapó knowledge 44
   What everybody knows 44
   Gifted artisans 45
   "Those who know something" 45
How the Kayapó learn 47
Factors affecting knowledge transmission 49
   Gender and the distribution of knowledge 50
   The status of knowledge 53
   Official and unofficial knowledge 55
   Age-grades 57
Summary 62

4 Living and Learning: The Everyday Setting 63
Everyday activities 64
Domestic organization 65
   Nuclear family 66
   Domestic group 69
   Interhouseholds 70
Everyday learning 72
   In the nuclear family 72
   In the domestic group 81
   Between households 88
Summary 99

5 Celebrated Knowledge: The Ritual Setting 103
Kayapó ceremonial life 105
   Ritualized activity 109
   Kôkô name-giving ceremony 110
Ceremony as performed knowledge 117
   Learning within ceremony 118
   Learning related to ceremony 127
Ceremony as schooling 130
The sociocultural context of ceremonial schooling 134
Summary 141

6 Onward and Upward: Education and Identity Building . . . 145
A foot in both camps 146
Bridges and backups 151
   The grandparent set 152
   Substitute parents 158
   Ceremonial partners 159
   Education and transformation 160

Accumulating knowledge: The strategies of learning 162
The educational value of trekking expeditions 167
Summary 169

7 **Changes and Chances: Education Outside of the System** . . 171
The Life Chance model 172
Life Chances and the Kayapó 173
   New options. 173
   New leaders and new networks 175
   New knowledge 177
Channels of outside knowledge in Kubẽkàkre 178
Traditional versus new attitudes to knowledge 180
Summary 183

8 **The Research Questions and Conclusions** 185
Summary 186
   Spatial organization and knowledge transmissions events . . 186
   Categorization, conceptualization, and distribution
     of knowledge 186
   The function of social relationships in transmitting
     general, everyday knowledge 187
   The pedagogical value of ceremonial activity 188
   The function of social relationships in transmitting
     traditional knowledge 188
   The effect of new knowledge on traditional patterns
     of knowledge transmission 189
Importance of this Study 189
   The Kayapó study 189
Future Research 190

Epilogue: The New Knowledge Transmission Ritual 191

Appendix A: Replication of Werner's Questionnaire 203

Appendix B: Kayapó Dietary Regulations 205

References 211

List of Tables

Educational settings in a Kayapó village 41
Comparison of Kayapó ceremony and Western secondary
   schooling 137
Education of a Kayapó person through time. 147
Production of the Kayapó person. 161

List of Figures

Geographical area of Kayapó villages. 3
Area of village and rough clearing 23
Kubẽkàkre gardens (based upon a drawing by Imã Kayapó) . . . 26
"Everyday" spatial orientation of Kubẽkàkre village 29
Ritual spatial orientation of Kubẽkàkre village 30
Kayapó age-grade divisions 58
Perceived direction of Kayapó knowledge flow 61
Male child's relationships showing proximity of
   mother's kin versus father's kin (and cross-kin) 83

Preface

Brazil's Kayapó Amerindians, raided Brazilian settlements as late as 1978. Now they are known for ethnic political demonstrations in Brazilian cities as well as their agricultural sophistication in managing Amazonian rainforest resources. The Kayapó have a strong sense of identity, tradition, and culture, which they successfully manipulate on behalf of the struggle for indigenous rights. How their cultural knowledge and sense of identity are transmitted from generation to generation, is the focus of this ethnographic study.

The Kayapó are particularly well-suited to a study of educational processes and patterns, since their culture has been the subject of many anthropological studies, T. Turner 1966, Bamberger 1967, Verswijver 1985, Vidal 1976, Werner 1980, Posey 1979, Lea 1986, Fisher 1991). The Kayapó are part of a larger cultural complex denominated Gê. The Gê cultures and languages are now among the best documented of Amerindian societies. This is due partly to a decade of coordinated research by seven anthropologists under the Harvard Central Brazil Project, directed by David Maybury-Lewis (1979), and resulting in several important published anthropological studies (Maybury-Lewis 1974, 1979, Maybury-Lewis and Almagor 1989; da Matta 1982; Melatti 1978; Crocker 1985). An extensive two-volume collection of the folk literature of the Gê has been compiled, comprising some 360 narratives (Wilbert 1984).

Taken together, the ample research on Gê social systems, the extensive collection of oral literature, and the ongoing documentation of sophisticated subsistence technology represent not only what is known about the Kayapó, but what the Kayapó know: a documentation of their knowledge.

The Kayapó recognize two broad knowledge domains: the general and the traditional. General knowledge, associated with life's daily routines and skills, is transmitted in the everyday setting, which includes parent and child transactions. Identity, person-defining, and traditional knowledge are primarily transmitted in the ritual setting and reinforced during ceremonial events when various village locations are temporarily transformed into ritual space. Indigenous education in these separate educational settings provides the basis for a Kayapó "dialectic of personhood."

Indigenous Kayapó education is learner-initiated and learner-centered, yet each person is ultimately responsible to pass on to certain others what has been received. Ritual-centered relationships, operating within and beyond the context of a ceremonial event, play a major role in the transmission of social, person-defining knowledge, without which the Kayapó individual is considered incomplete. The educational processes of ritual events could be compared with Western secondary schooling.

The processes of systematically transmitting knowledge between one another and from one generation to another is a basic requirement for the perpetuation of any human society. Kayapó social organization illustrates well the link between social structure and knowledge construction and transmission.

The connection between educational methods and social structure, however, is often treated rather generally in the literature. Numerous scholars appeal for more systematic studies of this connection as well as the processes transmitting knowledge, so that models of indigenous education can be developed (Mead 1949, 1978; Fernandes 1975; dos Santos 1975; Mélia 1979:13; Hansen 1979:30).

Models of indigenous knowledge transmission have become relevant to Western society, today. Global concerns, with multidimensional issues such as environmental problems, have led to the formation of broad-based interest groups including the environmentalists, the feminists, and peace-activists. These groups subscribe to a new paradigm of knowledge which is global, context-dependent, integrative, and holistic. Due to their influence, holistic learning is again coming into focus with a concomitant search for alternative educational models.

The Kayapó knowledge paradigm is not new but it does share the above characteristics; that is, it is global, context-dependent, integrative, and holistic. Kayapó society thus provides a model for holistic, integrated, antifragmentary learning, involving both the body and the mind, where knowledge accrued is seen as contributing to the wholeness of a person.

Nontraditional knowledge enters the village through contact with the outside world. It is a rapidly expanding domain which is clearly separated from, and presents a challenge to, the integrated traditional knowledge system, causing intergenerational tension.

This research which bridges the disciplines of education and anthropology makes the following contributions: it expands our knowledge concerning indigenous processes of education in the everyday context of village life; but more importantly, within the ritual context, it describes a model for holistic learning. In general terms, an understanding of this indigenous system of knowledge transmission, as practiced by the Kayapó, increases our knowledge of human learning. In addition, this ethnographic case study suggests a model for the analysis of a dynamic indigenous knowledge transmission system in educational anthropology.

First and foremost, I wish to thank the Kayapó people of Kubēkàkre who willingly "in their turn, passed on" to me their concepts of education. Special thanks to Bepgogoti for allowing me to live in the village and with his family. Also to Bepmotire, Bepkŭm, Nikà'iti, Imã, Irenapti, Bepkwynhkritkrit, and others for sharing knowledge and food with me.

The willing and able cooperation of my friend and colleague, Ruth Thomson, was fundamental to this study. Ruth generously shared with me all the benefits she had earned through twenty years of life with the Kayapó—her language ability, experience, friends, and family—giving sacrificially of her time.

The 1992 version of this study was presented to the University of Pittsburgh as a Ph.D dissertation. During the dissertation process, Dr. John Singleton supported, encouraged, and patiently guided with unfailing good humor; Anne Singleton eased my load with her involvement and practical helpfulness; Rolland Paulston, William Smole, and Seth Spaulding offered valuable suggestions and were always supportive; William Fisher, Terrence Turner, and Darrell Posey encouraged me with their knowledge of Kayapó; Sherwood and Judith Lingenfelter, Linda Flower, and Ronald Grimes offered encouragement and suggestions on the manuscript in its formative stages; and Shirley Breitigam guided me through manuscript requirements.

I am grateful to Earl and Ivy Trapp of the Unevangelized Fields Mission for their hospitality and for Earl's expertise in the translation of several Kayapó songs for which ethnomusicologist Thomas Avery provided a musical analysis. Robert and Dorothy Wright, Thomas Van Wynen, and James Albright of the SIL computer department, Brazil, spent many long hours creating programs, installing programs, and otherwise making me computer literate. Karesse Angelo and David Dinniny helped with diagrams. I thank them all.

This study was supported in part by a Tinker Grant awarded by the University of Pittsburgh's Center for Latin American Studies and a Doctoral

Fellowship Award from the University of Pittsburgh's Graduate Alumni Association. The Summer Institute of Linguistics (SIL), Brazil, graciously allowed me time away from my assignment and provided me with expertise and encouragement, and the Fundação Nacional do Índio in Brasília, Brazil, kindly authorized my research.

The support of my friends and peers in the writing process was essential. Words cannot convey my deep gratitude to two special people who believed in me: Margaret Sheffler, who has surely earned her doctorate vicariously by her loyal support and practical help throughout the long project; and my Brazilian "mother," Euridice Lima. I will be forever grateful to God for their unfailing love and support.

1
Introduction

Brazil's colorful Kayapó Amerindians, until recently one of the most feared peoples of the Amazon region, have a strong sense of identity, tradition, and culture which they consciously manipulate on behalf of the struggle for indigenous rights in Brazil. How their cultural knowledge and sense of identity are transmitted from generation to generation is the focus of this ethnographic study.

I conducted research on indigenous education—the structure and methods of knowledge transmission, as well as the types of knowledge involved—among the Kayapó in Kubẽkàkre village in the State of Pará. The major purpose of the study was to record the ways in which the Kayapó themselves conceptualize their knowledge and how they transmit it between one another and from generation to generation. We will look at Kayapó knowledge transmission as educational events which take place in particular settings. The secondary purpose of the study was to examine one education system, to develop a model for studies of cultural transmission and acquisition, and to augment studies in educational anthropology that focus upon culture-specific nonschool patterns of education.

Participant observation was the main research tool that I used during my eleven months with the Kayapó. This was coupled with directive and nondirective interviews conducted in the Kayapó language.

I used these and other ethnographic techniques to explore the connection between Kayapó social structure and knowledge-transmission mechanisms, since "the very structure of knowledge is conditioned by its sociocultural milieu" (Hansen 1979:1). The research shows that the formation of the Kayapó person as a complete physical and social entity may be interpreted as an indigenous educational goal to be achieved by definite means and specific sets of people who function as channels of knowledge transmission in relation to the learner. The contribution to the education of a child by people within the grandparent category, for example, is in contrast to the contribution of those in the parent category. The grandparent input involves the type of knowledge which is believed to make a person socially viable as opposed to physically viable, this latter being the responsibility of the parent category of kin. Kayapó knowledge transmission is directed towards unifying these two major components of the individual: the person as both physically and socially viable.

For the Kayapó, a desire to learn traditional knowledge denotes a good, socially cooperative person, whereas not desiring to learn may be indicative of an antisocial trait. In face-to-face societies like this, being judged as too antisocial often leads to social ostracism. The Kayapó goal for learning and teaching—the ideal—is the formation of good, sociable people who in turn should assure a well-ordered Kayapó society. Tensions arise when the learner does not desire the traditional knowledge the elder is expected to "pass on."

The people and their environment

The Northern Kayapó, numbering between 4,000 and 5,000, are one of the major Amerindian societies remaining in the Amazon region of Brazil (Verswijver 1985; T. Turner 1989; Bamberger 1979). The village of Kubēkákre, in which the major part of this research was conducted, is located on the Iriri, a tributary of the Xingu River, Pará State, Central Brazil. With a population of 347, it is one of the larger of the thirteen Kayapó villages: Bau, Kararaô, Catete, Bakaja, Metyktire, Pykany, Kubēkákre, Gorotire, Kikretũm, À'ukre, Kubēkrãkênh, Kôkraxmõr, Kapot. They are located on approximately 130,000 square kilometers of land between the rainforest of the Amazon and the central Brazilian plains (see figure 1). The closest distance between any two villages is between 50 and 100 miles. Kayapó men and families visit relatives in these far-flung settlements, and there is a government-provided wireless radio communications network linking many communities, manned mostly by the Kayapó. Yet village populations are basically endogamous, and no inter-village, political supra-organization exists. The village itself is "the basic social, political and ceremonial unit of Kayapó society" (T. Turner 1987b:3).

Figure 1. Geographical area of Kayapó villages
The enlarged area indicates Kayapó traditional land, including Kubēkàkre village.

Historically and until very recently, the Kayapó were notorious for warfare in the form of raids which probably expelled or exterminated other Amerindian populations in the area they controlled, including other Kayapó villages. Of medium to tall stature in comparison with other Amerindian peoples, the Kayapó notoriety among members of the dominant society and surrounding ethnic groups stems from their aggressive behavior, traditionally expressed in raiding and plundering. Their legendary fame was enhanced by their fearsome physical appearance, due mainly to a spectacular wooden lip plug inserted through a hole in the lower lip of the male warriors. With bodies freshly blackened with genipapo *(Genipa americana)* vegetable dye mixed with carbon, and the large, protruding wooden lip plug, they presented themselves as ferocious, formidable foes, no doubt intimidating to their enemies!

The Kayapó, and several other related groups who shared the same custom of the lip plug, were known locally as the people of the "wooden lips." The Kayapó referred to themselves, however, as *mebẽngôkrê* 'people of the space between—or hole in—the waters', perhaps, as Turner (personal communication) suggests, because their villages traditionally ranged between the Tocantins and Araguaia rivers. The term itself is also the generic for human beings as opposed to animals and other creatures; and it is the Kayapó autodenomination which confers an ethnocentric focus upon themselves as fully human in contrast to other non-Kayapó people, to whom they refer as *kubẽ kakrit* 'people of no account', or subhuman.

Until about thirty-five years ago, most Kayapó villages were largely inaccessible to outsiders, but the construction of the trans-Amazon highway system and the attendant immigration into the area has hemmed in the Kayapó and sharply curtailed their transhumant way of life (Maybury-Lewis 1979:129).

The Kayapó are often described as a seminomadic people who traditionally abandoned their villages temporarily in order to disperse into trekking groups for hunting and gathering, returning to their villages to practice horticulture and attend to their ceremonial activities.

The continuing encroachment of nonindigenous settlements into Kayapó territory means that the Kayapó are now cut off from the areas they formerly trekked, yet festivals and accompanying treks still occur year-round. Furthermore, the Kayapó have become accustomed to manufactured goods and medical services obtainable from outsiders, so they tend to remain closer to the sources of supply of these items and engage in activities designed to bring in some cash. Gold has been discovered in the region especially near the Kayapó villages of Gorotire, Baú, and Kubẽkàkre, and the mining company has agreed to giving the Gorotire Kayapó a percentage of its daily extraction. There is some wealth-sharing among the Kayapó of Gorotire village, but some of the leaders are refusing to share, becoming personally rich, which is contrary to the cultural norm. Other villages, such as Kubẽkàkre, are actively looking for their own bonanza equivalent to the Gorotire windfall, and this causes them to agree to lumber extraction, for which they can be compensated.

Clearly, then, the Kayapó are in a situation of accelerated culture change. There is tension between the elders and the younger generation, with traditional values being rejected by the young Kayapó men as no longer adaptive to the present, rapidly-shifting situation. For these reasons, this research began as a kind of "salvage" ethnography, where "little time remains to salvage the valuable information resulting from millennia of accumulated ecological knowledge" (Posey et al. 1984:104). Yet, in the course of this study, I concluded that the Kayapó people show strong adaptive responses to their changing circumstances, although their natural environment and the accompanying traditional knowledge may not fare as well.

Cultural knowledge, however, is more than content; it implies patterns and relationships of knowledge acquisition functioning in everyday and ritual activities, social rights and privileges, status and prestige, and a distinct Kayapó identity. It seems clear that some of this needs to be maintained for the Kayapó to continue to weather the pressures of acculturation.

Further, Kayapó ecological knowledge has, in the past, successfully contributed to the maintenance and balance of the delicate rainforest ecosystem (Posey 1982), but now several villages seem willing to forfeit their natural resources in exchange for material wealth. One benefit of this research may be to engender respect for the traditional Kayapó knowledge system among non-Kayapó and in so doing, rekindle respect among the younger generation of Kayapó as they see their traditions and the knowledge itself being valued.

Underlying theoretical issues

The theoretical perspective guiding my interpretation of Kayapó educational events is essentially functionalist within the equilibrium paradigm (Paulston 1977). Education is seen as process: the socio-cultural "making" of an individual as he moves from one emically-defined state to another. This actualization of the Kayapó "person" occurs in a dynamic temporal-spatial context which is transformed by human activity in both everyday and ritual events.

There are three basic issues underlying this study which challenge some prevailing ideas about (1) learner as object or learner as subject, (2) the influence of spatial categories upon knowledge transmission, and (3) ritual as education. This section will outline the relevant theoretical issues against which the data is applied in subsequent chapters.

Learner as object or learner as subject

Researchers have typically focused on cultural transmission (as education) with an emphasis on topics concerning what is taught, the teacher, methods of transmission, and the relationship of the content to the values of the larger society. Such interests were natural in view of an anthropological penchant for emphasizing content over process (Wolcott 1990:8). As a result, there has been less focus on the learner—how one selects from all the "noise" in the learning context, how one turns out more or less as expected/anticipated by society.

The content/process distinction is seen to be helpful in providing a contrast of focus between the teaching and the learning processes. But if teaching and learning are seen instead as an interactive event, as only one process where one action is inextricably linked with the other, then the former distinction between content and process is a false dichotomy (Hansen 1982:189). Such a distinction betrays a metaphorical "information-shunting" view of education and/or cultural transmission (F. Smith 1985:195).

Content is important to the Kayapó, but their primary emphasis of knowledge transmission appears to be the relationships through which knowledge transfers are validated and on the achievement of broad, socially-defined goals towards which these transactions are directed.

Most studies of culture transmission have focused upon the social transmission of information through a symbol system—mainly language, either oral or written. Boster and Mervis (1987) argue that focusing upon culture as learned, rather than taught "allows all potential sources of structure in experience to count as sources of cultural knowledge" (p. 7). Such sources of structure in experience include the structure of the human mind, structure in the environment, social structure, spatial structure, and lastly, perhaps, is the social transmission of information through the structure of a symbol system.

This emphasis upon the learner and his access to many sources of cultural information correlates nicely with the Kayapó view of learning. My persistent questioning about who taught what to whom, when, where, and how was usually greeted by the response that when the learner wanted to know something, he would go to the proper source of that knowledge and inquire. This led to a consideration of the relationships between a learner and the source of knowledge.

This focus leads to a Kayapó definition of education and shows their ideal to be experience-based, contextual learning, depending upon learner initiative. Interestingly, several studies (Lave 1988; Coy 1989;

Lave and Wenger 1991) describe learning as activity-based, following the theoretical orientation of Vygotsky (Wertsch 1985). Learning is seen as something that takes place in action and interaction, within a social and spatial context (often in spite of teaching). This leads to a second issue—the significance of spatial organization in relation to knowledge distribution patterns—at least among the Kayapó.

Influence of spatial categories upon knowledge transmission

Anthropological concern with spatial and temporal dimensions of human behavior dates back to the first formalization of theories of cultural evolution during the nineteenth century. The interactive nature of the relationship between society, culture, and the environment that man builds has always been of interest to scholars because, "...people both create, and find their behavior influenced by the built environment" (Lawrence and Low 1990:454).

Social theory has begun to focus anew on spatial as well as temporal dimensions of human behavior (Bourdier and Alsayyad 1989; Caraveli 1985; Hugh-Jones 1979). The built environment, including man's control over space in the natural environs, is seen as integral to the complex of cultural traits responsible for a group's adaptation to its natural environment. The particular forms of buildings, as well as the interior and exterior use of space, it is argued, mirror the cultures that produced them.

The cultural complex of Northwest Gê societies in Brazil, which includes the Kayapó, are distinguished by the circular layout of their traditional villages and the space surrounding the village. The theme of concentricity permeates traditional Kayapó society (Verswijver 1985:77): circular gardens themselves surround a circular village. Ceremonially-related treks into the surrounding forest are generally conducted in circular loops from the village perimeter.

The Cartesian notion of nature and culture (Levi-Strauss [1964]1983:28) or nature and society (Seeger 1989:192) is commonly applied by Gê scholars to spatial analyses of Northwest Gê societies. "There is thought to be a spatial grid onto which the relations between society and nature and the transforming influences of culture in remaking and defining boundaries can be mapped" (Fisher 1991:130).

This dualism refers to the linear association between center of the village ("society"), and the outer limits of the society's territory and beyond ("nature"). This has been described, not as a static dichotomy, but a dualism which recognizes "gradations of socialness in society and of naturalness in nature" (Seeger 1989:193).

The center of the village where the men congregate in the men's house is seen as the political and ceremonial hub of village life, the epitome of socialization, while the forest is its antithesis. The central political domain of men, CORE, and the surrounding domestic domain of the women, PERIPHERY, refer to distinctions made by society members themselves.

> I want to emphasize that all of these societies, irrespective of the paradigmatic shape of their villages, make a distinction between the center of the village and the periphery, which is correlated with the distinction they make between the sexes. The symbolic and social functions of men are clearly distinguished as being antithetical to those of women. These distinctions are reflected in the fact that the center of the village is thought of as a male sphere opposed to the periphery of the village which is a female sphere. (Maybury-Lewis and Almagor 1989:99)

However, the male sphere is not exclusively ceremonial and political; nor is the female sphere exclusively domestic. As Verswijver (1985) and Lea (1986) show, and my data seem to confirm, ritual elements such as *idji mex* 'beautiful names' and *nekrêx* 'ceremonial rights' are associated as much with the periphery as the core, i.e., as much with the female sphere as with the male sphere.[1] In fact, as illustrated in chapter 2, every concentric spatial division, i.e., house, village, rough clearing, garden, and rainforest, has two potential modes: the EVERYDAY mode and the RITUAL mode. In terms of educational activity, these modes can be regarded as educational settings where certain relationships are predominant.

The focus in the everyday mode is on the routine, more private, domestic-oriented activities, involving the input of the male to a significant degree. In the ritual mode, by contrast, different teaching/learning relationships are predominant and the focus of activity is concerned with communal, ceremonial events,[2] yet involving the female to a significant degree.

In terms of knowledge transmission, this view of the ritual overlay upon the everyday use of space is advantageous as an interpretive lens because it

---

[1] Since the purpose of my inquiry was not into the ownership of names and rights, I cannot attest to "matrilineal" transmission or lineages, which Lea (1986) proposes and Maybury-Lewis (1979) disposes, nor to households as "corporate entities" in the classical sense (Lea 1986). But my data seem to support the idea of ritual roles as belonging to households and names being returned to households, so I occasionally refer to these ideas in a loose sense throughout this study.

[2] These terms correspond to the public/private dichotomy in general; we could also say ceremonial setting versus domestic setting or domestic mode versus corporate mode. The dichotomy helps to target contrasts in educational interaction within the family versus community context.

Underlying theoretical issues 9

permits a sharper focus upon each gender in both the everyday and the ceremonial settings. For this reason, the spatial analysis presented in chapter 2 diverges in emphasis from previous analyses (T. Turner 1987b:4–6, 36, 37; Verswijver 1985:65, 77–88; Bamberger 1967) where core (village center) is seen as the hub of ritual activity and basically male-dominant and the periphery (households) as the hub of domestic activity and basically female-dominant. Yet, the use of space in each setting is clearly modified by gender as well as temporally.

Ritual as education

The third issue for Kayapó indigenous education is that learning occurs in ritual activity and includes bodily learning as well as cerebral learning. My thinking concerning ritual as education was stimulated by my fieldwork because the Kayapó in Kubẽkàkre were nearly always engaged in one ritualized activity or another. I observed, as did Jensen, "Even though festivals and myths offer a comparatively lower information load than direct teaching, they provide the philosophical base upon which all other information rests; the skeleton upon which the larger structure is built" (1990:114).

When the term ritual is used in this study, it refers mainly to Kayapó name-giving rites, which may be defined as ceremonies in the following sense:

> An elaborate, conventional form of expression of feeling...ceremonial may...be used to refer to those collective actions required by custom, performed on occasions of change in social life. Thus a ceremonial consists of a specific sequence of ritual acts, performed in public. (Goody 1961:159)

According to this definition, ceremonies are more than legal or civic rites, as in courtroom procedures or other rules of order.

For the Kayapó, name-giving ceremonies are specific, named, formalized enactments which they describe by the term *me rer mex*[3] 'crossing well' or 'passing along well'. These terms refer to the beauty of the decorated participants' activities in the village plaza as they pass on names to the children being honored. Dances *(me tôr)* and singing *(me ngrer)* are part of the activities. The name-giving rites, although structured and organized, are, at the same time, "emergent social constructions" (Schieffelin 1985:721) which "do not exist in a vacuum of structural scripts and frames. Insofar as they are

---

[3]Cf. Verswijver translation as "those who show off well" (1985:146); Lea translates *rer* as "to give," which I understand to be the same as "pass on" (1986:80); and Fisher feels it translates as "those who cross over a discontinuity well" (1989):10.

performed, they have historicity" (p. 722). A name-giving ceremony is, for the participants, "an event that they helped construct and to which they contributed part of the ambience, action, and final significance that it evoked from them" (p. 722).

"Ritual," Grimes states, "is not a 'what' or a 'thing'; it is a 'how', and there are 'degrees' of it" (1986:5). It need not be associated with religious action or even magico-religious behavior, although from the observer's perspective, Kayapó rituals and rites do include the latter.

The people themselves say that it is good to have ceremonies so that they will be happy. One ceremony may follow another almost without interval, and major ceremonies are often intertwined with minor ceremonies, dances, and rites. During the eleven months I lived among the Kayapó in Kubẽkàkre village, there were four name-giving ceremonies, each lasting several months, and several shorter dances. The Kayapó, then, provide a good case study for showing educational interaction in ritual activity.

In the field of ritual studies, both theologians and anthropologists have typically studied the symbolism in ritual, that is to say, the content, and have often assumed the participants' actual knowledge concerning the ritual they are performing and why they perform it. Ritual is shown to be linked to social structure, to social roles, to role reversals, to life transitions. While it is assumed that participants (active or passive) must learn the ritual in which they are involved, the "pedagogy" in/of ritual is rarely discussed.

Scholars are not in agreement concerning whether learning even occurs in ritual. Referring to initiation rites among the Gisu people of Uganda, La Fontaine observes that dances are "taught" to the initiates by an older man chosen for his knowledge and who is seen as an instructor; yet she does not believe this represents new knowledge. She argues,

> ...since all activity goes on in public and younger children tag along trying out the steps and learning the songs, it can hardly be said that the novices are gaining much knowledge. (1977:426)

Other scholars, however, believe knowledge is imparted to neophytes during ritual activity. Of initiation rites in West and Central African cultures, V. Turner observes,

> Many of these peoples have complex initiation rites with long periods of seclusion in the bush for the training of novices in esoteric lore, often associated with the presence of masked dancers, who portray ancestral spirits or deities. (1982:4)

and further,

> The neophyte in liminality must be a tabula rasa, a blank slate, on which is inscribed the knowledge and wisdom of the group, in those respects that pertain to the new status. (1982:103)

Perhaps the West African "bush" school as described by Watkins (1963) and Lancy (1975) is the most clear-cut example of learning occurring in the context of ritualized activities, vis-à-vis, secret societies and circumcision rites.

I believe the above viewpoints illustrate the Westerners' obsession with attempting to identify a temporal order in learning. It stems from a focus on the didactic mode rather than the experiential mode of learning, the didactic being sequential and linear, while the experiential mode is from the periphery of a task to the center. In the experiential mode,

> The apprentice doesn't learn something in a predetermined sequence from beginning to end. Rather she learns a bit here and a bit there, all the time able to fall back on the expert, and bit by bit becomes competent in ever-increasing stretches of the production schedule. Only at some advanced stage is she required to put the whole sequence together.

> This process of working from the periphery of a task complex to the center...stands in contrast to the ways in which such knowledge is transferred in training sessions. There we find no ordering from peripheral to central, from simple to complex, from inexpensive to costly. Rather, there is a (chrono)logically ordered sequence, each component of which carries the same salience and must be acquired in a linear order. (Jordan 1987:21)

The apprenticeship mode of learning and knowledge transfer correlates well with Kayapó ideas as to what is transpiring when the young are learning from their grandparents, or the younger ritual sponsor is learning from one more experienced. In chapters 5 and 6 we will see how the Kayapó perceive learning and teaching within their ritual events, such as name-giving ceremonies or specific dances.

Education and ritual are, I believe, intimately connected, even in an apparently nonritualistic society, but our thinking about education must be broadened to recognize the value of INCORPORATING practices in contrast to INSCRIPTIVE practices (Connerton 1989:72–73), as important and valid components of interactive, activity-based learning.

Even if learning is considered to occur in ritual activity, there is discussion as to whether it can be CEREBRAL, as well as CORPORAL. Some claim that what ritual teaches is learned mainly by the body.

> Ritual action does not primarily teach us to see differently but to act differently. It does not provide a point of view so much as a pattern of doing....Ritual knowledge is...the knowledge gained in bodily action, a knowledge which is a knowledge of bodily action. (Jennings 1982:117, 119)

Connerton takes the argument further, by stating that the embodiment of ritual is a principal means through which societies remember and as a result create tradition (1989). Grimes agrees with Connerton on this point, yet he believes Connerton "fails to comprehend both the creative and critical dynamics of the ritualizing body" (1991:4). While for Connerton, memory seems to function like a funnel or filter of tradition, with the body as its uncritical repository, for Grimes "the body is cognitive, not stupid; and conversely the mind is embodied" (p. 4). Grimes argues that although ritual embodiment, as Connerton proposes, is a primary means through which societies remember and thus create tradition, "rites do not 'transfer' either memories or knowledge," because "rites improvise; they reinvent" (p. 9), and often they are performative critiques of the very traditions they are perpetuating, thus implying a cognitive/corporal dialectic.

I agree with Grimes in rejecting a mind/body dualism in ritual events, where the mind is seen as an uncritical funnel and the body a passive container of societies' traditions. Obviously, both explicit and tacit ritual knowledge is learned, as much by the body as the mind in a holistic, integrated manner. If we can agree that ritual, whether traditional, modified, or newly-invented, is, as Bell suggests, "a strategic act with which to define the present" (1992:101), then we can acknowledge the immediate socio-cultural impact of ritual upon its participants and thus recognize an educational component of ritual which includes bodily as well as cognitive learning.

The Kayapó also have a concept of bodily learning which would seem to reject a mind/body dualism. They speak of people seeing, then doing, and point out that all the seeing in the world may not help if the person cannot do the action being taught. Dances are learned by watching others and by participating. Upon being invited to dance with the women, I remonstrated that I did not know how. Immediately one women came along beside me and told me to grasp her waist. Then she began to dance, telling me to follow her steps. After a few times of that, she launched me out on my own beside her (the way women dance that particular dance) and said

I would really know it well by doing it. Seeing was necessary, but so was doing.

So, for the Kayapó at least, ritual functions as a form of schooling, where the apprenticeship mode of experiential learning, involving both the body and mind, is the prime method of knowledge transfer. The advantage of this perspective on ritual, for my purposes, is to demystify it in order to see it for some of its practical, more pragmatic qualities. J. Smith says, "ritual is work!" (Bell 1992:viii)—something the Kayapó themselves frequently stated. Smith (1987:103) also said, "Ritual is, first and foremost, a mode of paying attention. It is a process for marking interest." This contradicts the notion that ritual is blind and thoughtless habit, a notion implicitly rejected by the Kayapó, as procedural and processual "rules" concerning the correct performance of ceremonies were constantly under discussion and, invariably, revision.

This study explores the role of ritual (especially name-giving ceremonies) in Kayapó indigenous education and the significance of learner/teacher relationships in ritual, as contrasted with closer kin relationships of knowledge transmission in the everyday activities. McLaren (1986) focuses on ritual in schooling, while this study considers schooling in ritual. Ritual is shown to be an important aspect of Kayapó learning and socialization, contributing to a Kayapó social memory of their heritage.

Research procedures

The main research strategy was participant observation supplemented by interviews, both spontaneous and structured, photography, recorded observations, regular house visits, field trips, and language learning, as well as brief, observational visits to the villages of Kubẽkrãkênh and Gorotire.

My twenty years' experience in Brazil facilitated my return to the Kayapó people (with whom I had spent three months, ten years earlier) with my colleague, Ruth Thomson. As Ruth's "sister" by their kinship reckoning, I gained immediate acceptance, sharing in Ruth's lifestyle completely. This meant living as part of a Kayapó family, eating meals in a variety of households, going to the gardens with the women (often my "sisters"), fishing with couples, joining in the name-giving ceremonies, trekking in the rainforest, and spending a certain portion of each day studying—either language learning, or working on my journals and data collection.

As part of the village leader's household, my colleague and I were treated as members of the family, with kinship terms and their attendant role obligations operating in our favor, and occasionally otherwise. Operating within the kin context meant that we had better relationships with all relatives of this family, and more formal relationships with others in the village unrelated to the family.

The Kayapó of Kubẽkàkre village are basically monolingual, speaking very little Portuguese. In order to understand and converse in Kayapó, I spent some time in language-learning activities, with the aid of a pedagogical grammar (Jefferson 1980) and other linguistic data (Stout and Thomson 1974). In spite of spending about one-third of my time in language learning, my language ability would not have been sufficient to elicit and analyze the in-depth interviews I achieved were it not for Ruth's invaluable assistance (see appendix A).

Since knowledge-transmission patterns reflect the social organization and structure of a society (Hansen 1979; Fernandes 1975; Meliá 1979), it was necessary to update a village census and prepare kinship charts for each of the twenty-four Kayapó households in the village. Mapping the village and surrounding area and comparing these with aerial photographs contributed to an understanding of the significance of the spatial organization as the kinship data were superimposed upon the map. The Kayapó also provided me with their conceptual maps of the surrounding gardens and of the village.

An analysis of the variety of subjects which constitute Kayapó knowledge enables one to categorize this knowledge according to the analyst's perspective. But the same information can be regrouped according to Kayapó categories. The ethnographic approach to data analysis is to combine these two perspectives, etic and emic. When this methodology is applied to all areas of the data, the result should be a more accurate account of Kayapó knowledge transmission than would be possible if just the outsider's or just the insider's view were considered. It has been my aim to combine both perspectives, yet retain a Kayapó essence and flavor in the description.

Included in this research is an analysis of knowledge transmission in one name-giving ceremony, the *Kôkô* ritual. The analysis was based on observation, participation, elders' accounts of the story of the ceremony, Kayapó explanations of what actually transpired, photographs and slides (viewed and commented upon by many Kayapó), and my account verified with several Kayapó ritual specialists. The analysis shows ritual to be of fundamental importance to every area of Kayapó social organization and knowledge transmission.

The study utilizes ethnographic methodology and analytic tools of cultural anthropology. The premise is that the knowledge transmission system of a society is better understood when considered in conjunction with the social structure and cultural values of the society in question. The researcher is constantly challenged to discover the meanings which a cultural community attaches to its behavior so that she may meaningfully communicate these to a different audience. The finished project—joining fieldwork and culture—is an ethnography of Kayapó knowledge transmission.

Data gathering and analysis

The Kayapó were always more than willing to cooperate in this research for two major reasons: (1) it provided some people with a way to earn manufactured items they particularly wanted, and (2) the leaders wanted the results of the study to be shared with outsiders, i.e., they believed the outsiders needed to learn from them. I endeavored to collect data and compare data from a wide variety of sources, both male and female, from different age-grades. I also interviewed children. The Kayapó, themselves, consider certain people authentic repositories of knowledge and would often be unhappy to see me asking certain people (especially women) for particular information. In order to authenticate my data from their point of view, I worked with several people who have helped other aspiring anthropologists with their data collection.

Taped interviews, combined with daily observations, provided the bulk of the database. Some of this recording was done in our study, and some done more spontaneously as we visited from house to house and people offered information in response to our questions.

For questioning, Ruth and I observed the following procedure: (1) we would discuss the list of interview questions I wished to ask, making them as concrete and unhypothetical as possible. (2) She would roughly translate these into Kayapó, and (3) we would then go over these with an experienced Kayapó language helper in an attempt to remove possible ambiguities. Sometimes such questions were asked relatively spontaneously as we visited from house to house. Other times it would be in the form of a more structured but informal interview. These would be taped. Often I would ask someone for his or her life history, or ask them to tell me everything they remembered learning from a particular person. Ruth and I would work on translating the taped data, first ourselves, then with a language helper. I would peruse this material, making a note of points to be clarified, or further questions to ask. We would then go over these with a second language helper, or return to the original provider of the data.

The eleven-month period was divided up into several shorter visits, and on one occasion I went in alone in order to hone my language skills. At that time I accompanied the Kayapó for eight days of trekking, camping with them in a different location each night, observing hunting, collecting, butchering, preparing food, nightly story telling, arguing, morning men's meetings, noting everything, as was my custom, in a daily journal.

The Kayapó practice herbal medicine combined with food restrictions, and on one occasion I was the recipient of their skills after stepping on a poisonous river sting ray. That was not the easiest method of gathering data on their medicines, but it was effective!

With a computerized data management program, the qualitative data was organized in a form that facilitated analysis. (For a listing of some of the data collected, see appendix B.)

It is not easy to describe analytical procedures on a qualitative data base. I relied upon Spradley (1980), Agar (1980), class notes on ethnographic procedures, and Singleton (1985) to guide me in the search for themes running through the data.

Research questions, gleaned largely from Hansen (1979), were always before me as I combed my data, and a large part of the analysis resulted from responses to these questions.

Research questions

The underlying, specific question of this study is: how do a so-called traditional people, the Kayapó of Central Brazil, transmit their knowledge between one another and from generation to generation? The inquiry is based upon the following set of questions suggested by Hansen (1979:30, 31) for studies of knowledge transmission.

A. What constitutes "knowledge" for the Kayapó?
   1. What knowledge do the Kayapó consider essential to their sense of identity?
   2. Is there a scale of values attached to types of knowledge?
   3. Is knowledge considered property?
   4. To what extent do myths, songs, and ritual serve as models of knowledge for the Kayapó?

B. How is knowledge distributed among members of Kayapó society?
   1. Is access to knowledge related to gender?
   2. Are there specialists in Kayapó society?

3. Are there restrictions on access to knowledge?
   4. Is control of knowledge related to prestige?
C. What are the main agencies and processes of knowledge transmission?
   1. Is the focus of knowledge transmission upon teaching or upon learning?
   2. What groups or individuals control which type of knowledge?
   3. How is knowledge actually transmitted? What senses are in focus? (Ours is a verbal society, another society might rely more on visual cues.)
   4. Are there rewards for learning and punishment for not learning?
   5. Is knowledge a commodity in the sense that one pays for it?
   6. What are the goals of the agencies of knowledge transmission?

In response to these questions a data base emerged leading, finally, to the broader questions addressed by the analysis. These are as follows:

1. What relationship is there between cultural constructions of spatial organization and knowledge transmission events? (chapter 2)
2. How do the Kayapó categorize and conceptualize their cultural knowledge? What factors influence knowledge distribution among the Kayapó people? (chapter 3)
3. What social relationships function to transmit general, everyday knowledge between people and between generations? What methods are employed? (chapter 4)
4. What is the pedagogical value of ceremonial activity within the Kayapó? (chapter 5).
5. What social relationships function to transmit traditional knowledge between people and between generations? What methods are employed? (chapter 6).
6. How will the introduction of new knowledge affect the Kayapó traditional patterns of knowledge transmission? (chapter 7)

My interpretative moves were largely inductive, based upon Kayapó commentaries, opinions, insights, and explanations in their own words, drawn from my interview data and other records. My challenge as an ethnographer has been to interpret this data in a way that is faithful to the Kayapó viewpoint and understandable to non-Kayapó readers. The Kayapó categories of knowledge uncovered by the research, provide the organizational framework for chapters 4–7.

Chapter 2 provides the background and setting of the area of research and includes a discussion of the dynamic and fluidity of Kayapó village space and its surrounds, as dependent upon the content and focus of

Kayapó activity within the environment. Everyday space is transformed into ritual space at given points in time, influencing social relationships and activity within the same social space.

Chapter 3 includes a description of the unique cultural influences which modify the distribution of knowledge, including types of specialists, age grades, gender, Kayapó ideology affecting knowledge transmission, and other related subjects. The Kayapó categorization of types of knowledge provides the framework for the next four chapters.

Chapter 4 deals with Kayapó knowledge within the everyday setting—knowledge which might be considered general knowledge, related mainly to subsistence activities in a domestic, family-oriented setting. The social relationships operating within and between Kayapó households is discussed primarily as these relate to child learners, although adult knowledge transactions are also discussed.

The Kayapó believe that parents and offspring share actual physical substance, enabling parents to influence the physical appearance and health of the child according to foods eaten or avoided. These "substance relationships" (da Matta 1982) influence Kayapó ideas concerning teaching and learning. People in the parent category in relation to ego (parent's siblings, either real or fictive), are assumed to be responsible for ego's physical growth including the transmission of general knowledge, survival skills, and other matters related primarily to the everyday setting.

Chapter 5 considers some of the generalized forms of learning which take place in Kayapó ceremony as the everyday spatial arrangements are transformed by ceremonial events. The learning which occurs in the socio-cultural context of Kayapó ritual is compared with that which takes place in Western schooling (Cusick 1973), and many similarities are noted. Finally, the ritual setting contrasts with the everyday setting in many ways: the use of space, the action of grandparents upon a learner in contrast to parental action, communal activities, reciprocity-based relationships between kin and nonkin, and ritual partnerships, to name a few.

Chapter 6 deals more specifically with some teacher/learner relationships which function both in the ritual and everyday settings. Kayapó education is seen as a process of identity-building where strategies are employed by the learner, or others on behalf of the learner. Knowledge is sought from elders considered to "know something," i.e., a particular remedy or specialty. Knowledge-transmission networks are discussed as well as the problem caused by ranking, where some knowledge is more esteemed, yet access to it is conditioned by a number of factors, leading to individual strategies of acquisition on the part of knowledge seekers.

An event which illustrates some of the knowledge transactions which occur "between" settings is the communal trek *(õtõmõr)* which takes place outside of the village. On this occasion, in which members of an entire village may participate, a wide variety of knowledge is made more widely available.

Knowledge which comes to the Kayapó from outside sources is the topic of chapter 7. In this chapter, Dahrendorf's Life Chances model (1979) is applied to a study of the Kayapó move from traditional to modern concerns. The Kayapó traditional method of incorporating new knowledge from (usually) hostile contacts with neighboring Amerindian societies is contrasted with the way outside knowledge is incorporated today. In addition, the influence of the Brazilian Indigenous movement and a pan-Amerindian consciousness is examined as it contrasts with or expands Kayapó traditional knowledge.

Chapter 8 summarizes and concludes the study, making recommendations concerning areas in which further study would be profitable.

2
Spatial Categories and Knowledge Transmission

From the perspective of a small, single-engine airplane, the huge expanse of dense Amazon rainforest seems like an unending plantation of broccoli, in spite of the gigantic height of the trees. In the midst of this, the sight of small circular clearings, like light green, blotchy polka dots on the dark green growth, stand out dramatically as a sign of human habitation. These "dots" are the Kayapó gardens, and signal the approach to a much larger, brown, circular clearing of a Kayapó village.

Just as a stage set provides a visual image of the imaginary world in which the action of a play takes place, so a description of the Kayapó set, the village and its people, provides the scenery necessary to comprehend Kayapó patterns of knowledge transmission. An emic model of spatial categories, within which certain knowledge-transmission relationships take place, represents a significant part of the set.

This chapter will describe the spatial context within which teaching and learning occur. Much more could be said about spatial divisions within a Kayapó village as these relate to Kayapó social structure, but my intention in this chapter is to show the dynamic nature of Kayapó social space as it is transformed by human activity from everyday to ritual use and to show the relationship between this transformation and Kayapó learning activities in both the everyday and the ritual settings.

We begin with a description of the village and its people followed by a portrayal of the village and its surrounding area as settings of contrasting activities within which context-specific learning takes place. These will be presented as two distinct Kayapó educational settings mediated by relationships considered INTERMEDIATE because they function in both settings. Yet, these settings are not to be construed as static location, so much as a dynamic two-way flow between everyday activities and ritually-oriented activity. When considering knowledge transmission, this view of space allows for an appreciation of the role of women in the ritual setting and that of men in the domestic setting.

Background and setting

Most Kayapó villages owe their origin to fission when conflict causes a breakaway group to start another village. In addition, ecological or health considerations may force an entire village to relocate.

An example of the latter is the area of research, Kubẽkàkre. The inhabitants of its predecessor, Mekrãknõti, relied primarily upon hunting, but being far from a major waterway, could not often supplement their diet with large fish. Some residents, encouraged by the government agency, the National Indian Foundation (Fundação Nacional do Índio or FUNAI), thought they should move to a location on the Iriri River where water and fish would be plentiful and access (mainly for government personnel and medical flights) would be facilitated. Many in the group which first attempted settlement in the new location were frightened back to Mekrãknõti by sickness and death, but those who remained founded Pykany village. Another group established itself about a day's boat-ride upstream and prospered. This became Kubẽkàkre with the majority of the former Mekãknõti population settling there by 1985.

Located beside the Iriri River, a tributary of the Xingu, Kubẽkàkre is situated high enough above the river so that the rainy season level will not flood the actual village. The water level, from dry to rainy season, might vary from forty to sixty feet. The village was constructed in the traditional circular pattern,[4] with each house having access to the main river for water, bathing, fishing, and transportation, although the families living on the southwest side of the village, away from the river, usually prefer to fetch water and bathe in a fresh, cold stream feeding into the Iriri (see figure 2).

---

[4]Not all villages follow the pattern today, although conceptually the circular layout remains a cognitive reality (T. Turner 1987b:85).

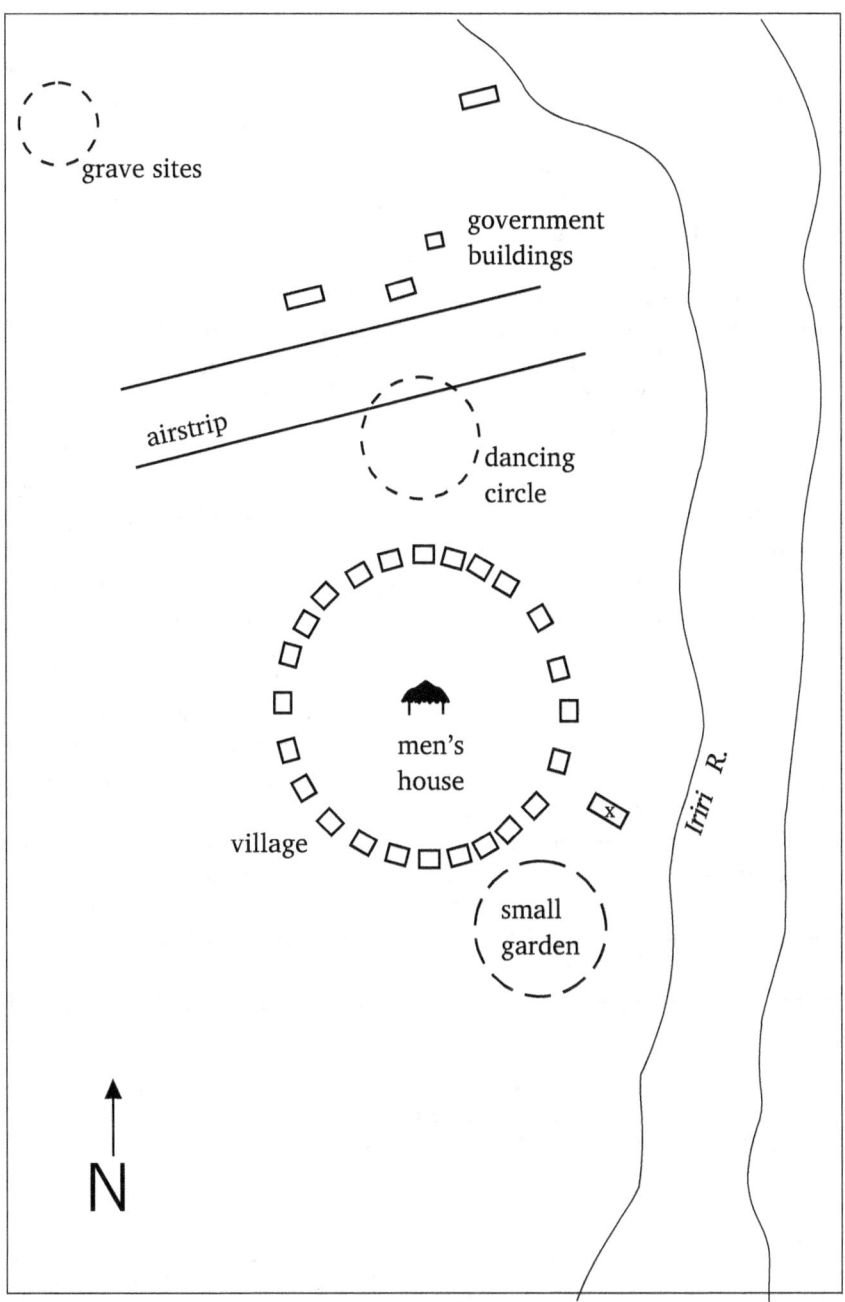

Figure 2. Area of village and rough clearing

Figure 2 shows the twenty-four houses with the men's house in the center. The airstrip is a grassy clearing maintained by the villagers. The squares or rectangles north of the airstrip indicate a set of mud and wattle houses which comprise the government "Indian Post" containing a clinic and house, a school, and another house for occasional workers. The rectangle marked X, to the east of the village, is a thatch and pole Kayapó construction which my colleague and I used as our study house, although we lived with a family in a nearby house. The village borders the Iriri River. The area surrounding the village is a semi-cleared zone (rough clearing) and includes the village grave sites, at least one small garden belonging to an elderly woman, and shows the "rehearsal" dance circle used in times of ritual activity.

Each Kayapó household is a matri-uxorilocal domestic unit comprised of a senior married woman, her husband, married daughters and their families, and single daughters and sons. Twelve of the twenty-four residences house up to twenty people, including the one in which I lived. Besides human residents, there are any number of "pets," including parakeets, macaws, pigs, chickens, dogs and their litters, and monkeys.

The people were nearly always friendly, cooperative, and eager to answer questions and explain their customs. Children were omnipresent; the teenage girls were giggly; the teenage boys usually attempted to be serious; young adults claimed not to know anything; and older adults were ready to work with me. Men found alternative phrases to explain something if I did not understand due to language difficulties; women usually repeated the same phrase with increasing volume until, in desperation, I was forced to "understand"—to their great satisfaction.

Although Bepgogoti, the grandfather in our household, is seen as the village leader, traditionally villages did not have one head chief. But after contact with non-Amerindians unaccustomed to dealing with decentralized leadership, "chiefs" were usually appointed, by one side or the other, in order to facilitate communication between the Kayapó and outsiders. Bepmotire, the old, white captive[5] says of Bepgogoti, the head chief of Kubēkàkre,

> Bepgogoti isn't really a chief...Claudio made him a chief by giving him goods. Then Mierelles came and really made him a chief by giving him a lot of goods.[6]

---

[5]Bepmotire was captured from a local nonindigenous rubber-tapping family during a Kayapó raid around 1923. About age eight at the time, he adapted thoroughly to Kayapó life, becoming an acknowledged expert in the knowledge of Kayapó customs and history.
[6]Claudio Villas Boas and Francisco Mierelles refer to well-known Brazilian Indianists who were instrumental in establishing Brazilian Government outposts among the Kayapó.

Nevertheless, Bepgogoti is considered the traditional head of the village, although no longer very active. Two of his sons act in his place.

In the center of the village stands the men's house, a thatched-roof structure without walls. This is the political axis of the village during everyday, secular life and a ceremonial focal point during times of festivities. Leadership in Kubẽkàkre is vested in the elders, particularly the leaders of the two men's societies, *me õtõti* and *me pã'ã kadjàt*. Each of these groups has an older and younger men's division since a system of age-sets is incorporated into the societies, and each division has leaders. There are also female counterparts to these societies.

The men's and women's societies, with their leaders, provide the organizational structure for political and civil action, both within the village and outside of it. The societies utilize kinship ties, both fictive and real, but transcend households by dividing the people into two larger groups referred to as moieties by T. Turner (1987b:33).

Traditionally the men's societies underwent volatile upheavals in terms of membership and action, warring with each other or with groups from other villages, or going on lengthy raids of enemy tribes (Verswijver 1985). Even today the societies are potential smouldering fires with various historical or political rivalries ready to spring into flames at some provocation.

When the men meet in the men's house, the most common topic of discussion in present times is the problem of achieving official territorial demarcation by the Brazilian government to ensure the Kayapó their traditional land. To attract attention to their plight, the Kayapó warriors may plan demonstrations to be enacted in state or federal capitals. Other topics of discussion may be questions of possible lumber concessions or alternative strategies for bringing economic wealth to the village. Upcoming traditional festivals are always on the agenda as well.

According to my "sister," Nhàktu, the women's societies of today provide a task force for village projects, such as clearing the weeds from the central plaza in readiness for a dance or getting gravel for the airstrip. They may also work in a chief's garden or even in the gardens of society members. When working for a leader, they will receive goods, but they do not get paid for working in society members' gardens. Some ceremonies also make use of the society divisions as organizing principles when competition is involved such as the Tapir Festival, *kukryt-te*, which culminates with a spirited tug-of-war between societies, using a dead tapir.

A village as large as Kubẽkàkre is able to sustain a number of festivals, most of which are ceremonies to honor children, bestowing upon them inherited names. It is a sign of a happy, well-functioning village to have many festivals.

It is also a sign of wealth and plenty, for festivals imply a good food supply, i.e., productive gardens and plenty of game and fish.

It is difficult to estimate exactly how many gardens the people of Kubẽkàkre maintain, since questions asking for quantities normally receive the answer one, two, or many. Every woman with children should have a garden, which ideally is cleared by the father(s) of the children. I was able to obtain a drawing by one man, of all the gardens he could think of, ninety-six, but he reckoned there were many more. From this map I was able to ascertain that the men's society leaders have more gardens than do others and to determine which families had more gardens. The drawing in figure 3 is based upon his map (it does not show all ninety-six gardens). The circles represent their circular gardens, and the lines represent the pathways leading from the village to the garden areas. The village, airstrip, and river are marked, and it can be seen that some gardens are reached principally by river. The entire garden complex encircles the village.

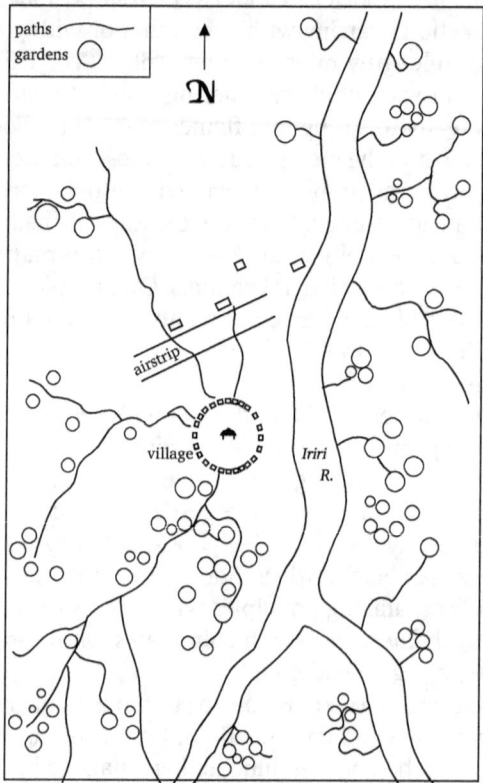

Figure 3. Kubẽkàkre gardens (based upon a drawing by Imã Kayapó)

The traditional village circle, with central men's house, the horticultural plus hunting and gathering economy, the historical political organization of societies and leaders, all belie the tremendous undercurrent of change which is sweeping through the whole society. Nevertheless, change is not happening overnight, and many customs of the old ones continue as guiding principles for the young. Women and men have distinct roles to play in the society, and spatial boundaries, in this traditional village layout, are imbued with meaning derived from century-old patterns.

Time and gender as spatial markers

It soon became apparent to me in a practical way that a relationship existed between spatial divisions and gender which effected a discreet avoidance pattern between members of the opposite sex in this face-to-face society. Certain areas and pathways were used predominantly by men, and other areas by women. Rarely did a woman walk straight across the village plaza alongside the men's house. The occasional exceptions were elderly women in the most senior age group or my colleague and myself attempting to avoid the fierce dogs which lie near the houses! Asked why she took the long way around the circumference, in front of the houses, a young woman replied that although she, too, feared the dogs, she felt "shame" to cross the plaza. Certainly women circumvented the men's house.

By the same token, men, who freely roamed the plaza, were not often seen in the area behind the houses where the women puttered and cooked and children played. Men would be shamed, and become the brunt of jokes, if seen too frequently in the domestic areas. This is especially true of young bachelors.

Little girls, when not helping their mothers in the gardens, stay around the houses, caring for, playing with, and teasing their younger siblings. The little boys, free of responsibilities, range much farther afield, playing in an area beyond the back of the houses. Clearly, the domestic houses and gardens are chiefly the women's domain, while the central plaza or core of the village, as well as the forest and its farthest reaches, are mainly the men's domain.

In addition to gender, temporal space markers are also in effect. For example, girls and especially boys play boisterously in the river, but rarely at the same time. Men and women bathe at different times, although occasionally a nuclear family or an elderly couple may bathe together.

At night, young boys of the "painted" age-grade, who have been through an initiation rite (between 8–12 years of age), take their hammocks and sleep in the men's house, although this custom is presently in a state of flux. Older teens, i.e., young bachelors of the "sleep new" age-grade, officially sleep there, although it is expected they will slip off to spend some portion of the night with a prospective wife. Fathers of newborns (especially a first child) are also required to sleep in the men's house. So, by day the men's house is chiefly, but not strictly, the domain of the older men and by night, of the younger men and boys.

Spatial map as social map

The above general description of the village, as well as spatial boundaries in relation to gender and time, leads to a further analysis of the concentric spatial divisions as these are regulated between everyday, secular activities versus ceremonial activities. Fisher argues that the main goal of most Kayapó activity is the control of all unbridled growth, or "nature." He, therefore, recasts "the concentric model as one of activity rather than a structure" (1991:314). He shows that part of the dynamics of social relationships is to control the physical by transforming it into the social. Of Kayapó ritual activity he states,

> What is crucial to understand, and becomes of prime importance when analyzing Xikrin-Kayapó ceremonials, is that the Xikrin-Kayapó regard "culture" as intervening directly in relationships. It is knowledge pressed into service for control of the contamination inherent in all growth and relations between living things that make society possible. (1991:314)

By looking at Kayapó use of space through the lens of a "transformative" model rather than a more static, structural model we are in a better position to appreciate the dynamics of Kayapó interaction with their social space, especially as this relates to teaching and learning events. Such interaction is expressed in productive and ritual activity, where specific kin relationships and special cultural knowledge combine to control and socialize the natural. The manner in which this control is operationalized has a direct bearing upon the ends to which teaching and learning are oriented in Kayapó society (see figures 4 and 5).

In the stylized diagram of the "everyday" use of space in the village and surrounding area (figure 4), we note that the squares representing the houses are surrounded by the front and back living spaces which translate to the equivalent of front and back "yards." These are the eating (front) and cooking (back) areas, where family groups gather privately, even though in public view.

Spatial map as social map

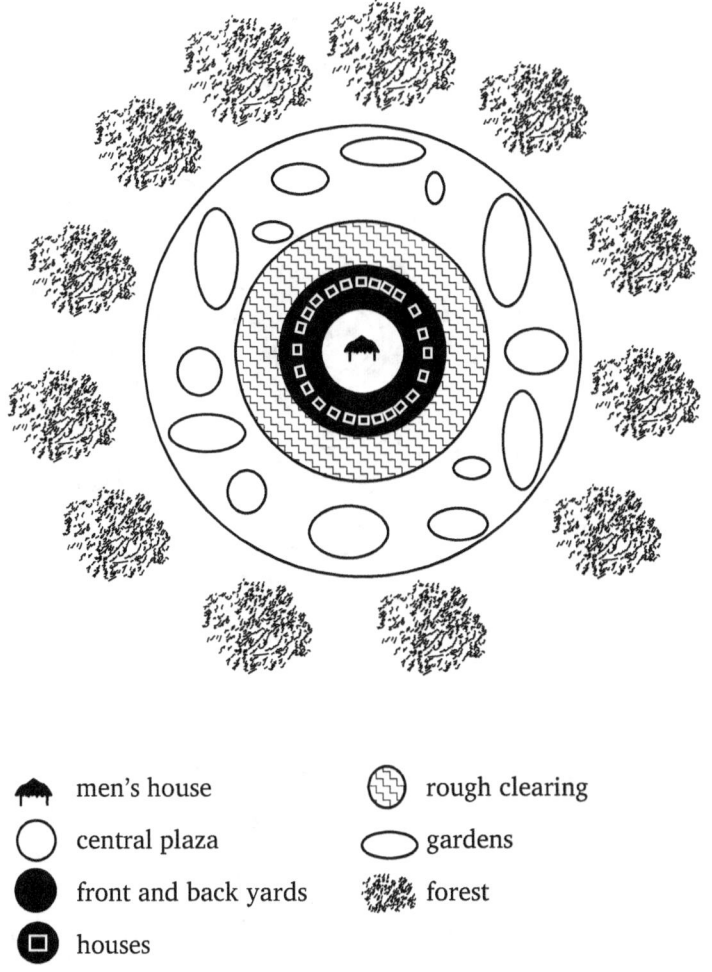

🏠	men's house	🌀	rough clearing
○	central plaza	⬭	gardens
●	front and back yards	🌳	forest
▣	houses		

Figure 4. "Everyday" spatial orientation of Kubēkàkre village

 The center patio surrounding the men's house is shown as clear space, but in fact it is often overgrown with weeds when ceremonies are not in progress. Except for men going to the central men's house and children playing near the house entrances, few people roam the plaza. The rough clearing area surrounding the back yard, flows into the garden area, which in turn is surrounded by the rainforest. The sense one has of the everyday use of space is that it is oriented towards household activities and is private rather than communal.

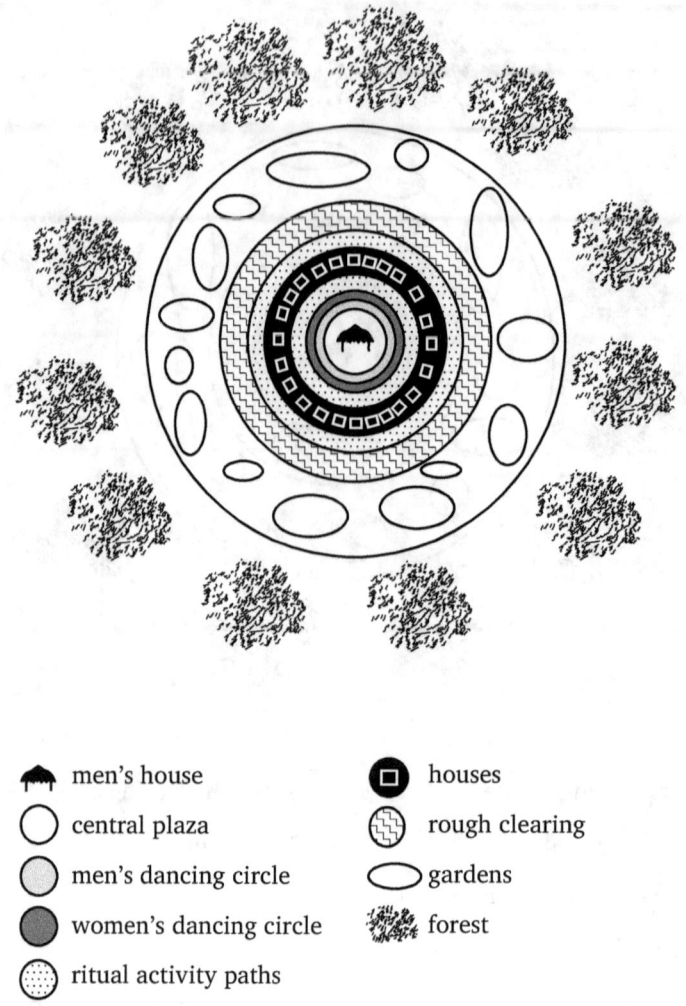

- men's house
- central plaza
- men's dancing circle
- women's dancing circle
- ritual activity paths
- houses
- rough clearing
- gardens
- forest

Figure 5. Ritual spatial orientation of Kubēkàkre village

In the stylized diagram of the use of space during ceremonies (figure 5), the plaza is etched with the men's dancing circle (1) surrounding the men's house, and the women's dancing circle (2) in front of the houses just beyond the eating area. In addition, the two circles immediately in front of and behind the houses are shown as paths of ritual activity because many public activities occur in this space only during ceremonies. What is otherwise private space assumes a more public nature during ceremonies, since some dances follow the inner circle relatively near to household entrances, especially those dances in which people from each house join as the dancers pass by. In addition, during the *Kôkô* ceremony, costumed young men saunter around the inner circular path of ritual activity, with a freedom they would not normally have. Further, when ceremonial sponsors distribute food at the climax of a ceremony, some of the distribution takes place in that area in front of the sponsor's house; and big, stone ovens are built there, where tortoises are killed, steamed, and distributed publicly. Some dance activities begin from the outer circular path of ritual activity behind the houses, and occasionally food is left in this area in a formalized transaction between a boy and someone from his "grandfather set" in exchange for the teaching services of the senior man who will instruct his junior. Although women often meet behind one or another's house to paint each other, many more congregate in this back area to paint each other's bodies during the "women's painting" ceremony. In other words, these two areas are used by more people, in a more public way, during ritual events. The rough clearing, gardens, and forest surrounding the village are areas used in certain phases of a ceremony for various activities pertaining to the ritual. A more detailed description of each spatial division as it relates to both everyday and ritual activities follows.

Village

In the village of Kubẽkàkre, twenty-four large houses, some of mud and wattle, others of poles, all with roofs of thatch, form the village circle, and spoke-like paths can be seen crossing the center plaza. Centered in the plaza is the men's house.

According to the Kayapó, the ideal village is very large, with many people, many festivals, and plenty of food. It should have two men's houses, one for each of the men's societies, and all of the houses should be located in their correct ceremonial position (see chapter 5). The older people refer nostalgically to the last of these truly large villages, Pykatoti, which was occupied from about 1870 to 1935 with an estimated population of between 3,700 to 5,400. By comparison, the largest Kayapó village today is Gorotire with a population of around 750. As one elderly man told me, in Pykatoti they really followed the customs correctly, implying that this does not happen now.

During ceremonially-related excursions through the forest, the Kayapó may refer to their village in festival as, *krĩ mex* 'beautiful village', whereas at other times it is simply "the village." A spatial analysis of a traditional village reveals the central plaza including the men's house as primarily a male domain and the surrounding ring of domestic houses as primarily a female domain, yet these categories are fluid as will be illustrated.

In ceremonies, the plaza between the centrally-located men's house and the houses is transformed from private wedge-shaped spaces pertaining to individual houses as domestic units, into a public "stage" invisibly etched with ritual markers which focus attention upon the house(s) as ritual entities. The circles in front of and behind the houses become visible when activated by the dancing. Other specific locations on the plaza become manifest as groups emerge performing a particular ceremonial role. The locations are specific to the role. Often these groupings are in a line with the "house standing place" which has the right to perform that feature of the ceremony. On the eve of a ceremony's climax, the entire village camps out roughly half-way between the houses and the men's house, each household group in front of its own dwelling place, and the plaza thus becomes the undifferentiated space for the whole population. The center, during ceremonies, is more frequently referred to as "village center."

The men's house is the central location where men and boys of every age group meet to receive food from the festival sponsors as payment for their participation. Dogs are routinely kicked and pushed away or have large objects hurled at them. Even in my role as photographer, frequently at the request of the people, I, as a female, was not invited into the men's house during some ceremonies. Yet, in the women's version of the "people's painting" ceremony, the women take over the men's house at dawn and late afternoon, to sing the songs pertaining to this festival. They will also dance with headdresses in the same circular pattern, although nearer the houses than the men's dance in a parallel ceremony.

The men's house, normally occupied by male elders when ceremonies are not in progress, is partitioned off in ritual, not by material divisions, but by the seating patterns of the men during a ceremony. In the one ceremony the women sing their morning and evening sing-songs seated in the men's house in five concentric circles, with the youngest participating age group in the center, surrounded by the puberty age girls, the "mothers of one child," the "mothers of many children," and the elder women on the outside (Verswijver 1982:46). In the men's version of the same ceremony, their groupings accompany the men's society divisions in part, but include the younger men who do not yet belong to any society. These young bachelors of the bachelor age-grade are in the center, and the oldest men of the elders' age-grade are seated on the outer rims of the men's house, with the middle age groups assuming gradient positions in accordance with their age and society. The people's perception is of an eastern men's house and a western men's house as it should be ideally even though it is under one roof.

Naming ceremonies are occasions when ceremonial partnerships are activated, and certain knowledge, rights to knowledge, and ceremonial privileges are passed down between the older partner to the neophyte. The men's house and the area immediately surrounding it is one of the main areas where ceremonial partners, both male and female, enact their ceremonial relationship.

In the everyday setting, by contrast, the men's house is occupied by a group of male elders and their canine companions, and even I was frequently allowed to step inside to observe the men weaving or just to sit and learn something. Young men and boys would mingle with the elders, especially when the latter were weaving, so that the space of the men's house was appropriated for informal occasions of teaching and learning between elders and their juniors. Even during ceremonies after sundown, when the last dance or song ended, the men's house would revert once again into the sleeping place for the young boys and men who normally slept there.

House

The word *ũrũkwuã* 'home' or 'residence' refers more to the totality of relationships incorporated in the residence than to the structure itself. The actual materials and structure of a house vary from village to village. In Kubẽkàkre, houses are rectangular and often constructed of mud and wattle and/or sticks, with thatching of palm fibre on the roof only in imitation of the houses of rural Brazilian settlers. The dwellings are still spacious enough to shelter a large extended matri-uxorilocal family comprised of several nuclear families.[7] The everyday aspect of the house may also be denoted by the term "oven place," referring to the actual hearths which are shared by domestic work-groups comprised of a mother and her daughters and the husband/father. This reflects the economic role and nature of the nuclear and extended families which occupy the house. Domestic relationships are in focus as well as the everyday, common knowledge which is transmitted through these relationships.

In the house in which I slept, there were several "hearth groups." The elderly matriarch and her husband had their pole bed in a walled off section, to the left of the entrance. Two of their orphaned granddaughters also had hammocks in that general section. In the daytime, however, the matriarch had a hammock slung by the entrance, and her husband would

---

[7]In Gorotire village, the prevailing pattern now seems to be separate (cement) houses for individual nuclear families (T. Turner 1987b:95).

spend hours at a time standing in the door-way weaving, or he might go into the room to rest.

One "daughter," a captive since infancy from the Kreen-Akrôre people, slept with her 4-year-old son, across from the matriarch's day hammock. She was an unwed, single mother. Her daughter, around 7 or 8, slept in a hammock beside her.

Next to them was another of the matriarch's daughters, an unwed, single mother, surrounded by her four children and her recently-married daughter, (the matriarch's granddaughter). These two single daughters and their children occupied about half the space in the house. The other half was occupied by a married daughter, her husband, and nine children, including her married daughter, the on-again, off-again husband, and their baby. They fit Ruth and me into the section of the unwed mothers since they have no category for "maiden aunt."

A strip of plaza in front of the houses is an area in which to socialize. In the evenings, these various families would sit as individualized hearth groups in front of the house, "eating their bit." The older siblings cared for the younger ones and often ran between groups carrying little tidbits of information or food from one group to the other. All around the village little groups would be sitting in front of the houses. It was the time and place to relax, to be public, to be seen by the others, to be accounted for. So eating, sleeping, weaving, and other routine, daily activities take place in and around the houses.

Although anthropologists tend to portray the houses in Gê societies as "just" domestic space, or "just" the women's domain (cf. Maybury-Lewis and Almagor 1989:101), humble houses assume their full status during ceremonies when members of each household enact ceremonial roles pertaining to, and often emanating from, particular households.

As a ceremonial entity, the household is a unit which may actually be comprised of several houses usually, but not necessarily, adjacent. The "good names" and ceremonial rights identified with these households are passed from people in the grandparent category to those in the grandchild category. The ceremonial unit is described by the term *kikrê djam djà* 'house standing place' which refers to a location on the village perimeter in reference to the particular name-giving ceremonies and ceremonial roles identified with the household matriarch. The term *abatànhdjà* 'growing-up place' refers to an individual's identification, both with the house as the place of his physical propagation and with the household as ceremonial location (see chapter 5). It is the place with which a Kayapó individual identifies himself or herself in terms of naming and ritual rights, and to which a man must return to pass on his rights to his sister's son.

On the abstract level, these "house standing places" seem to be consistent over space and time in each village. When a new village is being built, spaces are left for prospective occupants according to a pre-determined ritual order. When members of a particular household die out, their ceremonial rights may be taken on by others, but their household space and the last surviving members are remembered and spoken of, and attempts are made to trace some surviving grandchild to carry on rights which would have been passed to him had the people survived.

During the *Kôkô* ceremony described in chapter 5, the people frequently mentioned that the anteater dancers were not initiating their dance or finishing it in the "real anteater household," because that household had all died out. Instead, they were using the spatially adjacent household. But, they would emphasize, the rights to the anteater role did not really belong to the people of that household; it is just that the real owners had died out. No literal, concrete space is reserved for such a house as happens in the villages of the culturally-related Bôrôro (Crocker 1979:260), but conceptually the space seems to exist on the abstract level. One of the songleaders, Kutê'ê, said,

> There are no longer any grandmothers at the anteater's sitting place [household with right to anteater role]. Grandmother Nikotymre and they aren't living any more. There aren't any of the anteater rights' people left. They're all gone. They're really gone, and I look in vain for them. And so, after their deaths, others in their place, sit with the anteater masks—those in the house nearest to the missing ones.

In this case, one of the senior women attempted to claim the role of anteater for her grandson on the basis that her father had had the right in his life and would have, had he lived, transmitted it to her grandson.

Following the climax of the *Kôkô* ceremony our house was symbolically marked with a long, upright pole dug into the ground near the front entrance. This pole had been used in the climax of the ceremony to brandish a large body mask symbolizing an anteater. Our house had the ceremonial right to that pole following the climax of the *Kôkô* festival, because of the ceremonial rights of the matriarch owner which also meant the house occupied a specific location in the order of the houses on the village circle.

We see then, that the houses forming the perimeter of the village, while occupying one space, have several different roles and referents. Some terms refer to their everyday role while others refer to their omnipresent ceremonial role. In conversation, the terms may be used interchangeably depending upon what aspect the speaker wishes to emphasize (the ceremonial or the common), whether or not a festival is in progress.

Backyard

The area behind a house is considered private space where a woman has her own sheltered cooking area, where people go away from the houses to urinate and defecate, where lovers may sneak off together, and where women meet with members of their social group or "society" to paint one another and gossip. In short, it is a space where people do their own thing away from the watchful glare of potentially the whole village.

But the backyard may also be transformed by ceremonial activities. It is here that some phases of ceremonies first become public, such as the initial dance of the anteater costume in the *Kôkô* ceremony or the first appearance of the monkey costumes. In addition, the backyard is a place where food may be placed by prior arrangement for a grandfather by his grandson's mother in anticipation of a formalized transfer of particular knowledge. So even the ignominious backyard plays a role both in the everyday life and the ceremonial life of the Kayapó.

Rough clearing

The backyard fades into a large, partially cleared area surrounding the village, referred to as the *atykmã* 'rough clearing'.[8] This area is a transitional zone between the village and the gardens. Occasionally, a small garden may be planted in the rough clearing by an elderly couple who can no longer make the trip to a more distant location.

In the village of Kubẽkàkre the river banks constituted part of the rough clearing. Little boys thoroughly explore this area on a daily basis, discovering themselves, each other, and a part of the natural world. It is significant, perhaps, that these boys, who are in a transitional phase in terms of socialization processes, have the almost exclusive use of this transitional zone as their playground. The rough clearing, for the boys, is the site where peer learning is in focus. They go after small birds with bows and arrows or slings and may cook and eat their own catch there; they torment unfortunate dogs on their way to or from the river for a drink—all this away from the watchful eye of the adults. Yet parents seem attuned to what may be transpiring there, and if play becomes too out-of-hand there will be angry remonstrations when the sons come home for food. These things (and more) constitute the everyday use of the rough clearing.

But this locale, too, has a role to play in relation to ceremonies. Since it is a transitional zone, both in the everyday setting and the ceremonial setting, it seems appropriate that the rough clearing should be the place used

---

[8]This is often translated as the black or the dead zone (*tyk* 'black/dead') although *atykmã* is not the same word as *tyk*.

for the preparation stage of initiation rites and for the making of ceremonial paraphernalia prior to its use in the actual ceremony. In two specific ceremonies, *Bemp* and *Tàkàk,* the rough clearing becomes the solemn site for the male initiates to sit together as they are adorned with ceremonial goods and instructed by their ritual partners. A shelter is made in the rough clearing for the ceremonial partners to sit together while the elder partner makes ritual objects such as large bracelets. The neophytes are encouraged to closely observe the making of the bracelets so that they "in their turn" can make the items at a future time when they themselves will be elder partners.

Occasionally, festival dances are performed in the rough clearing. In many ceremonies, the men first dance in a circle in the forest, then repeat this between the forest and the village in the rough clearing, before giving the climactic performance encircling the village plaza.

Some anthropologists may see this as contiguous circles linking nature to culture through the performance of ritual, but it might also be a form of rehearsal before the dancers appear "in their beauty" before the whole village. In any case, each common area is momentarily transformed through ritualized activity and, some would say, socialized by means of the performance. The Kayapó themselves say they do what they do because that is what the ancestors did!

Spatially, then, the rough clearing is regarded as an area of transition in each aspect of Kayapó life: ceremony and everyday. If the Kayapó speak of the *atykmã* while a ceremony is in progress, one set of images is conjured up, and ceremonial relationships, especially that of ceremonial partners, are in focus. If they speak of the *atykmã* in relation to the young boys and their playing, another picture prevails where peer learning and the building of the concept of brotherhood beyond the boundaries of consanguineous relationships are in focus.

Garden

Beyond the rough clearing, the denser rainforest surrounding the village is interrupted with large, circular plantations or gardens *(pur)*. The men do the initial clearing; in fact, the gardens are said to be placed by the men for the women. These are domestic gardens belonging to women who are mothers. Married couples are said by some to be joint owners of a garden while others say the women are the owners.

The gardens are often in line, in a general way, with the female owner's house, but there is no perceived pattern. "People hunt or make gardens any place."

The gardens, as part of what is primarily a female domain, are a place of learning for young girls. Here they are shown how to dig sweet potatoes and carry heavy loads in baskets supported by a tumpline. They are expected to run errands for the senior women, to generally participate in the provision of food for their family, and to meet the reciprocal obligations incurred on a daily basis. They learn how to build earth ovens and stone ovens in which to roast sweet potatoes and other garden produce.

The gardens are also the place where couples rendezvous to have sex, not at night, but during the day.

Kayapó leaders have several gardens in which members of their society work periodically on a communal basis. The young bachelors of the older teens' age-set, *norny*, make these gardens for the leaders since as bachelors they do not yet have their own garden. In this way the young men learn clearing skills from older men, not primarily in the family gardens, but with their peers in the communal garden, under their leader. More importantly, they are building the social skills which enhance male solidarity and a communal outlook.

Produce from these communal gardens, cultivated by female society members, is used as currency by the leaders to enhance and maintain their leadership by showing generosity. When the produce is ripe, the chief's wife takes all the wives of her husband's workers to collect the produce which is then shared out among the workers.

The gardens are fundamental to the success of any ceremony, so they assume a role beyond that of sustaining a household and maintaining that household's reciprocal obligations. During a ceremony, the produce of many gardens will be shared communally, and the gardens of the families which sponsor a festival must be larger than usual. Reciprocity during ritual is played out on a grand scale. Extra gardens may be planted by a couple in anticipation of sustaining a naming ceremony for their child. Such gardens will be especially large, "as big as a chief's gardens." On some occasions, leaders may supplement needy families or help with supplies in naming ceremonies if the festival sponsors run short. In these ways, the gardens also have both a ceremonial and an everyday aspect.

Rainforest

The gardens are like sentinel outposts in the rainforest—the outer range which separates the village from the endless expanse of rainforest. Yet the dense rainforest is familiar territory to the Kayapó, where both men and women venture along barely visible (to my eye), yet well-known paths. Men go to hunt wild animals, collect medicinal supplies, and discover honey, while women collect fruits in season, gather wild banana leaves for steam cooking in the earth ovens, collect medicinal herbs, and bark and fruit for their painting, and perhaps also to discover the special treat of honey. Frequently, families camp out on these "everyday" pursuits for several days, even weeks. Such uses of the rain forest may be described as pertaining to routine, secular life, and constitute a time of valuable learning for the children.

The forest also figures prominently in ceremonial life, being used as a site for festival preparations or for initial performances of a dance or songs before the final performance in the village center. In the *Kôkô* naming ceremony, a forest clearing was the site of a shelter for the group whose responsibility it was to construct the two anteater costumes, and another shelter was constructed for the group which would participate as two types of monkeys.

In the "painted men" song festival the men gather together in the forest in the early afternoon. In a circular clearing covered with palm leaves, the men sit and paint each other with the red paste of crushed arnatto seeds and sing. This is a time for remembering and rehearsing old songs as well as for teaching these and new songs to the younger men. Later, from sundown until late evening, the men will lustily perform the songs in the men's house for all the villagers to hear.

In the women's version of the same ceremony, "painted women," I joined the women as they met in a forest location, close to the gardens. They cleared a dancing circle, beautified themselves (and me) with arnatto across the eyes and on the face, and danced and sang together for about half an hour. Then they made a mad rush for their canoes, paddling back to the village in order to perform, before sundown, individual songs to honor the festival sponsors in exchange for some food. Later, they gathered in the men's house to sing the songs rehearsed in the forest clearing for all the village to appreciate.

The forest is also a place for trekking. Families trek together, hunting and gathering, for several weeks at a time. This trek, *me y kôt* 'the people's trekking', is done at the discretion of individual families, usually with an objective in mind such as obtaining some seasonal fruit or honey. This is a period when children are shown basic skills necessary to survival in this environment.

In contrast with private family treks, common in nonceremony times, the culmination of a festival is marked by the majority of the village inhabitants camping out in the forest on a communal trek, *õtõmor*. For up to a month they search for game and the large land tortoises which are necessary for the climax of the festival.

On these occasions, they walk for several hours, then build an encampment from which they disperse to hunt and gather. Part of the purpose is the collection of large land tortoises *(Goechelene denticulata),* which are used as payment to all who perform their ritual duties in the climax of a festival. There is no time limit set for a ceremonially-related trek, since its duration depends upon the festival sponsor's judgment that the people have collected a sufficient number of tortoises to generously meet his ritual obligations.

On these communal treks, children of both sexes are exposed to the storytelling of a variety of elders which normally they are unable to hear in the village. (The layout and seating arrangement of the men's house is only a few yards from the temporary shelters of the group, so that spatial boundaries and the accompanying restrictions so effective in the village, are not operative on trek.) It is a time of generalized learning of traditional knowledge.

Like all other Kayapó space, the forest, too, hosts both everyday activities and ceremonial events, the individual pursuits and the communal endeavors.

Summary

The Kayapó male and female appear to have both a ceremonial and an everyday use of all the social space available to them. Male and female activity is regulated within this space by considerations of gender and time, but not confined exclusively to one area in opposition to another; neither can one area really be considered permanently more or less socialized than another.

In some cases different terms are used to denote a ceremonial or everyday reference to the same social space, as in the case of a house's location on the village circle relative to ceremonies known as "house standing place" and simply "oven place" as its domestic reference. In other cases, the same term is used but in relation to entirely different functions for the same space, as in the contrasting uses of the term for "rough clearing."

Space, then, is transformed by the action of the people through ritualized activity, and the behavior of the people is transformed by the significance attributed to space.

How the space is used, by whom, on what occasion, is relevant to patterns of knowledge transmission, and is an aid to understanding key teacher/learner interactions to be discussed more fully in the following chapters. Yet it is not the space itself which gives significance to

Summary

transactions between individuals, neither is it the spatial location which attributes (or withholds) a degree of socialization from an individual. All of space has the potential, depending upon the occasion, of being used for either ritually-oriented events or everyday events related to the daily routine, and people are not restricted by their gender to the exclusive use of only certain space, except as location may articulate with specific activities at a particular time. The use of space is summarized in table 1.

Table 1. Educational settings in a Kayapó village

Mode	Everyday	Ritual
Village	Loose spatial boundaries	Rigid spatial boundaries
Residence	Domestic house	Ritual household
Backyard	Work area	Transactional area
Rough clearing	Play area (mainly boys)	Transformational area
Garden	Family-oriented	Community oriented (for ritual sponsors)
Rainforest	Individual exploitation	Group exploitation

More significantly, a particular type of knowledge is conveyed through certain relationships when activities are oriented to the common daily routine and goals, so that what transpires in any spatial location when everyday activities are in focus is related less to the location than to the relationships which are in operation when everyday goals are primary. When ritual events are in focus, the same social space is transformed by these events, and the relationships which are in ascendance during ritual emphasize learning transactions which are contrastive, both in quality and purpose, to those which occur in the everyday setting.

In the next chapters, we will look at learning relationships as these operate (1) when people's activity is directed primarily towards everyday pursuits, (2) when they are directed towards ritual pursuits, and (3) when they bridge these settings—the everyday and the ritual.

3
Kayapó Ways of Knowing

One way to understand the basic dynamics of a Kayapó village is to see the transforming effect of ritual action upon social space. There is no sacred sanctuary into which the Kayapó person steps, to neatly divide his world into sacred and secular. Any given ritual transforms the existing everyday world into a ritual world. Within the everyday sphere, domestic relationships are in focus, but during ceremonies, another set of relationships takes precedence.

By focussing upon some typical relationships in both the everyday and the ceremonial (ritual) settings we note that educational interaction is modified by other social or ideological factors which need prior consideration. The social institutions which have some bearing upon the relationships are age sets and societies or moieties. Among the ideological factors which influence knowledge transmission channels are binary oppositions, including male/female, true kin/fictional kin, and official/unofficial (in relationship to ego) channels of knowledge transmission. Another ideological factor is Kayapó categorization of knowledge.

This chapter will touch on Kayapó ideas about knowledge and the various factors, both institutional and ideological, which influence the distribution of knowledge in order to lay a foundation for a discussion of education in the everyday and ritual settings.

Two main categories and several subcategories of knowledge or *mar* 'to hear' are acknowledged by the Kayapó.

Learning styles are both active and passive. The principal methods of learning are observation, imitation, and practice when a skill is involved, and simply hearing and listening when oral knowledge is recounted. Oral knowledge, *kukràdjà* 'customs', includes medicinal chants, songs, traditional stories, and myth/history. The transmission of more specialized knowledge such as cures for dangerous, life-threatening maladies, usually involves an economic transaction since the learner must be "introduced to the animal" considered responsible for the illness, an event fraught with possible danger. Learning occurs through social experience, social conflict, and play.

Categories of Kayapó knowledge

There are two general categories of knowledge for the Kayapó: (1) information that *me kunĩ kute omũnh* 'everybody sees' or *me kunĩ kute mar* 'everyone hears', where both verbs can be glossed as 'knowing' or 'understanding'; and (2) information that only specialists know: *me kute mỳjja mar* 'those who know something'.

What everybody knows

In the category of what everybody knows, i.e., common or general knowledge, are skills and information related to everyday living. For women it is gardening, collecting, food preparation, natural medicines, spinning, and body-painting. For men it is house-building; hunting skills; gardening; common medicinal remedies for headaches, stomach aches, stingray, diarrhea; "doctoring" dogs in preparation for hunting; and the list, in both cases, could go on.

These skills are passed along in the domestic realm of houses and associated areas such as the gardens and anywhere where household members may venture together, for example, fishing as a family or collecting in the forest. This everyday knowledge is channeled through key relationships operating primarily in nonceremonial contexts (cf. chapter 4). Such knowledge concerns the physical well-being and survival of a child. Appropriately, this knowledge is transmitted to a child by people associated with the literal formation and maintenance of the child's physical being: the child's parents and the parent's parallel cousins, categorized as the child's parents according to the Kayapó kinship system (see chapters 4 and 5).

Gifted artisans

Skills are considered common knowledge, yet certain people become renowned for their outstanding ability to perform a particular skill. These people are considered gifted artisans by the community.

Artisan skills include men's weaving and making of feather headdresses, and women's elaborate painting of their children's bodies in which people especially talented are spoken of as "having a good hand."

Men do their handiwork in the men's house where young, unmarried males are free to observe. The young man will ask his grandfather or perhaps even an older ceremonial partner to show him how to weave. If men do not learn this skill before they are married, it is said they will never learn it.

Women frequently beautify their young children in or around the houses. As mothers paint the elaborate, geometrical designs upon their child's body, they are closely observed by their young female offspring, who know they too will paint their own children one day. This skill is passed from mother to daughter without formal instruction. The children observe, then experiment.

"Those who know something"

In the category of more specialized knowledge, there are three main subcategories: "those who know a specialty," "those who know the (Kayapó) customs or ways," and "those who know outsiders' (nonindigenous) customs or ways."

Those who know a specialty. The same twenty to twenty-four Kubẽkàkre elders are generally recognized in every household, and often in other villages, as being able to save people from potentially fatal wounds or diseases such as snakebite. Their fame is enhanced by the cures they perform or the results they achieve mainly through the use of plants, but also through the use of insect and animal parts, bird feathers, and other things known for attributes the specialists desire to replicate. They are known by their specialty as "snake knower" or "fish knower," etc. In addition, there are specialists in fertility, both of humans and of gardens, and a few select people are "spirit knowers." Several people in Kubẽkàkre claimed to be a *wajanga* 'shaman' but the elders seemed to be in agreement that there were no longer any real shamans left.

This entire body of specialized knowledge is considered critical to survival. It is the privilege of the elders, both male and female, to practice.

They, in turn, pass it along to certain people, often in exchange for some payment. It includes among other things the recognition and ministration of medicinal plants with the accompanying songs and food prohibitions. The specialist is considered to have extra power if he or she was "introduced to the animal" at the time of learning the medicine. Whatever transpires when a person is "presented" to the animal is considered secret, but the effect is to achieve the cooperation of nature so that cures may be effected without endangering the curer. In my attempts to understand the advantages of being "presented" to the animal, I was told, "Fish specialists talk to fish, spirit specialists talk to spirits if they've been introduced. If not, they just know the medicines."

Being introduced consists of handling the animal. One man's father taught him the medicines, "but," he says, "I only know the medicine, I didn't handle the animal." This latter, according to him, means "seeing the animal face to face, touching it, listening to what it says. Animals speak in Kayapó face to face, like we're talking now."

Another person explained that learning these medicines as a young teen implies being introduced to the animal, but adult learners will not be introduced. Someone else stated that if an adult is introduced he must make a big payment to the specialist. The advantage of being introduced seems to be that the animal will know the person by name and become his ally in hunting, as well as his protector, by informing the other animals about him. This protection extends over the eating of game as well. Being introduced also seems to signify a thorough, complete knowledge of the medicine which counteracts sickness caused, however indirectly, by a certain animal or fish; the "diploma" at the end of a course.

It is the responsibility of the male grandchildren of these specialists to seek and acquire the knowledge possessed by people within the grandparent category of kin. Although both male and female grandchildren are exposed to basically the same knowledge, learning in this manner is validated by society mainly for the male children. Specialists may also transmit their knowledge to their wives, their sons-in-law, and their ceremonial partners.

Those who keep the customs. A second category of specialists is "those who know and keep the customs." Customs and tradition, in essence, the Kayapó way of life, include correct speech, a knowledge of naming customs, an understanding of the ceremonial life, including ceremonial rights, songs, dances, genealogies, traditional oral knowledge, and, in the case of the elders, being a good warrior. Some of this knowledge falls more within the sphere of ritual, yet a significant part of it is passed along through relationships in the household and between households, primarily from the grandparent category to the grandchildren category.

A common way for this learning to take place is when the grandson goes to the grandparent, lying with this person in his or her hammock, and listening to the stories. This often occurs in the context of an event—a ceremony or a pig hunt—so that the related knowledge is made relevant by the situation of an event in progress.

Those who know outsider's ways. A third category of Kayapó specialists refers to the people who know outsider's ways, meaning especially those of the dominant society. This is a relatively new category which has developed in the measure that outside material goods are valued and coveted. Those perceived as leaders in the struggle for demarcation of Kayapó land, who bring many outside goods in for general distribution, who understand money, are referred to as the new leaders, but not esteemed by the elders in the same measure as the traditional leaders.

Young unmarried men and newly-married men are the most avid associates of these new leaders, learning all the city lore they can from them. Although the elders agree that the old chief, Bepgogoti, is the one whose advice they follow regarding their traditions and customs, they also agree that Bepgogoti's son Bepkũm, is the one of all the new leaders who best knows the ways of the outsiders.

The above list is not, of course, a compendium of Kayapó knowledge but it does reveal Kayapó ideas about the organization of knowledge as well as a general idea of its content.

How the Kayapó learn

The Kayapó also have ideas concerning how the young learn, in what circumstances, and at what biological stage of life. Much of the knowledge accumulated by a child may be recognized by the Kayapó as incidental learning, if it is noted at all, because the important thing from their perspective is the particular channel of transmission through which knowledge is legitimized.

Learning which may take place as a result of social experience and conflict, by observation, or in play,[9] certainly does occur, but if the Kayapó acknowledge it at all, such learning would be taken for granted, much as we do in our society. Nevertheless, there are acknowledged ways of

---

[9]Dobbert and Cooke (1987:106–113), discuss these ways of learning as "learning mechanisms."

knowing, and learning takes place in a variety of contexts and situations in a socially integrated way.

Rather than seeing learning as a cognitive act in and of itself, the focus here is to describe how Kayapó learning is integrated with social experience. Learning and knowing, "take place in a social world, dialectically constituted in social practices that are in the process of reproduction, transformation and change" (Lave and Wenger 1991:123).

Learning through social experience by both children and adults occurs within the household, in visits to other households, and through the broader social networks in communal activity. For the girls, this will be in garden work. For boys, this social experience is gained in the men's house and in the home of someone outside of his personal kin network, that is, his "substitute father." For a newly-married man, this experience is further augmented by his move into the domestic realm of his wife and her family. In addition, social experience on the communal level is obtained by each gender through membership in a particular society or moiety, which functions as a political or economic group, and the cooperative work achieved by these groups.

The peer associations of young boys provide occasions for learning to handle social conflict because among their peers they are away from the protective environment of their own relatives. Since girls will always be together in their mother's household, they must, over the years, learn to handle their differences peaceably. Potential conflict between in-laws is controlled through rules of avoidance and deference on the part of a junior in-law towards the senior, but the appropriate behavior must be learned.

Play is a means whereby Kayapó children unselfconsciously reinforce social behavior learned by observation from adults. Play is also a way children have to incorporate and become familiar with new information, marginal to traditional values.

Learning by observation is a method well recognized by members of Kayapó society. Their expression for cleverness in skill learning is "good eye," while "bad eye" or "no eye" signifies a poor or slow learner of things requiring observation. The word 'to see', is used also in the figurative sense 'to know, understand' as is the verb 'to hear'. In fact, the verb to teach is actually a gloss for the more literal 'to show', so that questions about teaching inevitably led to descriptions of what people learned by being shown something. This included a knowledge of honey, for one has to be good at spotting the bee hives by knowing where to look for them, what trees, what height, what shape the hive, and so forth. Medicinal plants are also shown to the learner, since this implies a recognition of the plant, its ecological niche, as well as its preparation and uses.

I was inspired to learn about some of the medicinal plants when I had the unfortunate experience of stepping on a river sting ray! I kept track of the remedies which various people used to treat my wound, then questioned one of the elders concerning them. But when I tried to learn by my methods, that is, by getting the names and descriptions written down, my teacher, Bepmotire, remonstrated: "A snake bites them...(do you understand the names of the medicine that I would tell you and you would understand? Do you know medicines that you would understand the names)?"

An emphatic "no" was implied, as he went on, in a disgruntled fashion, to do it my way. I saw it was no use, so asked him if he could bring me some of the plants (since I was disabled at that time, and unable to accompany him, which would be the normal method). His face fairly shone, as he leaped to his feet, promising to bring me some plants, so that I could see, and therefore, really learn. His enthusiasm knew no bounds. To be shown something, is synonymous with being taught something which is observable. Seeing it, is synonymous with learning it.

Learning by hearing is equally important, for there are certain things that may only be learned by the ear or in accompaniment with being shown something. Kayapó boys traditionally had their earlobes pierced, in order to "open their ears" to telling, in order for them to "have understanding." As a boy's understanding is expected to increase, so the hole in the earlobe is stretched, though this custom is falling into disuse since the young men wish their appearance to conform to that of their counterparts in the dominant society. The expression for not paying attention is to have "no ear-hole."

The social learning so important to the formation of the social aspect of the personhood of a child is associated with a different type of intelligence which requires the word to penetrate the head in an almost literal sense. Therefore, the intelligence which is related to the learning of the Kayapó customs, is signified by the expression "soft head," meaning that the knowledge can enter. A "hard head" is not the same as stubborn; it implies an under-socialized or non-socialized person. So, to the Kayapó, learning by seeing and hearing are important ways of knowing.

Factors affecting knowledge transmission

Several social practices and factors which affect the transmission of knowledge within Kayapó communities are: gender and its attributes, the status of knowledge, as well as of its carrier, the authenticity of sources, and age and its relationship to knowledge transmission.

Among the questions I was seeking to answer by my observations of learning and teaching were:

1. What teaching/learning relationships are operative in a particular setting?
2. Do relationships in one setting contrast with teaching/learning relationships in other settings?
3. Is knowledge gender-oriented?
4. Is teaching directive and intentional or is the novice simply expected to pick things up?

Observations revealed that the female relationships with children were the dominant influences in the daily routine, irrespective of the child's gender. In addition, people categorized as siblings to a child's parents, whether real relatives or not, are considered as "fictive" parents to the child, and influence the child in the everyday setting. These relationships of fictive kin, for example, "fictive mother," "fictive father," are operative for both male and female in the everyday realm.

These roles contrast with teaching/learning relationships in ritual activity. In the everyday setting, relationships of people classified as children's parents are in focus, while in the ritual setting, the grandparent set and some nonkin relationships are predominant. In the intermediate category, intermediary relationships, as one would expect, are special relationships to a child ego which serve as mediating links between the everyday and the ritual settings. One such relationship is created for children of both genders during their initiation at puberty, when one of the "fictive" parents symbolically replaces the real parent—a mother replacement for the girl and a father replacement for the boy. For the male, this relationship of "substitute father" is very important in both the ritual and everyday world. Another intermediary relationship which may function as a channel of knowledge transmission is that of ceremonial partner (see chapter 6).

Gender and the distribution of knowledge

Gender influences both the content and context of learning throughout the life cycle. Girls ideally receive major input from close kin of their mothers. But boys begin early to form broader social ties, first through experiential learning with their peers by playing in the transitional zone of the rough clearing, then later, as young bachelors, through involvement in male-dominated communal activities.

Theoretically, there is a significant difference between the knowledge available to males versus that available to females. But in practice, females do have access to most of the same knowledge base. Yet, they themselves do not acknowledge this, and certainly their credentials are not recognized by others until they become elders. Young women, in the opinion of both themselves and the men, "do not know anything" or "only know a little." This evaluation would not apply to areas of recognized feminine expertise, such as body painting, but certainly to specialist knowledge and ritual knowledge.

One male elder, when asked what women know, immediately replied, "women don't know anything!," then proceeded to list a traditional female skill: "women know how to spin cotton and men know how to twist fibre" referring to men's weaving. This same person stated that some women are good at spotting beehives for honey, but all men are good at it. I inadvertently caused some embarrassment to one woman while questioning her about her own genealogy as she prepared manioc flour in the communal oven house. Along came one of the men to admonish me: "You shouldn't ask her questions like that; she doesn't know. You should ask her father." I replied meekly that I was asking everyone the same questions, and that I would be asking her father also. In fact, this prevailing attitude concerning expertise was a constant problem to my research, since younger people and young married women would say they did not know anything. I eventually discovered that their store of knowledge was considerably greater if there were no older person around while they were talking to me!

Another factor affecting the distribution of knowledge between genders is the Kayapó idea of tame and fierce. Women are considered tame, and men, fierce. I was watching a man prepare the ingredients for a medicine to be applied to dogs in order for the dogs to be better hunters. The medicine consists of parts of insects, fish, and other flora and fauna considered to have the attributes of fierceness. He consented to my picture-taking, but would not allow me to get a close look at the ingredients or touch them, muttering that women, being tame, should not see the dog medicine (which makes dogs fierce) because it will make women go crazy. Only men, who are fierce, can see it and handle it. Before I was aware of the tame/fierce attributes applied to gender, I asked a man if women learn about dog medicines. He looked startled, then answered, "I don't know. A long time ago our ancestors told the women about dog medicine. Maybe my mother-in-law knows. Ask her." In fact, no woman admits to knowing anything about mixing dog medicine.

This same idea carries over into foods which may be eaten by men but not by women. The jaguar is fierce, so women, being tame, should not handle it or eat it. Even married men, who may affect their children by eating jaguar meat, must not do so. The meat may be eaten by the old men and by young, unmarried men.

Children of both sexes are exposed to the domestic environment with its predominantly female role models up to the age of about five years. Here, both sexes play together under the watchful supervision of their older siblings. Infant boys and girls are usually treated equally, although each will receive play things appropriate to its gender. A small carrying basket is made for the female toddler by her father or grandfather; she carries one or two sweet potatoes, as she sees her sisters and mother(s) doing. Tiny boys usually receive a small bow and arrow from their father or grandfather. In each case, specific gender-related roles are being reinforced by these basic symbols of the male versus female tasks, "foreshadowing what they will do as adults" as one grandfather commented.

When boys reach the age of around five years, they begin to gravitate away from their households to play with peers and older boys, while girls begin to become serious contributors to the female economic production unit in a variety of ways. At this stage, peer learning becomes a very significant factor in the learning environment of both sexes, but especially for the boys.

In general, children are expected to learn simply by observation and practical endeavor. Many skills are appropriate to one gender or the other, and children are strongly encouraged in roles appropriate to their gender. All see, all observe, but all do not learn everything. Little boys watch their mothers spinning cotton or body painting, as much as little girls do, but do not learn to do body painting whereas little girls do. Each proceeds to try the skill exhibited by the same sex role model, and so learns by doing. All learning by observation is reinforced by imitating socially appropriate role models.

Small children commonly model their behavior after their elders, and the Kayapó adults seize the opportunity to provide instructive verbal reinforcement. A child handing an object to an adult will frequently be instructed about his relationship to that person, what vocative term is appropriate, and what phrase is correct to accompany the gesture.

While I was learning the Kayapó language at a considerably slower rate than my three-year-old Kayapó "daughter," child of my sister Nhàkti, I suggested to Nhàkti that perhaps she could teach correct speech to both Inhôr and me at the same time. She laughed and immediately told me how to ask my child to fetch water for me. Both Inhôr and I were learning not only the correct speech and attitude towards one another, but role expectations as well. This teaching method was commonly applied in the socialization of the children and me as we struggled to learn the language.

A favorite teaching method of adults in this context is to put words into the learner's mouth. "Tell him such and such." The child parrots the phrase. A reply comes shooting back, and they are supplied with a response. Many conversations or good-natured arguments are carried out in this vicarious manner, so that children soon learn how to hold their own in any situation.

For the Kayapó, learning is an activity in which the environment and social context are as important as the information being absorbed. The context is more than merely occupational; rather, social roles and relationships form an integral part of the learning experience. Some knowledge is gender oriented, observable to all, yet not socially sanctioned for all. In addition, certain relationships serve as channels which make knowledge transmission official in a particular setting. The question of the validation of knowledge by society is another aspect of Kayapó ideology which must be considered.

The status of knowledge

Some knowledge within Kayapó society is imbued with a validity that gives it status and gives status to the possessor of that knowledge. There are two main ways in which knowledge and skill equate with prestige. One is in the domain of what "everybody knows," where those who excel in a particular area are recognized and respected for their skills. Secondly, and by far the most discussed among the Kayapó, specialist knowledge must be transmitted through socially validated relationships from "one who knows something" to a "layman." The status of some knowledge is derived from its bearer. Knowledge also derives status from its source.

Of nineteen respondents representative of the elders in households, seven were in agreement that the woman Ngrenhkômex was the best body painter, a patently female skill.

Although all men know how to build houses, without distinction, two in particular were noted for their ability to measure. All men know how to hunt, but seven of eighteen said the man Bep'ôrôti was the best hunter. This formal survey was borne out with spot questions to a much wider cross-section of people, young and old, as they dropped into our study house for a visit or literacy classes. These general results also agree with a quantitative study by Werner (1981a:360–373) which I used as a guideline (see appendix A). Those who excelled in a skill were recognized and admired by a wide consensus, seemingly without envy, and thus enjoyed a measure of prestige in accordance with their abilities.

Concerning ceremonial knowledge, the general consensus was that "the old ones" know all about ceremonies. Of those, the songleader Kutêê was recognized as possessing more knowledge in this realm, even more than the oldest chief. This was perhaps due to the fact that he was the object of three naming ceremonies in his childhood and, therefore, had acquired more knowledge and status and more "beautiful names" than had his peers. And since he was one of the two official songleaders, one would expect him to know more about the ceremonies. Except for him, others named as experts in this area were among the oldest in the village and included women.

The acknowledged specialists have acquired their knowledge through legitimized channels, such as one or more people from their set of grandparents and, as stated above, must transmit this knowledge to their grandchild.

Many times a legitimizing chain would be traced. One elder, commenting on another elder's knowledge of a particular song said, "If Bepmotire knows Ipreri's song he got it from Bepbakati who taught it to Bepbanhãti, who taught it to Bepmotire."

He lamented further, "If I had been old enough I would have heard (learned) it." The elders' idea of who is truly a leader (whether leading a group or not) is based upon whether he possesses knowledge of a form of ritualized speech called *bẽn*. The transmission of this knowledge is traceable:

> Katàmkrãme told his child Mekàr; Papre told Kretire. Mekàre was really a chief. Kretire was the other who just started to learn and he taught Mrykrãnre. They went around houses doing the *bẽn*.

The above list names "the old ones"—ancestral in quality. This was followed by a list of those who know the *bẽn* today, accompanied by the common disclaimer: "these days no one 'places' the *bẽn*," i.e., the ritual blessing does not have the power it once did.

The status of knowledge may be further defined by a linguistic feature which distinguishes the authority of the past from the authority of the present. Past events, legends, or Kayapó history are marked with the particle *we*, which says, in effect, "that's what the old ones say." This is not so much a disclaimer, "I wasn't there so I don't know," as an appeal to the authority of the elders. The source of the information is the elders or ancestors whose authority and veracity is being cited, not questioned.

In contrast, there is the authority of the present—of living eyewitnesses. "I saw it myself." The appeal of the eyewitness account allows the hearer to equate the information with the source and thus evaluate it.

The distinction between past reality versus present reality is a question of source acknowledgment linking the information and knowledge to an authority.

There are other legitimate channels which will be considered in more detail in later chapters, but these examples should serve to introduce the Kayapó idea of official versus unofficial knowledge.

Official and unofficial knowledge

The Kayapó have a concept which is central to an understanding of their ideas of knowledge transmission. The concept, expressed by the term *kajgo*, is used in a variety of ways with many possible glosses, but the underlying common denominator seems to be at least partly connected with whether or not some form of payment is expected, intended, or required in a particular situation.[10] Knowledge that is obtained by means of some form of reciprocal exchange seems to be regarded as more official than the same knowledge learned outside of a relationship where reciprocity is expected.[11] Knowledge, as object of some reciprocal transaction, is confirmed as commodity, or asset, ratified by the mutual fulfillment of a social obligation.

For example, someone is singing songs related to a particular festival when the festival is not being performed, i.e., just for pleasure, and they will say that they are "singing *kajgo*." In other words, if they were singing during the festival, they would be exchanging their song as commodity or property for some "payment" of meat or produce. Outside of this specific reciprocal transaction, the song is being sung *kajgo* because it is sung without the expectation of material return.

Headdresses made by the men for sale in the city, rather than for the ceremonies for which they are normally intended, are made *kajgo*. That is to say, the headdress is not made for the people of the household which

---

[10]Special acknowledgment to W. Fisher (personal communication) for this helpful insight.

[11]My use of the term RECIPROCITY refers primarily to the Kayapó use of the terms *o djuw mex* 'to look after well' and *pãnh* 'cost, payment, or price'. The term *o djuw mex* usually refers to agreed upon or expected transactions between people. Some relationships have this expectation of exchange as a basis for interaction. Exchanges may include tangible for tangible or, as in the case of knowledge, food for knowledge, where knowledge is treated as a tangible. The Kayapó term *pãnh* 'payment' is also a form of reciprocity, where the contract may not be between people who have some obligation, as is implied in the term 'to look after well'.

has the right to dance in it, therefore not made as an item to be exchanged with those people within the Kayapó system of reciprocity.

During my stingray ordeal, many Kayapó men and women came to my aid with various topical medications. Later I was asking one of the elders about the qualifications of some of the people who ministered to me. He acknowledged the older specialists, especially the men, but said that two of the younger women in particular had learned from others, but that their knowledge was *kajgo*. This could mean that he thought the knowledge was picked up, overheard, but not obtained from specialists in the formal way, where they would give meat and food over a period of time, in exchange for the knowledge. When he saw my wound healed he said, "Well, maybe they touched the stingray," meaning that the young women had perhaps been "introduced" to the animal officially by a specialist and, therefore, had completed a training course in the accepted manner, thus gaining the knowledge-power in that domain through some legitimate channel.

The above illustrations of the concept of *kajgo* are related to either ceremony or specialist knowledge, and indeed, the term does seem to be more widely applied in these domains. But it is also utilized in other areas connected to learning, such as skills learning.

When the young men are learning to weave manioc baskets or baby-carriers, they do not work with the palm fiber normally used. Instead they plan it out to themselves with some other palm material, and they state that they are weaving *kajgo* 'not for real', using material that is not the real thing. Actually, at this point they are only learning, and the weaving is not being done as part of the obligation they will later have to a mother-in-law for whom they must provide a manioc basket. Only when they attain to a higher age-grade and marry will they weave for this purpose. Therefore, their weaving now is *kajgo*—not in fulfillment of any reciprocal obligation; not for the benefit of any exchange.

Knowledge which is attained through socially validated channels is treated as a commodity, something which can be exchanged for something else. It becomes an asset, similar to how names and rights are regarded as assets or wealth. There are certain acknowledged channels of knowledge transmission where knowledge is passed on in exchange for meat or honey. These are the accepted channels by means of which children should learn traditional Kayapó customs. In return, the elders will be looked after with food, often provided by the parents of the learners. The learning and teaching which occurs within these accepted channels of reciprocal exchange will not be considered *kajgo*. It is knowledge transmitted in a socially validated manner, and as such, the person receiving it increases in social wealth and viability. This is not to say that learning does not occur outside of such channels. It does, all the time. Such knowledge is said to be *kajgo,* which may be interpreted as knowledge which was not received as commodity, not confirmed in a relationship of reciprocity, and cannot, therefore, be considered officially part of a person's validated repertoire.

It is important to note that learning can and does occur, according to the Kayapó, whether or not it is made official by some standard even though the knowledge acquired through the acceptable channels is considered the real knowledge and is treated with more respect. This concept will be elaborated upon in later chapters dealing with ceremonial rights and knowledge transfer.

Age-grades

In addition to gender and the status of knowledge and knowledge-bearers, I have alluded to the influence of age upon the right to transmit and receive knowledge of all types. The Kayapó have an institutionalized system of age-grades. Based upon biological stages and applying to each sex, the age-grade system also determines when one is expected to acquire particular knowledge and when one is expected to transmit it.

Age-grade divisions (which could more appropriately be referred to as stage grades) reflect Kayapó perceptions of the biological development of each sex, including ideas about what type of knowledge and what kind of behavior is appropriate to either gender at a particular stage in the life cycle.

In figure 6 I have arranged the eldest at the top and the youngest at the bottom as the Kayapó conceptualize the categorizations. All male or female infants up to the walking stage are classified as babies or "little ones." A synonym for the elders is "old head"; synonyms for the infants are "foot" and "new head." The growth of new plants, particularly corn, is compared to the ascending order of these biological stages.

Male *(me my)*		Female *(me nire)*
old men *(me bêngêt)*	ELDERS *(me tum re)*	old women *(me bêngêx)*
parents of many *(kra krãptī)*	ADULT *(me krare/krapdji)*	parents of many *(kra krãptī)*
fathers of new child *(kranyre)*		mothers of one child *(kra pỹnh)*
sleep new *(nõrny)*	NEWLY ADULT *(arym abatanh)*	old thigh-blackened *(kraxtyk 'atum)*
new penis sheath *(mydjênyre)*		
painted ones *(me 'ôkre)*	BOYS AND GIRLS *(me bôkti/me kurerer)*	new thigh-blackened *(kraxtykny)*
moved to men's house *(bêngàdjy)*		big little ones *(prĩti)*
big boys *(bôkti)*		big girls *(kurereti)*
babies *(prĩre)*	INFANTS *(me prĩre)*	babies *(prĩre)*

Figure 6. Kayapó age-grade divisions

For females, the girls and newly-adult division include the walking/talking stage of "big little ones" and young developing, "new thigh-blackened" or painted signifying puberty and marriageable age, and "old thigh-blackened" or puberty plus. These are not rigid stages in terms of age, reflecting as they do biological development. A girl may skip the old thigh-blackened stage if she has her first child shortly after becoming new thigh-blackened, i.e., at around twelve years of age.

The boys division is subdivided into three stages: "big boys," roughly corresponding to the female "big girls" stage; "moved to men's house," corresponding to the female "big little ones," and "the painted ones" equivalent more or less to the female stage of new thigh-blackened or puberty. When boys reach puberty they customarily acquire a penis sheath, so "new penis sheath" is the title of that stage. The title of the "sleep new" age-grade, refers to the custom of the young bachelors beginning to sleep in the house of a potential wife which should eventually lead to a more permanent union upon the birth of a child.

The male and female adult divisions consist of two stages representing early and later parenthood, and finally, members of each sex attain to the esteemed category of "elders."

> From birth to death, all males and females are classified through a series of conceptual categories of social age called age grades. Each age grade is named, is ritually distinct, has a peculiar set of behavioral rules, and is visibly distinguishable by specific ornaments, body painting styles and hair cuts. (Verswijver 1985:88)

Kayapó adults use the age-grade system as a device to define social expectations for a child, much as North American adults appeal to age or school-grade standards to cajole their children into line. That is, children are made aware of roles and expectations which correlate to age and maturing.

A North American child might hear, "When you're six, you can go to school like your big brother. You'll learn how to read." A Kayapó boy will be told:

> You're already a *bôkti,* so now learn something! Ask about the things from those who know. So be a *bôkti* and know something thoroughly. Then when you're 'ôkre, too, thoroughly know something! Learn the old things (traditions).

In fact, the younger boys (about 6) are not expected to learn much. "The young *bôkti* aren't smart," said one man. "They can't learn anything. But when they're *bêngàdjy* (about 8 or 9) they'll learn about dog medicines." Another person said,

> When they're *bêngàdjy/'ôkre,* (between 8 and 12), they just watch and learn. After they've had their penis tied (around puberty) they go off and do the things they've learned. They're already adult.

The girls, too, when they are *kurererti* (between 6 and 10) are admonished to accompany their mothers and sisters in their work. The adult women say,

Come with me and see my work. Then, when you're adult, you can go alone [to the garden] and get something for yourself: field produce for yourself. Thoroughly look at their [adults'] work. Go along with them and learn something!

If the children do not heed these admonitions, they become the butt of scornful remarks. They are called lazy or worthless. Mostly, the adults encourage them to feel proud of their status, and since older children are soon appointed caretakers of their younger siblings, they are happy to progress to the next stage and become the bosses instead of the bossed.

The attainment of puberty is marked for both sexes in a ritualistic fashion involving the child's close kin. In the case of males, the boy is taken over by a nonkin person who "symbolically supplants, for all public purposes" the boy's father (Turner 1987b:19). This may happen in an initiation rite embedded in either the bẽmp or the tàkàk naming ceremonies. Or it might be a relatively small, semiprivate ritualized activity, where the boy is painted[12] by his "substitute father," and sits in the men's house as a junior member of this man's society. The false father becomes a type of tutor to the boy, taking him hunting and raising him until the latter becomes an adult. (More will be said about this relationship later.)

For the girl, puberty is marked by a thigh-painting ceremony, hence the name, "newly thigh-blackened ones." The girl, too, receives a false mother, a nonkin girl from the next ascending stage, and these two become like close friends, working and playing together. Once the children have passed this phase, sexual activity is the norm.

Sexual play and experimentation by both sexes is acceptable, even encouraged by adults, but a good mother, according to the elders, tries to control her daughter's exploits in order to reserve her for a proper husband—one who will weave for the mother-in-law according to their traditions.

In general terms, children are expected to complete their official training by the time they have passed puberty and are expecting their first child. The transition between junior and senior adult, for the men, is the young bachelor stage. Once the young man acknowledges fatherhood and has his first publicly-acknowledged child, he moves into the senior gradations which shift from father of one child, to many children and finally, elder. Similarly, the woman's transition to full adulthood comes with her first child. From this she progresses through stages which parallel the men's stages.

---

[12]Men paint others with broad hand-strokes, not with a stylus, a strictly feminine skill. The paint is supplied by a female relative of the painter.

The Kayapó life cycle is made explicit by each member's progression through the age-grades or life stages. Simply by virtue of becoming elders both men and women are considered to have attained full knowledge and status in the community. They are the treasure-store of the Kayapó way of life and are required to officially pass their knowledge along to their grandchildren and other junior members of society. In fact, members of any senior stage are encouraged to pass along knowledge to their juniors, with the implicit provision that the wisdom of the most senior person in the learning environment is automatically privileged (see figure 7).

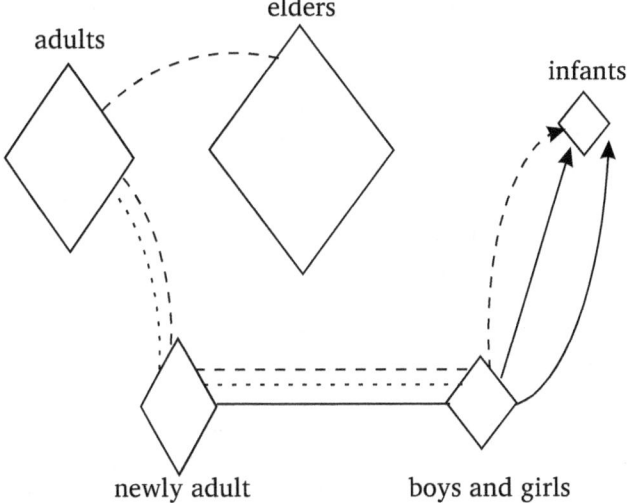

Figure 7. Perceived direction of Kayapó knowledge flow

Any senior elder, male or female, may transmit knowledge to any person, male or female, in a junior position on the age-stage hierarchy. The flow of knowledge is perceived to be unidirectional, with each age group influencing each of the junior groups, though knowledge flow between peers may be bi-directional on any level. The elders, therefore, exercise the most influence, relating to every age-grade. There is a tendency for knowledge-transmission relationships to be stronger between members of the same sex than across sexes.

Summary

This chapter has dealt, in general terms, with Kayapó ideas about knowledge and knowledge transmission. The categorization of knowledge into information that "everybody knows" and that which pertains to specialists; knowledge which is geared to the physical formation of a child, in contrast to knowledge geared to the social formation of the child, is basic to an understanding of the relationships through which particular knowledge is transferred. General learning modalities: observation and modeling, social experience, social conflict, and play are seen to be modified by Kayapó cultural contexts, because learning does not take place in a social vacuum.

Ideology, such as ideas about what knowledge is appropriate to which gender, what knowledge is official, or made official by the proper channels of transmission, has a distinct bearing upon the dispersion of knowledge throughout Kayapó society and an incontrovertible effect upon the status, influence, and authority of the elders. The institution of age-grades, correlating with significant biological advances in the human life cycle, is used to further control the transmission of knowledge by specifying what is an appropriate time to learn particular information and from whom.

For the male, the relationship with his fictive father includes him in relationships with this man's family, as well as his society or moiety. The girl's fictive mother, does the same thing in a more modest way. An individual's knowledge base is expanded as adulthood is approached in the measure that social interactions move from relationships of immediate kin and those classified as parents, within the everyday setting to include relationships with the grandparent set and some nonkin in ceremonial roles in the ritual, communal setting.

4

Living and Learning
The Everyday Setting

In the everyday setting, the transmission and acquisition of skills and knowledge by a Kayapó family spatially includes the houses, the gardens, and specific areas of the forest, and does not imply an exclusively female domain.

Three principal social groupings account for the key relationships utilized in knowledge exchange within the everyday setting. Within these groupings children are free to—indeed expected to—copy their elders and participate in whatever is going on to the best of their limited abilities. Most of the teaching and learning events which occur in the everyday setting are routine in nature, fulfilling the respective role expectations of parent and child. In contrast to individualized knowledge-transmission events in the ritual setting, no formal exchange or transaction is involved between parent and child in the everyday setting, although the child is included in the economic production groups where the principal of generalized reciprocity is in operation.

Parents, bonded to their children by the belief that they share actual physical substance with their children before and following the birth of the child, must observe certain food restrictions in order to benefit their children physically. This self-abnegation by parents on behalf of their children contrasts with the relationship that people in the grandparent category have with the same children. The dichotomy created, with the children as pivotal between parent category and grandparent category, is expressed literally in ritual events as will be seen in the next chapters. In relation to a child's learning and development, this dichotomy is significant; for people of the parent category are responsible for transmitting the general knowledge, i.e., information and skills that pertain to the natural (physical) nurture of a child, while the grandparents are responsible for the transmission of traditional knowledge pertaining to the cultural (social) aspect of a child's formation.

For the female, households and gardens comprise the context of a large part of her life's activity, and most of what she learns pertains to the daily work tasks and is immediately applicable. For the male, in addition to gender-related skill learning in the domestic environment, he moves towards the wider community through relationships formed in play. To appreciate more fully what is meant by the everyday setting we set the scene by describing an average day in the life of Kubẽkàkre residents.

Everyday activities

On any given day, activity begins at sunrise with some men going off with their dogs to hunt or fish and most women and nursing babies heading for their gardens, often accompanied by one or two dogs. Older men come and go between their houses and the central men's house. Here they sit around puffing on their funnel-shaped, hand-carved wooden pipes, watching the day's events unfold, and perhaps doing some weaving while chatting amiably among themselves.

The older women occasionally go to the gardens, but more often they stay around the houses keeping an eye on their grandchildren whose mothers went to the gardens. The elder matriarch in our house was no longer very active, but many young women would come to her throughout the day for her medical ministrations. Her medical specialty was to stroke people, in a special way that soothed aching limbs, thus earning her some reward, perhaps food, perhaps some cotton thread from the city.

The matriarch's husband, estimated to be in his eighties (Verswijver 1985:188), would stand for hours weaving a sleeping mat, occasionally stopping to eat sweet potatoes or some meat brought to him either by relatives or in payment for some service. Pet macaws, roosters, chickens, ducks, and ever-hopeful emaciated dogs scavenge incessantly for scraps of food on the earth floor. The young boys can be heard in the rough clearing surrounding the houses or playing in the river.

Around midday the younger women return, heavily laden with manioc tubers and sweet potatoes, the main staples; they also bring other produce such as corn, bananas, or watermelon, depending upon the season. They grab pots and rush off to the river for a refreshing bath and to fetch water.

Soon the sound of grating fills the air, as mothers and daughters together grate manioc, often just inside the front door of their houses where the light is good (and they can keep an eye on the neighbors). The energetic, rhythmic grating produces a pulp which is used to make a thick, chewy bread or pie, into which meat or fish may be placed, and steamed in an earth oven for a substantial meal.

Some of the pulp may be dried and mixed with another type of dried manioc pulp to be converted into farinha. This process takes place in one of two or three oven houses, where an entire family congregates to roast the grated manioc, transforming it into thick granules of fibrous flour. Husbands help in this task, stirring and turning the large, yellowish lumps with a round canoe paddle, separating them into toasted, golden brown hard grains. The oven houses, where manioc is roasted, and the water's edge, where women gather to eat and exchange roasted sweet potatoes, are two favorite places to catch up on the village gossip.

Before sunset, the husbands return one by one, some with fish, others with meat, others without anything. They bathe and many go off to the men's house to socialize.

As darkness approaches, the families move to the plaza in front of their houses and sit around in family groupings, socializing and eating. If the moon is full, activities may continue as if it were daylight. Gradually, people saunter off to their beds or hammocks; young couples mysteriously vanish into the darkness; "gangs" of young boys, flit from place to place or play together near the men's house where some of them will eventually hang their hammocks for the night; dogs bark and fight for scraps.

After dark the droning of simultaneous conversations between husbands and wives can be heard, or the women chatting with each other while husbands doze or listen. Generally, one or two radios are blaring, rarely on the same station! Noises, such as coughing, spitting, radios, and roosters never seemed to bother anyone but me, and it was not good etiquette to complain about such impediments to sleep. In an apparently communal situation, certain things are regarded as private to an individual or family—as if they could neither be seen nor heard by others.

Little by little the air cools and relative silence envelopes the village. Another day ends.

Domestic organization

The members of one or more households comprise a domestic group which in turn is composed of several nuclear families. Within the everyday setting, the three groupings in which relationships function to transmit common, everyday knowledge are (1) the nuclear family, (2) the domestic group, and (3) interhouseholds.

A brief description follows of these three groups in order to better appreciate the context within which teaching and learning occur in the everyday setting. This is not to imply that learning does not take place outside of these groups, but the influence of relationships within the groups is constant in the life of the average Kayapó child. Also, there are additional learning relationships in the everyday setting which do not involve children.

Nuclear family

The nuclear family is the basic unit: husband, wife, and offspring. But among the Kayapó, single motherhood is common, so that a mother and her children, while not literally a nuclear family, nevertheless function in many respects as though they were.

Nuclear families are the building blocks of Kayapó society. That the Kayapó implicitly recognize this is evidenced in at least two ways. First, most Kayapó knowledge is directed to the maintenance of this specific unit, and second, the unit is bound together by a philosophy of common substance. There are several stages explicit to the formation of a family within the Kayapó society.

The young man is already in the sleep new age-grade of marriageable bachelors, and his wife-to-be is in the newly thigh-blackened or old thigh-blackened parallel age-grade for females. They have begun seeing each other regularly, he, stealing into her house to share her hammock for awhile, signalling (to her mother) their intention to marry.[13] If the girl becomes pregnant and if he decides to acknowledge paternity, he will make this announcement in the men's house, particularly to his substitute father, a man who has sponsored him since his initiation. At this point, the relationship between the sponsor and the young man terminates, for the former has seen the latter successfully reach manhood (T. Turner 1987b:19).

Now the new father-to-be must form a new set of relationships, moving into his wife's household. The average, traditional household in Kubẽkàkre houses is around twenty people. The junior son-in-law enters into a respectful avoidance pattern with his wife's parents, inhibited by a formalized respect or shame in speaking to them. If he is a good weaver (and he will be

---

[13]This pattern is also in flux. The girl may now move into her boyfriend's home until her first child is born, at which time she may return (with husband in tow) to her mother's household.

Domestic organization

more popular with the in-laws if he is), he will weave a special basket for storage of manioc flour to present to his mother-in-law. Naturally, the more industrious he is, the more a mother-in-law will be interested in the success of the marriage! Lately, the quantity of trade goods a man may acquire by one means or another is becoming an additional criterion for a desirable husband or son-in-law.

Prior to the birth of the first child, the expectant parents, "pregnant ones," are supposed to observe specific food restrictions. They believe that the fetus is an integral part of each parent, based upon a concept of shared substance. The child, according to the Kayapó, "makes itself" from the fluid or substance of the father's semen, yet within the mother, so that each parent is uniquely and substantively bonded to the child.

When the parents partake of food, therefore, the blood or substance of certain animals may be dangerous when incorporated. If the person is weak or otherwise susceptible to the dangerous qualities of the animal's substance, the person becomes ill. The parents observe restrictions most carefully in the early stages of pregnancy when the child is still "liquid." A newborn child is also considered especially fragile. As part of the parents, even following birth, the child is believed to be affected by what the parents eat either for good or ill.

An analysis of the dietary regulations reveals a set of values relating as much to the child's appearance, especially the head, as to its health (see appendix B). For instance, a mother should avoid eating monkey meat so the child will not have a round, monkey-like head. Paca *(Cuniculus Paca)*, on the other hand, should be eaten in order that the child have a wide, flat forehead. In fact, while eating this meat, the parents rub themselves with the animal fat on the back and thighs to ensure a transfer of this desirable attribute to their child. Summarizing from a text given me by a male elder:

> It is undesirable for a child to have a round head or black skin. Its head should not be thin-skinned. It should not have flakiness on it (like dandruff). The forehead should be flat without a cowlick or a "tail" of hair at the nape of the neck.

To avoid such physical aberrations in their children the parents should avoid round-headed animals like monkeys or bees which have a black skin. If a Kayapó child had these characteristics, they would look like the foreigners, the regional nonindigenous people, and that would be undesirable, since these people are considered to be nonsocial beings. They will not eat certain fowl because of the flakes on its skin nor the part of a tapir or palm heart which has protrusions like a cowlick. In order for a child to walk well, they will avoid deer meat, because a deer "walks poorly," and the list could go on.

One significant thing about such food regulations is the control the parents perceive themselves to be exercising over the physical formation of their child through their own self-denial. This control pertains to the physical-social formation of the child because if the head is physically good, *mex*, the chances are greater that the social knowledge later imparted by the grandparents will enter so that the child will be physically and socially complete. Another significant factor is the hierarchical structure which is reinforced within the household, as the soon-to-be grandparents strongly influence their expectant child and spouse to observe the food regulations.

Another practical and social consequence of this belief in the common substance of parents with their children is to set the unit apart, psychologically and physiologically, from the surrounding relatives. Since the restrictions are especially invoked upon the first pregnancy, this could be because the union of the parents, which implies the incorporation of an affine into each of their families, is considered a tenuous, threshold-type relationship needing constant reinforcement. All crossing of social boundaries (as we will note later), especially in the direction of affines, is considered a risky business worthy of special precautions, often ritual. As the nuclear family increases, becoming more stable, the dietary restrictions for the third or fourth child are considerably relaxed in practice, although not in theory.

It should be mentioned that this substance relationship exists only between parents and offspring, especially while the children are young and relatively unsocialized. Siblings may affect each other by what they eat, as parents affect their children, but the direction is from strength to weakness in terms of health and generation; i.e., children do not jeopardize the parent's condition by what they eat. If a parent is sick, that parent's father, mother, and siblings may observe food restrictions, but his wife and children can "just go ahead and eat meat."

Those of the child's grandparent set, whose relationship with the child is very close, are nevertheless not bound by food restrictions. They are not believed to share a common bodily substance with their grandchild. A grandmother will, however, be careful to make sure she rinses her mouth and hands after eating meat so the smell of the meat on her breath will not harm her grandchild or the animal's blood figuratively touch the infant. And in times of a child's grave illness, relatives of various degrees of proximity to the child may, to show their concern, voluntarily forego foods believed to be causing the child's illness. A main topic of radio conversations with people in other villages is to appeal to a relative of a sick child to avoid certain food.

The degree to which food prohibitions are actually followed may serve as an indicator of change and modernization in the society. A constant refrain of the elders is that the young pregnant ones just disregard the prohibitions to the detriment and puniness of their children. Certainly any misfortune, a miscarriage, for instance, will probably be attributed to the parents' failure to follow restrictions and, no doubt, cause the parents to approach the next pregnancy with greater adherence to the rules.

It is appropriate to refer to dietary restrictions, at this point, for these emphasize the importance of the Kayapó nuclear family to the society as a whole. The dietary code, while underscoring the Kayapó belief in the commonality of the bodily substances of each parent with its child, may also point to the centrality of the nuclear family to the Kayapó by its focus upon a metaphysical bond between a parent and the child.

It becomes clear that the importance of the nuclear family in terms of a study of knowledge transmission is not only due to the teaching and learning accomplished within this unit. It is important also because the content and focus of a high percentage of Kayapó wisdom channeled through all the relationships which connect a child to society is germane to the continuation and survival of the nuclear family. Yet this body of knowledge has two distinct aspects: the physical and the social/spiritual. Those in the parent category (a child's real parents as well as those considered his parents' siblings) are responsible for the transmission of the knowledge that pertains to the physical nature and survival of the child and the child's own future nuclear family, as will be illustrated later in this chapter.

Domestic group

The nuclear family is surrounded by the larger domestic group to which the mother's parents and sisters pertain. As a child develops, it is in constant contact with this wider social group.

Most households in Kubẽkàkre are comprised of extended matri-uxorilocal families, i.e., domestic groups. In some villages this is beginning to shift to separate nuclear families, or the young bride may leave her household to live in the house of the groom. While there are such instances in Kubẽkàkre, it is, nevertheless, still the norm for several nuclear families to constitute part of a domestic group or household.

All children within a household, including their parallel cousins, are considered siblings, but their primary loyalty is to their own parent(s) and brothers and sisters. They should listen to (obey, respect) all their mothers and fathers, but only their biological parents may take measures to encourage this.

The women of the household are the producers and suppliers of garden products and staples such as manioc flour and bread. Every woman with children has at least one garden which provides for her family and other social obligations. An unmarried daughter works in her mother's garden.

Knowledge of swidden horticulture is not trivial. Most older women could list, with little trouble, twenty-five varieties of sweet potato, fifteen types of bananas and plantains, and ten varieties of manioc. In addition, one must know types of soil, when to plant what, and where to plant it in relation to other plants.

> The Kayapó practice concentric ring/crop segregation agriculture based on sweet potatoes, manioc, yams, and perennials, periodically intercropped with maize, beans, cucurbits, introduced rice, and numerous other minor crops and ritual plants. Kayapó swiddens stay in active root crop production for about five years, and continue to contribute these products at reduced levels for as long as eleven years. (Hecht and Posey 1990:79)

Any Kayapó child is most frequently exposed to, and learns from the female members of the households: mothers and mother's parents, especially the grandmother. Somewhat less frequent is its contact with the male members of the household: fathers, brothers-in-law, and the grandfather, who pays special attention to his male grandchildren. Peer relationships, for the children, include nuclear and extended family siblings, as well as parallel cousins and cross-cousins, who are members of other households.

Interhouseholds

Once married, a young woman will expand her social network to include members of her husband's household, particularly her mother-in-law and sisters-in-law. Her husband's sister, who will become an important cross-family link to her husband's children as a member of the grandmother set, visits her brother's new wife, thus confirming a relationship between the two households.

Over time, visits between sisters-in-law are frequent and as a result, their children, actually cross-cousins, establish relationships, playing together. In addition, the kinship tie between the sister-in-law and her brother's children is strengthened.

Women will occasionally visit the homes of members of their own working society, as well as go to each other's gardens and work in communal gardens. The children, of course, accompany them and in this way their social horizons and learning opportunities increase as interhousehold relationships are formed.

Another set of relationships which link households is the expanded network of a child's parent's fictive siblings. Both parents have a set of people who are considered their brothers and sisters and by extension, become fictive parents to each other's children. The father's false or fictive brothers are inherited patrilineally, and the relationship is expressed publicly when a young couple has its first baby. When a child (male or female) is born, all of the men considered to be the father's brothers are painted black and stand together in each other's "first baby ceremony." By means of this action, they become fathers to each other's children. Their collective offspring become siblings to each other. This entire network of relationships is important, not just in the everyday realm, but in the ceremonial realm, as a parent's siblings, both real and fictive, cooperate with each other in sponsoring festivals for their children. The ceremonial partners for their children will be chosen from among the collective fathers' ceremonial partners. The Kayapó view the expanded network of false fathers in very practical terms, as my Kayapó brother explained:

> My fictive father and my real father make each other real brothers, and they blacken themselves for our ceremony [baby ceremony held for himself and all siblings when they were infants]. And so I make them my fathers really well. Then, when my real father is dead, they look after us with meat.

This underlines, too, the parental role of providing physical sustenance to children, thus contributing to their positive physical growth and appearance.

Men in the child's father's generation control, to some extent, the educational, social, and material benefits and potential of the fictive brother/father relationships on behalf of their children. Materially, the system functions as a safeguard against their children being hungry, since hopefully one person's hunting success might cover another's failure, with reciprocity expected in like circumstances.

A male child will also establish close ties with the household of the man from among his father's brothers, (i.e., his fathers), who becomes his substitute father. This relationship begins when a child ascends from the boys-age stage to the moved-to-men's-house stage and one of the fictive fathers takes him on as a son, becoming instrumental in the boy's transition to the men's house. This man's kin becomes a set of fictive kin to the boy, and he calls them by the terms he would call his own parents, grandparents, siblings, etc. This important teaching and learning relationship will be described in more detail in chapter 6.

Everyday learning

Teaching and learning naturally occur in each of the groupings detailed above. A child in its natal home deals primarily with the relationships within its nuclear family and, secondarily, its extended family within the domestic group or household.

In the domestic group, since the household organization is matrilocal, the women are dealing primarily with consanguineous relationships and secondarily affinal. In contrast, the male is dealing primarily with affinal relationships. The conduct of the male in this environment is subject to more social rules of behavior than are in operation for the female, such as a prohibition on speaking directly to his father-in-law. Yet through the mediation of his wife, the son-in-law may communicate with his father-in-law.

We will now look more closely at learning situations in the everyday setting. The transmission of general or common knowledge pertaining to the daily routine will be considered as it occurs within the nuclear family, then the larger domestic group, as well as between groups. We will see the role that play and discipline exercise in reinforcing Kayapó values.

In the nuclear family

Within the natal home, teaching and learning take place in the sweat and toil of everyday activities where the smallest variation constitutes variety, where rumor and speculation provide conversation and drama, and where the youngest learners are constantly surrounded by attentive, talkative, indulgent, if not bossy, caretakers.

The family members closest to a child are subsequently the child's teachers. The subject matter is related to the daily living routines and varies according to gender. Examples of knowledge transmitted in this environment include: traditional stories, medicinal knowledge, cultural values, hunting, spinning, body painting, gardening skills, kinship terms, and villagers' names.

The channels of knowledge transmission in this unit are between husband and wife, between parent and child, and between siblings, yet the acknowledged flow of information is not considered by the Kayapó to be multidirectional.

Everyday learning

Any senior person, male or female, may transmit knowledge to any person, male or female, in a junior position on the age-stage hierarchy. Knowledge flow between peers may be bidirectional on any level. There is a tendency for knowledge transmission relationships to be stronger between members of the same sex than across sexes.

From a Kayapó perspective, a husband will teach his wife something, but rarely does the reverse hold true. A father and mother will each teach a daughter certain things and a son other things, and although children do undoubtedly bring new knowledge to their parents, this is not recognized by the Kayapó as legitimate knowledge transmission.

Siblings definitely "instruct" one another, and elder siblings inevitably pull rank. The knowledge that an elder sibling has acquired from a parent is constantly being reinforced by its retransmission to a younger sibling, since soon after infants can crawl the parents place them in the care of their siblings, especially the female siblings. It is a common sight to see little girls five or six years old cheerfully staggering around with a chubby toddler clinging to their hips. When they "hush" a baby to sleep, they do so with the loud ã ãããã breathed directly into the baby's face just as they see their mothers doing.

Within the household, small children commonly attempt tasks they see being done by their elders. They are operating within an affectionate and supportive climate where siblings and other close kin watch and encourage them, an important condition to learning. With amazement I observed Inhôr (about age three) collecting little dry sticks, placing them in a pile on the floor, lighting it, and watching as the smoke made a small, grey cloud. At just the right time she blew on it, slowly adding more twigs. In no time she had a fine fire going, exactly as she had seen her mother doing. I thought of the horrified admonitions to which any North American three-year old would be subject if caught doing the same thing! Not only was Inhôr praised, but her mother then handed her an unlit pipe requesting her to light it for her. Placing the pipe stem between her teeth, Inhôr held a smoking ember to the strong, homemade tobacco and puffed until smoke curled from the pipe, then handed it to her mother. (Yes, children are generally confirmed smokers by the age of six!)

I asked Inhôr's mother, if she had taught her daughter to do these things. "No" she said, bemused. "She just saw it and then did it."

Since girls are constantly with the women in their household, they are exposed to little else except female domestic routine. Everything their mother(s) or sisters do, they watch and try themselves, but are not formally taught. Nevertheless, there is a pecking order where the more experienced at a task feel perfectly free to offer endless, unsolicited advice;

and being bossed around by what seems like everybody just goes with the territory of learning by doing.

Between mother and child. Domestic skills, including grating manioc, preparing food, the proper distribution of meat portions, and female crafts, including spinning, fashioning festival ornaments, and body painting are all learned by daughters from their mother(s) by observation. The standard response, almost verbatim, to my questions concerning the acquisition of such skills implied that the child watched how the mother did it and when she was older "just went along doing it." The reverse also holds true. I noticed that a common excuse for lack of knowledge in a female skill is "my mother died when I was young." Mothers do not overtly make a point of teaching such skills, yet the effort of children to learn them by experimentation is respected and acknowledged. Body painting is a case in point.

It is common Kayapó practice for mothers to paint elaborate designs on their son's or daughter's body. The baby must be healthy and strong, otherwise, as one elderly woman stated, "the painting, if a child is sick, will make it sicker." Adults, too, will not be painted unless they are well.

The mothers prepare a mixture of carbon and genipapo seeds and pulp *(Genipapa americana)*. The bitter genipapo is chewed to provide the juicy, clear liquid which turns dark on the skin. The child, often half-asleep, is laid on a blanket or woven mat on the floor, and the painting begins, generally on the child's back. The geometrical designs are drawn with the flexible inner spine of a large leaf.

The designs vary in complexity according to the ability of the mother and are idiosyncratic. Some of the designs represent "beautiful animals" such as the land tortoise and armadillo whose shells are patterned and the striped anteater. No two children will be painted alike even by the same mother. In this way, the mother's unique bond with a child is signified. Similarly, there is no typical pattern establishing any commonality between children of other households. This reflects the social situation of the infant within the nuclear family as "unintegrated into communal society above the level of its particular family" (T. Turner 1979b:18).

Painting a child takes several hours, and mothers often use this means to quiet, soothe, and control the infant when it is feeling fussy and irritable.

Young mothers are usually less skilled than their seniors for lack of regular practice. Their first child immediately becomes the "canvas" upon which they can improve their technique. "The child's body is the laboratory, the canvas for the young mother to learn body painting. It is in using and reusing her child's body that a woman practices, learns and becomes qualified as an artist" (Vidal and Müller 1986:129).

But body painting is more than an idle pastime. There are elements of communication, not only in the use of certain designs, especially when applied to adults, but also in the manner and occasion of the painting as well as the relationship between painter and painted.

Just as the absence of body paint is a mark of social isolation due to sickness or mourning, so the application of paint signifies social integration and participation. For example, in the first week following a baby's birth, all close relatives of the child, as well as the child itself, will be painted with the red arnatto paste which signifies that the people so marked are in a precarious, liminal position in terms of social integration because of an infant's fragility and the danger of its mortality. About a week later, if the infant is healthy, the parents and grandparents will be painted with the black genipapo, each relationship marked by a different design. This painting signifies the end of certain birth restrictions which the parents had been observing and the reintegration of the family into the community.

I mention these details, not in an attempt to analyze the intricacies of body painting, but rather to illustrate that a mastery of this skill, in addition to the artistic factor, is a mastery of a socially recognized metalanguage expressed through the painting.

The Kayapó women, of course, take all this for granted. They acknowledge that they gained their abilities by observing their mothers (or another female caregiver in the case of a mother's death). The elder Nhàkti told me:

> I learned it from my mother. As a child I sat watching her as she laid on the sticks, and then when I had my child I painted her. We learn from our mothers and we pass it on. I learned it from my mother. It is my mother's way of doing it, my mother's design. I saw how she did it on me and how she laid the sticks on me. And then when I became an adult I did the same—my mother's (designs).

Nhàkti went a step further, pointing out the advantages of having a talented artist for a model:

> And those who have mothers who are not good at painting, then they aren't good either, because the mother doesn't paint well and so the child doesn't see and doesn't learn and doesn't pass it on. But those who have mothers who have a good hand, they learn from their mothers and they in turn are good and they pass it on.

While acknowledging that she copied her mother's designs, she also said she created designs of her very own.

Frequently, several women would crowd into our study house with their painting supplies and family in tow and would settle down to paint their children where the light was purportedly better. The mother would often begin with the youngest child, as her elder daughters would, less seriously, begin to paint a younger sibling. The older daughters would cast furtive glances at their mother's designs and progress, but never attempted a total imitation. They would laugh in frustration at their thick, wavering lines in comparison to their mother's thin, straight lines, but the mother rarely, if ever, commented or criticized. There seemed to be no need to either encourage or disparage, since experimentation is considered a private thing even when done in public, and comments are usually not forthcoming unless specifically solicited by the learner.

Although both sons and daughters are the objects of their mother's painting skills, only the daughter will learn the art. The preparation and use of the black genipapo paint is the exclusive domain of the female.

The growing, spinning, and ownership of cotton is also an exclusively feminine task. When a man finishes weaving a sleeping mat for a woman, usually his wife or daughter, he must get the red-dyed cotton from her in order to finish off the mat with cotton binding and tassels.

In my visit to the Kayapó in 1973, one commonly saw women spinning white cotton into thread with a small, hand-held spindle. By 1987 it was a rare sight because purchasing brightly-dyed, manufactured red cotton yarn is easier and satisfies the requirements for body decorations and artifacts. It is still female property, however.

The women who do spin cotton are mostly from the "many children" age group or the elders. They learned from watching their mothers, they say, lamenting that their own daughters have no interest in learning this feminine occupation.

Body painting, spinning, and other skills are not expressly taught, that is, there is no intent on the part of adults to intervene in the child's own timetable for experimentation. There is, however, an expressed consciousness that these skills are being passed along and it is assumed that when the child becomes an adult, he or she will be able to perform the appropriate task.

In other words, things which may be learned by observation are generally allowed to happen according to the child's initiative. But there are other types of knowledge which are expressly taught. Learning which occurs principally through hearing must be encouraged, either by admonishing a child to go and learn (hear) something from someone who knows something or by the deliberate recounting of information.

Women, especially the elders, are the official repository of a very complex knowledge base concerning names and naming practices among the Kayapó. If ever a question about naming arose, I was referred to Pãnhõr, one of the oldest women in the village. It was her prerogative, and that of other female elders, to keep track of the treasure-store of names pertaining to the various households and which are bestowed upon children in naming ceremonies. Although men may know the long list of their child's names, they will usually defer to their wives to recite these.

In addition, women are generally the best sources to consult concerning complicated kin relationships between villagers. Lea (1986:177) observed that if men have no living uterine relative to whom to defer on this knowledge, they do, in fact, know the information. This may explain why certain male elders, and not others, were able to give me satisfactory data concerning these matters. But it is considered women's knowledge.

It is not surprising, therefore, to hear a mother teach her son or daughter the names by which the people in the village are known; or the relationships and terminology (vocative terms) a child must know in order to properly address any given adult.

One evening, as I was trying to fall asleep, I could hear a young mother in our household carefully instructing her three-year old son on people's names, household by household, around the village circle. As he lay with her in her hammock, she would say a name, and he in his childish way, conscious of an audience, would repeat it. Listening to her was, for my part, analogous to counting sheep. I fell asleep! But my colleague assured me that the young mother and son managed to name everyone in the village. Over three hundred people!

Between father and child. Fathers, especially the elder ones, will lie in their hammocks after dark, and tell their children some of the traditional stories. If a festival is in progress, the myths of origin connected to that ceremony are recited, or accounts of bigger and better festivals in times past are told, emphasizing Kayapó ideals of beauty, riches, and generosity associated with dances and naming ceremonies.

One man, who had learned the old stories as a child of about seven or eight from his grandmother (his grandfather had died), never told the stories until he had his own children. "Are your children wanting to know?" I asked.

> I tell them, but they (female children) don't want to hear. I tell them, but when does she ask me, "Dad, tell me about the customs?" But some lie down at night and want to hear. Only my younger child shows any interest. At night she says, "Tell me something, Dad. Tell me about the old ones." So I lie in

my hammock, telling her about the rainmaker (and other cultural heroes). I know some stories but I've forgotten some.

Younger fathers do not often tell the old stories to their children, most likely in deference to the father-in-law in the household, and partly because they should be "fathers of many children" and perhaps even a grandparent themselves, before they are considered ready to tell these. This has to do with the idea of knowing how to speak well, a quality that is considered highly socialized as well as a skill that is associated with age.

Fathers also teach their sons skills such as basketmaking, the lengthy process of fashioning a dugout canoe, or making round canoe paddles, if these are special skills of theirs; and all fathers will take their young sons hunting. Said one hunter of prowess, a young father himself:

> My father told me. About the forest he said, "Let's go and kill some meat." So I walked after him and in the afternoon we returned. And I saw how he killed animals, then I also killed animals. He showed me how to fire a rifle. He put the bullet in the barrel, and I shot it off and killed the animal.

Others described their fathers teaching them how to track animals or how to recognize an animal's food so it can be ambushed when it comes to eat. They were told about an animal's "pet," another animal that shares the same habits or food, which may be found near each other. The tortoise, for instance, is said to be the armadillo's pet, because when you dig out the armadillo, invariably there will be a land tortoise nearby.

A father may also teach his child about herbal medicines. A son or daughter must be at puberty age before being taught this information. They will be shown the plants and told how to prepare and administer them for numerous common afflictions.

Through the father, children learn the importance of attempting to preserve social relationships at all costs. If a father gets very angry with someone within the household, as the outsider, he has no way to express his anger without causing grave social consequences. The outlet for anger, therefore, is the scapegoat dog. Usually, dogs are kicked or tossed about in someone's fit of anger. Not infrequently, a father will encourage his children to kill a dog on his behalf in order to appease his anger. The dog itself need not be guilty of anything. This is a rather graphic way for the children to learn the cost of keeping a human relationship together.[14]

---

[14]In another village, an outsider, rebuking a child with a slight tap for treating a puppy cruelly, was shocked when the father of the child came at her with his shotgun. He shot the puppy, he explained, instead of her because he liked her too much to kill her, but she had struck his child.

Everyday learning

When the children are old enough, families commonly go on fishing or gathering excursions, camping out for several nights, even weeks. The Kayapó enjoy this partly because it is also a way to escape the tensions of living within a household and providing for relatives. It is a time when the adults are free from the constraints of deferring to elders and are at liberty to show and tell their children all they know about survival skills. Children, too, are away from the collectivity of elders and cousins and have a chance to interact more closely with their parents and siblings.

Between siblings. Younger siblings are constantly in the care of elder siblings, especially their sisters. But older brothers will make toys such as clay animals or wooden airplanes for their younger brothers. They will show them how to swim (normally under the supervision of a parent).

The interaction between female siblings mainly takes place in the house or garden and usually not far from the presence of some adult. But once little boys reach the age of about six or seven, they will go off with their older brothers and become part of the boys' gangs which are allowed considerable autonomy and freedom in comparison to the girls.

The age difference between siblings implies an elder/younger relationship and precludes the type of peer interaction that is more common between cousins of roughly the same age. What a younger sibling learns from its elder is invariably practiced upon the next junior member. The younger children are allowed, even encouraged to hit their older brothers and sisters, while the reverse is not considered acceptable.

Discipline in the nuclear family. There does not seem to be any idea of molding either a child's skills or character. What a child has is considered innate or preexisting. A person grows up either bad or good, less because of parental or societal influence than by its own choices.

Young children occasionally have screaming temper tantrums which are handled with the utmost calm by mothers who just let the child exhaust itself. Older children have verbal exchanges with their parents which turn the air the proverbial blue, yet no action is taken against the child. The main forms of social control are loud conversations among adults about a child's behavior, as if the child were not present. Laughter at a child's temper is also an effective deterrent.

If a baby or toddler cries, wanting something, it must be indulged. There is no denying an infant, and often a young mother's excuse for getting something she herself wants is to say her child was crying for it. While this strategy may be viewed with a measure of skepticism, no one will question it.

Corporal punishment is considered a major aberration of social norms. If a mother were to hit her own child, her husband would be considered within his rights to abuse or even kill his wife for such an offense. Children are rebuked verbally, but never struck physically by adults. Nevertheless, it is common for adults to incite younger children to hit older children, if the latter are being problematic.

I witnessed a small incident escalate into a rather major one as a mother became extremely provoked with her teenage daughter's behavior. The daughter, in the thigh-blackened age group, was arguing with a younger sister over the baby sister and ended up hitting them. The mother told her young son to take a stick to both girls (not the baby). This he did with great brotherly gusto, and the oldest sister hit him back while the younger went off crying. At this point, a real fight ensued, with everyone present siding with the boy. This, perhaps more than the physical assault, grieved the teenage daughter, and she went off in tears of rage. The mother pontificated that the daughter had had this coming for a long time, that she was bad and angry towards everyone, and that she could sleep in the house that night, but she could get out the next day. The daughter went off with a hoe in her hand, intending to hit someone with it later. An elder sister, noticing this, physically tussled the hoe away from her. Meanwhile, the brother, upset that he had been hit, revengefully took apart his sister's pole bed, piece by piece, and dumped it outside. When the girl returned to this, she, in her turn, chopped her own hammock down as well. Her mother said, "Is it yours that you should do that?"

Later, an older "sister" (parallel cousin), helped put the bed together, and someone from the next house offered asylum, which the teenager refused. The next day, all was calm, and the daughter remained in the household, and for awhile she seemed more cooperative.

Fathers admonish their sons against smoking. They are told to pay attention and not be bad or angry. They tell their sons of the painted age stage to go and learn a medicinal specialty (an animal medicine that protects against harm from certain animals) from a grandfather or uncle instead of lying around doing nothing:

> You just think of sex all the time. You just fool around! Would you learn an animal medicine from them (grandparents) so that you could, for the sake of your wife and the sake of your children, know it, and without fussing, go and doctor your wife with it for yourself; doctor your child for yourself?

Mothers admonish daughters not to be lazy since daughters should be their helpmates, assisting in gardening, caring for siblings, carrying water, and other chores.

Theoretically, the parents require payment for the first sexual act performed with their daughter. So a good mother keeps her daughter by her side and watches her at night to see who might slip into the house and into the daughter's hammock.

This was graphically confirmed as one mother publicly scolded her young daughter (around ten) for promiscuity. She did not want her daughter to just "wife anyone" she yelled. She wanted a useful son-in-law—one who could weave and hunt. This admonition was meant, no doubt, as much for the unwanted suitor as it was for the daughter.

The foregoing descriptions of learning relationships within the nuclear family possibly give a false impression that the unit is isolated. In fact, nested as it is within the household, the nuclear family is merged with others to form a network of extended kin which may be labeled domestic group.

A husband may also teach his wife medicinal remedies she has not already learned from her father, but a woman will not be taught the "magical" chants which accompany many ministrations, such as the song to call a child into the womb for a woman desiring to become pregnant. Only men know these. A wife is not expected to teach her husband anything.

In the domestic group

Children's relationships within the household include the families of their mother's sisters and especially the mother's parents. The main relationship a male or female child has outside of the household is with its mother's married brothers and their wives and its father's parents—all people categorized as "grandparent." The relationships cultivated between the grandparent set and the grandchildren set are especially important in terms of the child's education. This is also the relationship through which a child will receive a selection of names and rights, to be discussed in the following two chapters. In addition, a male child, may form a relationship with some of his father's fictive brothers, i.e., learning from them what he would learn from his own father.

People in the child's grandparent set act in a child's life as a mediator between the child and the broader society in both ritual and everyday contexts. This and other mediating relationships will be treated in chapter 6. The relationships which remain on the consanguineous level are adult sisters with their children and on the affine level a father-in-law will teach a son-in-law and brothers-in-law may teach one another. Domestic knowledge is the subject matter between mothers and daughters, while knowledge of medicines is the main subject between in-laws.

Between adults and children. Sisters often work together in one or the other's garden, and their children may accompany them. For the child, the interaction is between parent, cousins, aunt—all of whom are regarded as mother or siblings—and himself. The didactic interaction is, therefore, basically the same as that between his own parents and siblings. That is, there is no new or special knowledge that is transmitted between a mother's sister and a child, except what might be of an idiosyncratic nature. The influence of this person upon a child is nevertheless pervasive in that each is so often in the other's company.

The same is true of a child's cousins who are regarded as extended siblings. But some behavioral rules are different and bear mentioning. For instance, when arguments and disagreements occur between true siblings; they are allowed to hit each other; in fact, a younger sibling may be incited to hit an older sibling, as noted earlier. But between families, this is not the case. When Djatire, a girl of about ten, hit her parallel cousin, Kôkôba, about six, Kôkôba's mother (also Djatire's "mother") spoke sharply to Djatire, "All right! Go ahead! Do like the adults do! You're wanting me to leave the house I see." She meant that if such a disagreement had occurred between adult sisters, one or the other would leave the house, establishing another dwelling. The implication was that Djatire's behavior, if Djatire had been an adult, would have caused such a split.

I witnessed many verbal tirades directed at children, which, had they been directed at me, would have crushed my spirit, yet they had no apparent effect upon the child. In this case, however, Djatire was visibly shaken, and it took her several days to get over it. She had learned the hard way the possible consequences of friction between families within a household.[15]

---

[15]Following this incident, I was told of an occasion where someone hit someone else's child, precipitating a family feud which took seven lives! And the village of Porori split up over thirty years ago, just coming together again about ten years ago, because someone in a household hit another household member's child.

Everyday learning

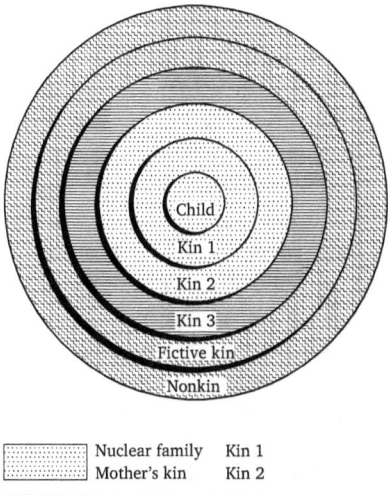

	Nuclear family	Kin 1
	Mother's kin	Kin 2
	Father's kin and Crosskin	Kin 3
	Nonrelatives	Fictive kin Nonkin

Kin 1 = M *(nuã)*, F *(bãm)*, Z *(kanikwynh)*, B *(kamy)*

Kin 2 = MM *(kwatyj)*, MF *(ing't)*, MZ *(nuã)*, MZD *(kanikwynh)*, MZS *(kamy)*

Kin 3 = FM, FZ *(kwatyj)*, FF, MB, MBS *(ing't)*, FB *(bãm)*, FZC *(tàmdjwy)*, FBS *(kamy)*, FBD *(kanikwynh)*, MBD *(nã)*

Fictive kin = "FB" "fictive fathers" *(bãm kaàk, kr" 'ã bãm)*; "F" substitute father (initiation) *(bãm kaàk, kr" 'ã bãm;* ceremonial partner *(kràmdjwy)*

Nonkin = F's and M's ceremonial partners

M	mother	MB	mother's brother
F	father	MBS	mother's brother's son
Z	sister	FB	father's brother
B	brother	FZC	father's sister's child
MM	mother's mother	FBS	father's brother's son
MF	mother's father	FBD	father's brother's daughter
MZ	mother's sister	MBD	mother's brother's daughter
MZD	mother's sister's daughter		
MZS	mother's sister's son	"FB"	"fictive father"
FM	father's mother		initiation father
FZ	father's sister		

Figure 8. Male child's relationships showing proximity of mother's kin versus father's kin (and cross-kin)

Adult conversation is not private, and a child is never considered too young or too high-strung to see, hear, and participate totally in every aspect of life. In fact, children are the eyes and ears of the community. With fewer social constraints upon where they are allowed to go, children are actively encouraged by adults to find out a neighbor's business, for example, what did so-and-so bring back from the city with him? Did they get any meat today? What did they get? My efforts to administer a questionnaire from household to household were thwarted by the children running ahead and telling the adults in the next household how the ones in the present household were responding to the questions.

When meat arrives, children learn about reciprocity, since there are rules concerning which relative gets which portion of the butchered animal. One of the most exciting things that happens in the village on a fairly regular basis is the call for wild pigs. If a lone hunter has spotted a herd of wild pigs within reasonable distance from the village, he returns and calls for others to join in the kill. Some of these pigs have dangerous tusks and so require a cooperative effort to hunt. Every man rushes to his house for a rifle, and young teens race off with their seniors. Women stand at the doors of their houses shouting encouragement to their men. The air crackles with anticipation.

Later, a successful hunt is greeted by whoops of approval by the elder men who remained in the village. Children will watch as an animal is butchered, then be told to run with portions to the mother's various relatives. When there is enough meat, it is portioned out to a mother's children, married or otherwise, and to her parents and grandparents. Some may also go to the husband's family. As children participate in this sharing, they are learning what particular part of the animal is given to which people and which relationships are reciprocal. Another time, they will be the recipients, receiving from the same relatives.

Since there is usually something going on with one family or another in a household, children are exposed to all facets of life and death. If a member of a household is sick or dying, children are present throughout all the agonizing, watching as various elders administer medicines, or smoke and sing for long hours beside the infirm or dying person. When death occurs, the children will see their mothers and others gash themselves on their heads with machetes, as an expression of grief. A child of seven or eight has probably witnessed two or three deaths firsthand. Death, separation, recounting the death of a relative in another village, and arrivals after a prolonged absence are all occasions for a stylized expression of emotion the Kayapó call "good crying."

This is a social skill which children learn in the context of the household through observing the emotional and dynamic performances of parents or grandparents. In ritual wailing, the women both dialogue and cry in a high, falsetto voice. Ritual wailing is a status maintenance or interaction rite (Grimes 1986) showing deference and decorum. It carries a heavy emotional load. The men's form, a weeping dialogue alternating with a partner, is also performed in a hiccoughing, slightly falsetto fashion upon similar occasions.

There are several facets to ritual wailing. First, it is a long-standing tradition, the origin of which dates back to mythical times, when two brothers, avenging the death of their grandmother, were said to have begun the good crying.[16]

> They were the ones who started the good wailing for the people. They were the ones who started the crying. So they (Kayapó) quit the other kind of crying *(tônti jabôr nhy)* and already cry well now *(arỳm myr mex)*.

Secondly, ritual wailing is a particular linguistic or sociolinguistic form which must be learned and produced. Rather than the standard vocative terms, other terminology is used, and men's and women's wailing terminology is distinct (Lea 1986:243).

Thirdly, ritual wailing is a communicative, social signal which must be learned and properly executed as such. In a study on ritual wailing in Brazil, Urban comments that wailing is "designed to communicate to visitors a desire for sociability by signalling the grief that was caused by their absence" (Urban 1988:393).

He adds that for the signal to communicate properly,

> the ritual wailer must wail under circumstances in which other members of the community would find it appropriate for that individual to be experiencing a feeling of grief or loss and the actual wailing itself must suggest that feeling, at least in some measure. (p. 393)

According to the Kayapó, one should wail under the following circumstances:

> If a stick pierces one then they cry for each other. If a pig bites them they cry for one another. Then when they go off away from each other, then arrive, they cry for each other. When sickness kills them, and they lie there dead, they cry for each other. Kukrytwir told them the good crying and according to

---

[16]When Kukrytwir and Ngõkõnkry blackened their eyes in order to kill the bird responsible for their grandmother's death, it apparently gave origin to the (black) pupil without which good crying was impossible. Before that, the ancestors' eyes were just the whites.

that custom, the people still do it. If an animal kills their pet, then they'll cry for it.

Not only must a person wail at the appropriate time with the proper emotion, but also with the correct person. The following dyads are expected to wail with each other: parents with child; sisters on behalf of each other's child; sister-in-law with parents-in-law; son-in-law with parents-in-law; grandparent with grandchild; and ceremonial partners.

How do children learn all this? The Kayapó say that the custom is passed along from generation to generation. That is, the elders tell the younger, thus giving authority and importance to the process. The children, however, observe the adults.

> The children watch it for themselves and then, when they're adult they can already cry. When the girls reach the thigh-blackened age stage, they already know how to wail.

The skill may be taught to both male and female children by the mother or maternal grandmother. When I asked one man how he learned the different terminology, he replied, "When I was a child my mother told me and I went listening and when I was an adult I understood." Another man explained, "My mother's mother taught me how to do the good crying (greeting). She said, 'You say this; you do like this'; and she taught me all the parts of it."

He also said he and his wife would teach their own children how to do this, since the children had no maternal grandmother. He will teach them when they reach puberty age.

Peer learning is also acknowledged:

> The children, as they get older, tell each other and cry/wail. They tell each other about the crying ways. And the men, too. They don't know about crying when they're little, but when they're adult, they know and already cry.

Because ritual wailing is an emotional, as well as a sociability signal, and "emotions can be the cause of social breakdowns, it is especially significant when they are in fact socialized" (Urban 1988:393). Ritual wailing, therefore, is more than meets the eye. By learning all the socially significant facets—voice quality, correct greeting terminology, appropriate context with correct person—the Kayapó child is learning to adhere to the collective norm, signalling thereby the desire to be and to appear sociable—an important quality in a face-to-face society.

Between adults. An incoming husband often establishes a very friendly relationship with his wife's younger brother, teaching him things, taking him hunting or fishing, and behaving like a benevolent older brother towards him. But one of the most important teaching relationships among the Kayapó is that between the incoming junior son-in-law and his father-in-law. For the Kayapó the same kin term *(ydjwỳ)* applies to brother-in-law as son-in-law including also the brother of the daughter's husband (ZH, DH, DHB).

This relationship has been underestimated as a teaching relationship, perhaps because of the prohibition which exists concerning their speaking to one another. In fact, the junior man must not directly address his father-in-law, avoiding even eye contact. Yet he will approach him through the mediation of his wife:

> The fathers lie in their hammocks, telling about the medicines, and their sons-in-law who have married their daughters say to the wife, "Ask your father to tell me all about the medicines against the foreigners, and the indigenous medicine, and the dog medicine."[17] And so the war hero, who killed enemies, who knows the medicines, who was asked to tell about the medicines, tells it to his son-in-law. So he lies in his hammock, telling it to his son-in-law. And so they second-handedly tell it to each other.

This last phrase refers to the custom of citing authorities. "Second-handedly telling" means the information has come from the ancestors down through the generations and across kinship boundaries. Another man, referring to the custom of a father teaching from his hammock after dark when everyone is in the house, said, "Those who know the medicine for doctoring dogs also tell their sons-in-law about the medicine for dogs; they lie in their hammocks, telling their children and grandchildren."

One of the elders told me he had learned some remedies from his father-in-law and had taught some medicines to his son-in-law. I asked if there was any payment for this and he replied that his son-in-law did not pay him but that he would bring him sweet potatoes to eat as he was teaching him, saying to him, "Eat your bit and then tell me." So he taught his son-in-law everything about the snake medicine, "told him thoroughly and finished it up." Telling thoroughly means knowing the antidotes against one's own medicine, "Otherwise the medicines will turn on the person, come back on him, and make him soft." Did he tell everything he knew, I asked. "Some things I didn't teach him. I'm the only one who knows," he replied. He said that his son-in-law was really smart and very motivated to learn, "He said, teach me, then I'll save people and they'll give me things."

---

[17]Referring to the past custom of raiding nonindigenous and other indigenous settlements. The medicines would be thrown at the houses and dogs in the settlements to "make them soft," thus controlling the opposition.

If a newly-married man shows no interest in learning from his father-in-law, he may be berated by his young wife:

> Some wives sit saying to their husbands: "You just think about your (illicit) lovers! Are you from the old ones (have you learned the traditions)? Would you know (see, hear, understand) or learn one of the animal medicines for your wife, for your child? Learn something from them! Then when your wife or child is sick, then you would be able to stroke them, then you could stroke them for yourself and doctor them for yourself. You could go around doing that for them."

This same type of speech, as we saw above, is used to motivate young bachelors to learn "for their wife and children," underscoring the importance of the nuclear family in that certain knowledge is considered crucial to children's physical survival. It would be safe to infer that a son-in-law is proving his good intentions towards his father-in-law's daughter and grandchildren by asking the senior man to teach him how better to care for them.

Between households

The interaction that constitutes learning and teaching between members of different households includes consanguineal and affinal relationships from the perspective of both adults and children. It also includes the category of the child's fictional parents. In addition, we may include intracommunity type relationships, such as the elders addressing the whole community, discipline by grandparents and elders, or relationships formed through the interaction of boys (and girls) from various households playing together.

In consanguineal relationships. Aside from the grandparent/grandchild relationships and the ceremonial partner relationships (see chapter 6) as mediating between households, the main educational interaction between people of different households will be with members of a child's father's family and mother's brother's family. The father's brother is also a child's "father," and as such, may teach the things a father teaches: hunting, medicines, and so on. The father's brother's children are considered siblings and relate to each other as such, especially male children as they run around in gangs after moving away from the sphere of their own household. I say the adults "may teach," as a reminder that the burden of knowledge transmission rests less upon the elder than the younger person who must actively seek knowledge. Most of the elders regularly complain that the young people do not do this any more. When questioned, many young people admitted that they had no desire to go to their elders, although some said that they did.

In affinal relationships. Men will teach their sons-in-law's younger brothers, also considered sons-in-law to them. One elder told me he did this for his daughter's husband, teaching the younger brother at the son-in-law's request. He taught him the same medicine he had taught his son-in-law. In other words, the senior men, the "ones who know something" are increasing the younger men's legitimate knowledge base by teaching them through authentic lines of knowledge transmission.

A woman and her husband's parents and sisters interact, and their respective children accompany them in various tasks. For the children, these are consanguineal relationships, but for the adults, affinal. No doubt there is some new knowledge transferred between the women of the two households, but the women do not acknowledge this as a particular line of transmission. For the children, it is a relationship between grandparents and themselves, a key relationship for the Kayapó.

Between fictive parents and child. Any person classified as sibling to a child's parents may interact with a child as though he or she were its parent. A boy may go hunting with any of his fictive fathers and learn from him as he would from his biological father. A girl may help take care of one of her fictive mother's children, classified as her own sibling or sit and watch as the mother paints her biological children. In general, the closeness of the relationship between the child and the fictive parent will be determined by the degree of closeness the child's parents have with their respective fictive siblings. There is a potential material benefit from these relationships, since children have the right to request food from any of their fictive parents, when they are hungry. In terms of knowledge transmission, the child may learn something from a parent, but most commonly the type of information imparted is advice concerning acceptable behavior. In this sense, the relationships function as a form of extended but loose parental control over the behavior of children (see figure 8, page 83).

In this diagram we see that the people closest to the child (center) are members of his nuclear family (Kin 1), but in the same household he is surrounded by his mother's kin (Kin 2), whom he also calls mother (MZ), sister and brother (MZC), and grandparents (MM, MF).

For the male, his father's kin and cross-kin relationships (Kin 3) in other households are also important, especially the grandparent relationships (FM, FF, FZ, MB, MBS). The relationships cultivated between the grandparent set and the grandchildren set are especially important in terms of the child's education. This is also the relationship through which a child will receive a selection of names and rights.

In addition, a male child may form a relationship with some of his father's fictive brothers, learning from them what he would learn from his own father. Finally, he establishes relationships with nonkin people, especially those who will be his ceremonial partners.

From the time he is born the male child is educated away from the household of his birth, through the formation of teaching/learning relationships involving kin and nonkin from other households. This is in contrast to the female who receives most of her education from her mother's kin, the female members of her household of birth.

In community relationships. On the community level, elders are able to interact with all the households by means of a stylized oration. The message transmitted will then be picked up for discussion among members of households. In addition, elders have a role to play in the discipline of all boys in the general boys age-grade category. Children's play, especially among the boys, is also interaction among members of the broader community.

Verbal instruction by elders. The male elders have a generalized way of teaching the entire population, which is the harangue, sometimes referred to as "good talk." This stylized oratory consists mostly of exhortation to one group or another to adhere to certain social norms, and is often quite negative, i.e., "don't, don't, don't...." Theoretically, all the male elders qualify as haranguers, but not all are skilled orators. Thus, only certain of the elders actually engage in this form of oral communication, and those who speak the best are considered to have "big speech."

> Public speaking, in an ornate and blustering style, is the most characteristic attribute of senior...(authoritative) manhood, and the essential medium of political power. (T. Turner 1979b:13, 14)

The huge, wooden lip plug that the senior men wear is symbolic of this power and "a physical expression of the oral assertiveness and preeminence of the orator..." (ibid.).

The harangue usually takes place at dawn or in the late afternoon or early evening, when most people have returned to the village from their gardens. The men will have gathered in the men's house after eating something in their houses, and an elder will step outside of the men's house, perhaps leaning on a walking stick or club, and begin his exhortation in a loud voice, walking as he does so, his voice carrying through the dawn or twilight air. Conversation in the households may subside depending upon the novelty of the speech, or people tune in or out. No listener is obliged to do anything personally about the admonitions of the elders, but expectations are being voiced, and social sanctions may follow.

On one occasion, as my colleague and I were eating with Irenapti in her house, a loud harangue began. I recognized the voice of 'Êkêtti, Irenapti's brother-in-law, and noticed Irenapti listening intently and urging us to listen. The stylized speech is difficult to understand, let alone hear clearly, so Irenapti patiently reiterated the complete oration for me. In essence, 'Êkêtti was challenging the young boys to go to their elders and learn something. Of course, I was interested and the next day asked 'Êkêtti to repeat into the tape recorder what he had said the previous evening. His speech was as follows:

> What will you do to doctor your child? With your lust, with your intercourse, will you doctor your grandchildren? Smarten up! To save yourselves, ask us, for your own sakes; then when we're gone you can doctor your son, daughter, grandchild.
>
> Who will, at night, lie asking Bepgogoti? And who, at night, will lie asking Bàykàr? Who, at night, will lie asking Karadja? Who, at night, will lie asking Katemã? Who will, when it's night, lie asking dear 'Ypo? Who will, at night, lie asking old Bepnhô?
>
> The only thing you understand is your playing. Go according to the ways of our grandfather, your father, your grandmother, and quit your play and smarten up and learn (hear) something. So then you can, when we're dead, take our place and doctor your grandchildren.

The next day, when a group of boys came into the studyhouse to look at books, we asked, "Is it true what 'Êkêtti said about you, that you're not asking to learn things?"

"Yes, it's true," they replied cheerily.

"Why don't you want to learn?" we continued.

"Because."

"Because what?"

"Because...we don't want to go."

Then, in typical Kayapó fashion, they proceeded to give the names of five among them who were going to their grandfathers to learn something! Later on, one youngster, sensing my keen interest and possible distress, came in and volunteered to tell what exactly it was that he was learning from his grandfather 'Êkêtti.

The subject matter of exhortations, especially as these relate to the children, will be discussed and reinforced in the households. Irenapti assured us that she would discuss things with her son and try to orient the young man better. But another elder, upon hearing this, said, "They talk to the young in vain. They don't want to listen." In the case of the above harangue, everyone in the village would know who were the delinquent grandsons of the named elders. To name the elders was almost as good as naming the particular boys themselves.

Little boys as a group are thought of almost as a unit, not only in terms of the age groups they represent, but in terms of behavior. They are addressed as a group by haranguers, although occasionally the behavior of an individual might be singled out. But the unit is rarely punished for misdemeanors, the most frequent discipline being a public, verbal rebuke which brings shame to the families, followed by a second scolding at home. Apart from the power of words, there are other ways to call attention to adults' displeasure with children's behavior.

Discipline by grandparents. Grandparents do not directly discipline their grandchildren. Yet there are times when the children go beyond the bounds of what is considered to be reasonable behavior, and the grandparents believe some control is in order. Taking advantage of their shared identity with the offending grandchildren, the grandmothers get together and say, "Let's dance like our grandchild," implying the fooling-around behavior of the children. Then they dance to the houses of all their own children, i.e., parents of the misbehaving grandchildren, and ask for the containers of precious hair oils. They take these and spill the oil all over their heads "and the liquid just runs down all over the woven sleeping mats," and then they dance to another house and do the same thing,

> just ruining the wife's things. When it rains and there's mud, they rub the sleeping mats into the mud and take down the containers of seeds used to make decorative paint and chew them and throw them around.

The mothers and fathers just watch and the grandmothers say,

> Tuka! There you go! You who wanted to dance so much. Your grandmother has thoroughly smeared and ruined your parent's sleeping mats. What are you going to lie down on now? You who are always wanting to dance!

After this has taken place in several houses, the chagrined parents pay the grandparents with meat! This signifies the parents subordination to the grandparents and conveys that, at least publicly, there are no hard feelings. The parents will not admit to being bothered by these actions, but the desired effect is usually achieved as children are brought into line, at least for a little while.

I asked if the destruction of the property was meant to influence children's behavior by shaming them. "Do the children have shame?" was the retort, implying an emphatic "no." Was it to shame the parents, I enquired. "Yes," my friend answered, smiling. "The parents just watch and laugh," but the signal has been given to take more control over their children's behavior. This does not happen without some warning, since the grandparents will threaten these actions for awhile, before actually embarking upon the apparently radical behavior.

Such destructive actions taken by the grandparents are justified by the concept of doing things "according to your grandchild." For instance, when a child passes to an ascending age-grade and has his hair cut as a marker, the grandfathers will also have their hair cut by their own children (parents of the child in focus) and receive payment for it in the form of meat. When children participate in name-giving ceremonies, the grandmothers are "doing according to their grandchild" when they join in the dance. These actions confirm the shared identity between grandparents and grandchildren, but in the case of the ruining of the parent's goods, it gives the grandparents a socially acceptable way to express their opinions about the children's behavior.

Physical discipline by elders. From time to time, the boys are required to submit to the scraping of their calves and thighs, perhaps even their arms, by the elders. Girls are not scraped. The scraper is made from the sharp teeth of certain fish, and following the scraping, medicinal fluids will be rubbed into the long gashes. This method of control has two purposes: (1) to discipline boys who are considered by the consensus of the elders to be "bad" or "angry" and (2) to make them strong. Sometimes both reasons are given for a scraping event.

In fact, the formation of scar tissue seems to harden the skin's surface over time, rendering it more impervious to cuts and insect bites, but the toughening of the skin is more on the symbolic, social level than the physical. The skin, as a "shell" or boundary between the "inside" (*karõ* 'spirit') of the person and the natural world, must be strong to keep the spirit in and thus ensure the social nature of the person.

One day, just after several of the elders had assured me they don't do scraping any more, a gang of boys came running to me proudly showing off large gashes on their calves. "Tomorrow," they said brightly, "we will have our thighs done." "Who scraped you?" I asked. "Old man Bepnhô," they replied. "Why?" I countered. At this there was a jumble of replies, some saying because they were bad, others saying it was to make them strong. Later, one of the men intimated that the boys were "just going around" getting into trouble, so, when the men discussed the problem in the men's house, the scraping was suggested. This followed an incident when the boys broke into the government buildings, stealing crayons, which they used to decorate their toy airplanes. A public harangue, followed by the scraping, were the results of their misdemeanor, which was not considered merely boy's play.

The apparently conflicting replies concerning the reason for scraping, i.e., because they were bad or to make them strong, are really not so contradictory, since the boys behavior had an antisocial quality, and "being strong" is the equivalent of being socialized—that is, having a strong "shell" which ensures keeping the physical and social being united.

Play. Play, *bixaêr,* refers to children's activities in contrast to adult, goal-oriented activities. It may also mean "to tease," as, "I was only playing when I did that."

Another term used to express a type of playing is *kukãm* or *kajmã'ã* 'to foreshadow', as when children model some adult activity—playing house, making flour—foreshadowing what they will do as adults.

Still another expression referring to an attitude of play, but usually with negative connotations, is "to just go around." This is a rough equivalent to the English expression for "fooling around," and is often uttered with reference to young teens who ought to be settling into more adult roles, but are not. This term expresses the divide between legitimate play and inappropriate play. As children reach puberty, they are encouraged more and more against playing, and fooling around and told to smarten up and learn something from their grandparent, before it is too late. In other words, as far as the Kayapó are concerned, learning begins when playing ends.

From the perspective of social and educational theory, however, learning clearly takes place in the midst of play activities. Children are learning social roles, gender-related activities, motor and cognitive skills, to manipulate social relationships, and to deal with social conflict, all as they play.

> Playful routines provide predictable interactions within which novices learn sequences of action and disposition and complementary roles, and experiment with what is acceptable and what is not within a particular frame. (B. Schieffelin 1990:222)

As is often the case in so-called traditional societies, boys have fewer social responsibilities and more freedom to play until a later age than do girls. Tiny nursing children of both sexes play with each other, within easy access of their mothers or grandmothers. Girls play mostly with female age mates in their own household, but also may play with cross-cousins in the father's sister's household as well as the mother's brother's household. When boys are about five or six, they begin to play with a set of age mates from various households and range further from home than do the girls. Generally speaking, girls have constant access to adult role models in the midst of their play, whereas boys do not.

In playing with their younger siblings, girls are also caregiving, thus foreshadowing what they will do as adults. Most girl's play is of that nature, and as such, is legitimized in the eyes of their elders. Little girls from about two on make fires, carry a few sweet potatoes in scaled down baskets slung from their foreheads onto their backs, carry puppies or dolls around in a baby sling, and perform other acts modelling adult behavior. They are also given toys to play with, a favorite being fledgling birds or baby mice, which soon succumb to the attentions, causing no apparent distress to the child.

Older girls, in the five to seven-year-old range, help to carry water and small loads of garden produce, yet still love to carry manufactured dolls around in baby slings. They also model their mother's behavior and begin to pay attention to expressly female roles, such as body painting. For this they take advantage of leftover paint to experiment on their own.

One day several girls came bouncing into our study house with large, green gourds in their arms which they referred to as "my child." They sat around on the floor and proceeded to cover the gourds with designs. Some were very good, and I grabbed my camera to capture the results. My admiration of the most outstanding work (according to me) caused the others to quickly erase their gourds and begin to paint by hand, as opposed to painting with the stick, the latter requiring more skill. The young girls exhibited enjoyment and pride in their work and appreciated each other's efforts, and if the less able ones were aware of "shortcomings," their peers did not draw attention to them. I sensed that I had inadvertently caused some embarrassment by showing a preference.

Self-evaluation by comparing their results with those of someone else is not normal. The tendency, when experimenting with a skill, is for learners to proceed confidently and uncritically, and they are not at all embarrassed to say they think their work is good. If something causes them to feel their work is not very good, they will divert attention from themselves and their work in some way, and their peers cooperate with this strategy. As I discovered many times, in this and other contexts, any focus on shortcomings is an extreme embarrassment and is deliberately used for discouragement.

For the girl, then, the playing that meets with adult approval is the type that foreshadows her adult role. I observed young girls playing house, calling each other mother, and making a little shelter as their house. I have also seen them making manioc flour out of some of their mother's grated manioc. They had built a fire and were roasting the manioc on a wide flat pan, just as the adults do. Following this they sat around and ate it, supplemented by some other food. Sometimes, one of their brothers, say, age ten or eleven, will bring them a small fish, which they will take and cook for themselves, eating together, instead of with their nuclear family.

In households where there are several adult women, the pressure on the younger girls is diminished, and they have time just to enjoy themselves. A favorite pastime is playing in the river. They frolic in the water, climb up on tree branches and leap off, and would stay there forever, if mothers did not admonish them to fill up their pots with water and come home.

Play, for the boys, is under much less adult scrutiny than female play, because the boys play further away from the households in the transitional area of the rough clearing. Here the young boys, who are in transition from their households to the wider public arena, are relatively free to pursue their own interests, but they do so in a typically Kayapó way. They follow a leader. Just as adult male leaders are recognized by the consensus of a following, so are the male child leaders. The status of this person evolves as he attracts a following. He is the one who "gathers the others around him" and thus is recognized as the leader of the boys as much by the adults as by the children.

The leader suggests daily activities, and much of their play also foreshadows adult male roles. Perhaps they will hunt for birds today, and if they all agree, they pair off in pursuit of birds, kill them with arrows or slings, build a fire, cook the birds, and eat together as a group. Or they may go fishing after collecting grasshoppers as bait and either eat their fish or give them to their sisters.

Traditionally, the boys as a group were supposed to be up earlier than everyone else in the village and call from the rough clearing to awaken the people. They acted like sentinels, assuring everyone that enemies or animals were not threatening the village. But today, the elders complain, the boys don't do that anymore. This was a continual complaint of the adults, when speaking of the boys' group. Nevertheless, the boys are occasionally expected to render services to the village. They will be called on to cut a new path to the river, for instance, or to search for a sunken dugout canoe. The mother of the leader will often offer her son's group for these types of activity. A boy is considered a good leader by the adults in the measure that he leads his group to perform activities which meet with the approval of the adults. When this does not happen, the adults will begin to complain about the boys being bad, and soon their behavior will be the subject of a harangue from the elders.

Play often incorporates new information. One day we heard the boys playing "Going to the city." The main topic was what they would order to drink. Proud of their mastery of the Portuguese language, one said, "Fanta," another, "Guaraná"—soft drinks. Another said, "Cerveja"—beer, perhaps not knowing the difference! Then they started to pretend they were taking pictures with a camera.

Outside things are a huge attraction, working themselves into themes for play. The small airplanes that land on the village airstrip, are no exception. Trips to the grassy clearing to watch the frequent landings and takeoffs, are a common part of the young boys' daily rounds. They especially like to stand behind a plane as it revs up its propeller. They lean into the hurricane-force draft, with eyes closed and hair blowing, their squeals of delight drowned out by the crescendo of the motor. Such encounters inspire the older boys to create toy wooden airplanes with fancy propellers for their young brothers to play with. Just as girls are expected explicitly to care for their younger siblings, the older boys are expected implicitly to keep an eye on their younger brothers once these have joined the boys' gang.

Normally, older boys and girls do not play together because each go their separate ways during the day. One evening, however, we heard lots of laughter behind one of the houses, and found adults and children gathered to watch a wrestling match. There were three groups, two boys' groups and one girls' group. One child would challenge another from a different group. They would step into the center, and to cheers and jeers, try to throw each other to the ground. The next challenger came from the loser's group, to take on the one still standing. The hilarity came when the girls joined in, with the mother's of the boys who lost to the girls, making excuses for their sons, "He's been sick lately," "he's not strong yet."

One of the mothers later explained how the children had organized themselves:

> They divide themselves according to the men's societies. They defend each other. The ones who can't overthrow the strong on the other side are defended by the strong on their own side. No side wins or loses. When they sit waiting, they

are saying, "Go get him, go to it, fight him." Mothers stand around saying, "You'll break your neck!" "You'll have to go off in the plane!" "You won't be able to eat meat!" The children decide for themselves if they want to wrestle. The adults fear for their children.

This game illustrates several cultural values: men's societies, as an organizing principle; loyalty to group; the stronger defending the weaker, thereby neutralizing competition; no group winner or loser; parent's concern for their children; children's relative autonomy. In other words, Kayapó norms and patterns are apparent in games.

In summary, the words "to play" (or to foreshadow what they will do as adults) denote the Kayapó attitude to the activity of play as pertaining to children of both genders: enjoyable and experiential. When children become young adults, however, such activities are not considered play but rather, fooling around, and older adults take every opportunity to remind the youths that they are no longer children.

By the time girls reach puberty and have their thighs blackened, and boys have progressed to the sleep-new age-grade, sexual experimentation is a norm, but other forms of play in which they may engage begin to be criticized by the adults. Parents endeavor to channel their children's promiscuity towards a single partner, and eventual marriage, by means of many social pressures and admonitions. One pressure is expecting them to participate seriously in communal activities: women's society activities, such as clearing the village plaza of weeds in preparation for a dance or helping in a chief's garden; and the boys, as they move into the sleep-new age-grade, are expected to participate in communal endeavors pertaining to men. The reluctant young man or woman is strongly criticized, to the point of being practically forced to participate.

Another way good parents put pressure on their children is to chaperone their children when they participate in western-style dances in front of one house or another most evenings, whenever a Kayapó festival is not in progress. Parents who do not oversee their children's sexual activities are considered lax by the more righteous ones.

Hart distinguishes two phases of education in traditional societies: prepubertal and postpubertal. The evidence provided by my observations of the Kayapó lead me to strongly disagree with Hart's characterization of prepubertal education as, "rarely if ever standardized, rarely if ever regulated around known and visible social norms" (1963[1955]:361, 362). He states, "In asking for a uniform cultural pattern in such a laissez faire, anything goes area, we are asking for the inherently impossible, or at least the non-existent" (p. 405).

Hart's evidence to support the judgment that "prepubertal education in the simpler societies is relatively so variable as to be virtually normless" (ibid.) is that adults cannot give straight answers to questions about how children should be brought up. But, the following account reveals that the Kayapó have a clear idea how a girl should be raised.

Good women, according to the Kayapó, are "nonsleepy ones,"

> who made themselves good when they were children, and are still good. Those who go with their mothers to work and, together with their mothers, carry their burdens. They go with their mothers to get firewood and the mother splits the wood for them and they put it in their baskets and with their mothers they go back and throw it down and go together with their mothers to the water and bathe and return, and get *py* and redden themselves with it and sit like that and wait for their husbands on their bed.

"Waiting for their husbands" refers to the ideal of a girl's mother knowing the identity of the daughter's suitor so that payment can be claimed from him when he sleeps with her.

And the public harangues, often directed at children's activities and parent's duties with respect to their children, leave no doubt that the Kayapó have general and expressible norms for their children's upbringing.

Play may be considered as contributing to prepubertal education in that much of the activity in play, according to the Kayapó, foreshadows what will be done as adults and requires at least a subconscious notion of modeling on the part of both adult and child. Such play meets with the adults' approval in that no admonitions are forthcoming, and adults even encourage this type of play by providing food for their offspring when they play house, or gather to eat together. When play, especially boy's play, becomes bad, public notice is given. In addition, the adults begin to discourage teenagers' frivolous play as "just going around." The increasing public criticism of promiscuity, laziness, or anger (rebelliousness) is meant to channel the young teenager into his or her appropriate adult role. In many societies, such channeling of the youth is done by means of initiation rites, but for the Kayapó, ritual, as we shall see shortly, appears to have a much broader focus.

Summary

The daily activities which are enacted in the everyday setting, provide the educational milieu for Kayapó children and young adults. A child's most intimate relatives, the nuclear family and the household occupants, are the child's first teachers, and much learning is done by means of modeling adult behavior. But adults also intervene in children's education through the medium of the public harangue by elders, which is subsequently followed up with further instructions from parents. Learner initiative is the ideal towards which children are being motivated as adults verbally express values placed upon the acquisition of particular information which the child will negotiate with its grandparent set. Educational interaction is from the top down in terms of age, gender, and experience, the elder males having the most authority on the village level and the elder females having the most authority on the household level. The nuclear family is bonded together by the Kayapó notion of the common substance shared between each biological parent and its offspring, and the importance of this basic societal building block is emphasized by the abundance of knowledge that is directed towards the maintenance of this unit, as well as to the survival of individuals within the unit. This includes food restrictions and medicinal plants, survival skills, body painting—knowledge related to what the Kayapó define as within the physical, natural, everyday realm. A significant characteristic of this general knowledge is that it is transmitted freely, i.e., not with any expectation of a reciprocal exchange of any kind. This knowledge is not viewed as a form of currency, an asset which can later be given in exchange for something else. This is the type of knowledge which the parents are responsible to share freely with their children. What reciprocity there is occurs as the child becomes a contributing member of the family as a production unit.

The material that children learn in the broad, domestic environment is gender related. Girls' learning is more in focus than boys' within household settings. Here they are exposed to predominantly female skills, such as body painting or spinning and female roles and domestic routines, such as collecting garden produce and making manioc flour.

In the everyday setting, boys learn from their fathers and older brothers and perhaps a sister's husband, but much learning takes place with their age mates in play activities which mainly occur in the rough clearing area. In addition, boys will learn from persons who stand as mediators between their kin and wider nonkin relationships.

Contrary to the notion that most indigenous children are left to bring each other up, Kayapó adults have constant input into their children's upbringing. The female children, especially, are rarely away from the watchcare of female adults and role models. All children have many additional fictive parents who are actually the fictive siblings of their biological parents. These people have the authority to intervene and influence a child's actions and behavior. The boys may appear to run freely within the security of a gang, but the *bôkti* 'boys' age-grade is a regular subject of adult conversation. Adult opinions concerning their comportment are clearly verbalized to individual boys for the benefit of the group, and the elders keep a vigilant eye on the boys' group, the members of which are mostly their own grandchildren. Harangues and the discipline of scraping, are a form of control exercised by the elders over the behavior of the boys. The grandparents' actions of ruining precious objects belonging to their children to express displeasure concerning the behavior of their grandchildren is an indirect control over the children's behavior and a form of control exercised by the elders over the parents.

5

Celebrated Knowledge
The Ritual Setting

We have seen how Kayapó children learn the daily routines of life in the everyday setting. Kinship relationships within the household and between households are the main channels of learning the general knowledge related to everyday activities, and most of the daily routine is performed within the household family groupings.

In contrast to this, ritual performances, especially name-giving ceremonies, involve a network of relationships expanded to include nonkin members of society. Most activity related to Kayapó ritual events is performed in an interhousehold rather than a single household context, emphasizing cooperation between the extended siblings of the sponsors of a ceremony. The sponsors and siblings, as parents, are working on behalf of the grandparent "givers-of-cultural-patrimony," and the children, as receivers. Thus, relationships and experiences of teaching and learning take on a new dimension.

Normally, rites of passage, particularly for male members of traditional societies, are seen as a means for more structured instruction—something equivalent to the western concept of schooling. This chapter will show that Kayapó ceremonial activity, as the performance of traditional knowledge, is indeed, a form of education. We will see that ceremonial events for the Kayapó are not mindless, repetitive action. They imply a body of knowledge and practical information which is being actively and consciously constructed and reconstructed by all participants, and in the process being transmitted between people and from one generation to another. Concerning learning, the Kayapó themselves recognize that both the body and the mind are involved, so that learning is experiential and does occur in Kayapó ritual activities.

Learning within ceremonies contrasts with knowledge transfers in the everyday setting, not so much because of the formality, in and of itself, as because of the types of relationships which are in focus; because of different meanings assigned to the same space; because of formalized exchanges which are often involved, and most importantly, because the traditional knowledge which is transmitted through these relationships is directed towards the formation of the sociocultural and spiritual aspect of a child's being, just as general knowledge transmitted in the common routines of life contributes to the physical and biological aspects of a child's being.

The ritual context does not always represent the initial exposure of an initiate to special skills and information. Much of what the initiate is being taught has been learned already through prior exposure to rituals. But at one point in time, it becomes official for him or her. Part of the function of Kayapó ceremonial activity, therefore, is to legitimize or confirm certain knowledge transactions by utilizing special relationships which are considered by the Kayapó to be the correct channels through which traditional knowledge must pass. Participation in ritual confers upon the participants, especially children and those learning the ritual obligations and roles connected with their households, the right to the knowledge they are being taught over time. The specific children being honored in a name-giving ceremony are officially acquiring *kukràdjà* 'culture-stuff'—their names as well as some ritual rights and wealth. The honored children thus symbolize the reconstitution of their household as a ritual entity in the public sphere, yet they are not singled out more than others for special learning activities within ceremonies.

The subject matter to be learned in ritual is acquired in a holistic, integrated, and experiential way. Ritual activity provides an emotive context for the confirmation of skills and knowledge specific to ceremonies, but which has application in everyday life. Novices are exposed to the craftsmanship involved in the fashioning of ritual ornaments and costumes. The elder Kayapó teach songs and dances to their juniors. Myths and stories related to ritual traditions are recounted by elders to their grandchildren. Ceremonies ideally activate and revitalize interhousehold and nonkin relationships, some of which are utilized to convey special knowledge from a senior to a junior ritual partner. Ceremonies express and celebrate a hierarchical opposition between people in the grandparent category and parents (including fictive kin), where the former are the bearers of the social knowledge crucial to the formation of the parents' children. Name-giving ceremonies focus on the knowledge of female elders concerning the system of ownership and transmission of "beautiful names" and ceremonial rights and/or ritual wealth, as well as of the Kayapó customs or social knowledge which is the essence of Kayapó being and personhood.

Social space is redefined in ceremony, and the transmission of knowledge is illustrated by focusing on educational interaction within ceremonial activities themselves, as well as interaction related to ceremony, but not part of it. Bodily learning is seen as a viable way of knowing, in addition to verbal instruction.

Finally, a consideration of the sociocultural characteristics of Kayapó ritual illustrates that certain implicit information is communicated through the structure of the ceremony itself, some intentionally, some unintentionally. I argue that the sociocultural context of ritual is similar to that of a Western high school (Cusick 1973), in that pupil learning is not always cooperative, the authority of the elders must be reinforced, tacit as well as explicit knowledge is conveyed, and in the case of the Kayapó, the structure of society and its values are reinforced by the educational content of ritual activities.

Kayapó access to Western economic goods is seen as a strategy for making possible more ritual performances, which reinforces the existing patterns of knowledge transmission through ritual and seemingly ensures, rather than jeopardizes, the value and vitality of ritual as a form of Kayapó education (Siegel 1963:540).

Kayapó ceremonial life

We have seen that the domestic, family-oriented routines of Kayapó daily life are common to every household. The labor and productivity of individuals is relatively undifferentiated from one family to another. In the everyday setting, in other words, one house and its daily domestic routines is very much like another.

As the Kayapó move through time into the ritual setting, however, the apparent uniformity is transformed into a rich outwardly-displayed diversity. Rituals, such as name-giving ceremonies, ideally transform the private domestic units into a public, cooperative community in which each household, as a ritual entity, publicly displays the ritual wealth of its members. This happens as the household members are adorned with distinctive ritual decorations for the dances and enact ceremonial roles received from grandparents.

One general function of Kayapó ritual life is the linking of the private everyday sphere with the public communal sphere by socializing young household members from the biological to the social realm; from members of the household as a domestic entity to members of the household as ritual entity; from family to community. Thus, ceremonies celebrate the category of relations who are responsible for this transformation in a child—the child's parents' cross-siblings and parents of the same.

> Ceremonial names are bestowed by senior consanguineal relatives of the "cross-family" category...The ceremonial organization is thus preeminently identified with the assertion and celebration of this category of relations. (T. Turner 1987b:25)

This "assertion" and "celebration" recognizes the grandparent's role of contributing to the social component of a child by transmitting cultural patrimony—*kukràdja* 'the customs'. This status of grandparents is articulated in ceremonies in opposition to the status of parents as nurturers of the physical component of a child.

> Corporeal reproduction is not contrasted on the same level with the reproduction of knowledge for to do so would give it a sort of symbolic equality between the corporal and the cultural. Instead the system of kin classification contrasts the child's "mental nurturers" with "physical nurturers."...
>
> During ceremonies the circuit of cooperation is based on the child's classificatory parent's working in benefit for the child's mentor relatives [i.e., grandparent set]. (Fisher 1991:314, 386)

Some of the above social contrasts and oppositions are also expressed spatially, as private space is transformed into public space for ceremonial performances. For people of many different cultures, ceremonial activities take place in an especially constructed ritual environment, such as a temple, church, or ritual place of some type. As Smith observes, this marked-off space "serves as a focusing lens, establishing the possibility of significance by directing attention, by requiring the perception of difference" (J. Smith 1987:104). For the Kayapó, however, the common places are redefined by ritual, perhaps even recreated in ritual, from private domestic-oriented space, to public ceremonially-oriented space.

During festivals in a Kayapó village, it is tempting to see the central plaza as a large stage exclusively for the performance (particularly by the men) of colorful, vigorous dancing and lusty singing. Less obvious is the fact that the women are fully involved in the festivals, and the houses typically regarded as a female domain are as much a major focus of ritual events as the central plaza or men's house (Lea 1986:399; cf. Maybury-Lewis and Almagor 1989:101). Houses are the dominion of the senior matriarch, and names inherited from the grandparent set may be as much the patrimony of their household as a ritual entity, as they are of any individual. Houses are referred to, especially in ceremonies, as the place where particular rights are kept, yet rights and names also belong to individuals.

A major part of Kayapó ceremonial life is concerned with the grandparents' transmission of "beautiful names" and ritual wealth and privileges identified with a child's parents' birthplaces to the male or female child/children being honored. Children so honored become *me mex* 'beautiful people', a social category signifying that they have literally "slept with ornaments" (Verswijver 1985:151).

Kayapó ceremonial life includes nine name-giving festivals, *me rer mex* (Lea 1986:152), varying in duration from several weeks to several months. These are the *Bẽmp, Tàkàk* (m) and *Nhàk* (f), *Kôkô, Me my bijôk, Me ni bijôk, Kwỳrỳkango, Pãnhti, Ngrer,* and *Bekwynh*. The names which are confirmed in these festivals are considered "truly beautiful names" and bear the ceremonial prefix corresponding to a particular ceremony. For example, in the *Kôkô* ceremony only names beginning with the prefix *Kôkô*, such as *Kôkômatí, Kôkôbẽ*, will be placed on the nominated child. Three of the nine ceremonies, however, allow the transmission of any name, regardless of the prefix. The rule is that the name-giver, one of the child's grandparents, will pass along names by means of the ceremony in which that person received the names as a child.

Many times ceremonial names are not confirmed in ceremonies so remain simply good names. Not all people receive ceremonial names, having names considered either common or play names. And those with ceremonial names, may also have these other types of names. In 1980, twenty-eight percent of the adults had been honored as children in at least one ceremony, eight percent of these in two, with the numbers being almost equally divided over the sexes (fifty-one percent male, forty-nine percent female). In another village, thirty-five of ninety-three men had been honored as children, and twenty-six of ninety-three women, for a total of sixty-one beautiful people out of one hundred and eighty-six (Lea 1986:153).

Two name-giving festivals (*Bẽmp* and *Tàkàk*) include a male initiation ceremony and are therefore considered more prestigious. All name-giving festivals include the actual rite of name confirmation to both male and female children being honored.

The frequency of certain ceremonies in any particular village depends on a variety of factors: not only the size of the village, but also its composition in terms of the ritual components represented. Not all villages have equal ability to perform all ceremonies. The ideal is to have a large enough population, with a sufficient number of qualified ritual participants to perform the ceremonies adequately. When this is not possible, villages will unite to perform name-giving ceremonies. Kubẽkàkre is one of the larger villages, and ceremonies there appear to be on the increase, a trend observed by Verswijver during his field work in the early 1980s (1985:151).

Name-giving ceremonies are not strictly seasonal, barring a possible preference for holding them in the dry season. The Corn festival, however, is related to the corn's growing season. During the Corn and Tapir festivals, ceremonial rights/wealth are transferred, but naming rites do not occur. In addition, there are dances, such as the enemy dance, unrelated to particular festivals. The people also perform numerous rites, including the painting of a father's brothers upon the birth of his child, the painting at puberty of a girl's thighs, and many other such ritualized activities.

For the Kayapó, the significance of general everyday knowledge and enterprise is enhanced by its contrast with traditional knowledge ritualized within festivals. Actions, such as reciprocal exchanges of food between kin, which may seem mundane in everyday life, are transformed within ceremony to important gestures strengthening more tenuous and distant relationships. Activities not normally regarded as dangerous in everyday life become dangerous in ceremonies, and precautionary measures must be learned and taken. Common routines, such as gardening or eating, enacted in intimate groupings in the everyday setting, become public and communal during ceremonial activities.

In a word, the nature and essence of life's daily routines is brought into sharp relief against the backdrop of ceremonies. The significance of reciprocity, for example, can only be fully appreciated when it has been practiced both in nonceremonial and ceremonial contexts. "Routine giving plays off ritualized giving and vice versa; they define each other" (Bell 1992:91). "Ritual serves as a paradigm for all significant action" (Jennings 1982:118).

Ceremony is essential to the Kayapó way of life, not only in terms of the broad social functions it fulfills, but, in more pragmatic terms, because they believe the ritual property of names and rights must be circulated by means of a festival to be authenticated. That is, otherwise good names not confirmed in ceremony are considered *kajgo* 'in vain', since they were not conferred in exchange for the payment of a festival. In fact, the most generic term for *me rer mex* 'festival' refers to the tradition of passing on names and ritual privileges from grandparent to grandchild by means of name-giving rites and ceremonies.

Ceremonies also provide occasions for some to expend material wealth in order for the ritual wealth within every household to be displayed. In this sense, the ceremonial wealth pertaining to people as members of a household as a ritual entity is an important focus of ritual, with children receiving their own particular inheritance of names and ceremonial privileges and other household participants enacting or displaying their received rights.

It should be mentioned that ritual may or may not achieve its own ideals as stated by a community, such as unity, happiness, lots of food, and beauty. Many Kayapó ceremonies have erupted in feuds as the tensions of negotiating a wide variety of relationships with the accompanying transactions of reciprocity, payment, role obligations, and the like, prove too volatile. Yet, the ritual occasions which are considered to have reached a successful conclusion, according to the Kayapó, are the ones where complaints are minimal and where the sponsors of the ceremony are considered to have achieved the ideal of Kayapó behavior, i.e., generosity, and where the honored children, adorned in an abundance of ritual paraphernalia, were truly beautiful.

Name-giving ceremonies are a major part of Kayapó ritualized activity, requiring advance preparation. But many rituals may be invoked upon the spur of the moment, illustrating the high accessibility of an underlying ritual structure or organization which facilitates the dynamic process.

Ritualized activity

Within minutes, the Kayapó can step from the everyday to the ritual setting. I observed this on one occasion when a spotted jaguar invaded village space near to a stream where people regularly bathe and draw water. The animal killed one of two dogs although they put up a valiant defense, and upon the call, "jaguar!," all males, both men and teenagers, raced for their guns and converged upon the large cat. Each man put a bullet through the jaguar's skull, and the carcass was brought into the village and tied in an upright position to a pole placed near the men's house. Almost immediately, these same men, who moments before were hunters, appeared with their heads decorated in white feathers and their bodies hastily blackened with paint by a female relative.

The new fathers led all the men in the enemy dance. Circling the men's house, they sang in a high falsetto voice. Each time they passed the carcass, they mocked it verbally and physically. The song leader ended the dance with ritual wailing in front of the animal. Then the carcass was carried off to be skinned and butchered. Only unmarried boys and the elders could eat the meat. Women would allegedly go crazy if they so much as touched the carcass, and fathers would harm their children by eating it.

The Kayapó reasoning behind this incident was that the big cat had made himself their enemy by coming into village territory and threatening the people. Something natural had gone beyond its boundaries, stepping into Kayapó social/cultural space. The invocation of the enemy dance was to reassert Kayapó control over these boundaries. Once the carcass was removed, the men dispersed, and everyday routines were resumed in the houses. The excitement lingered, of course, and the story of the jaguar's sudden appearance on the river path grew with each telling.

The Kayapó have a name for all their ceremonies, as well as for dances within ceremonies. Each ceremony has special activities which contrast with those in other ceremonies, while also sharing some common elements. Not only are all ceremonies, name-giving and others, differentiated one from another, but ceremonial activity is differentiated from everyday activity, most especially in terms of goals towards which activity is oriented—wider community enterprise versus family enterprise; the relationships which are in focus—nonkin versus kin; the use of space; festival leaders versus political leaders as the main focus of leadership; elaborate and frequent body decorations of all participants versus less frequent painting; communal dancing and singing—only in ritual activity.

These differences and others aid the Kayapó and the outsider in distinguishing ritualized activity from nonritualized activity.

The main things which Kayapó ritualized activity share with everyday activity are the economic pursuits of both men and women, albeit with broader distribution patterns.

The following description of the *Kôkô* name-giving ceremony illustrates what is meant by ritualized activity, and highlights some of the knowledge which is performed in ceremonies. This illustration provides a context for the ethnographic observations to follow concerning the educational aspects of ceremonial life in general.

Kôkô name-giving ceremony

Presenting the *Kôkô* name-giving ceremony as consisting of four general phases—preparation, commencement, continuation, and climax—not only facilitates description, but corresponds directly with Kayapó accounts of the event.

Some general features of this ceremony to watch for, which have a bearing on Kayapó education, are: the planning and anticipation which accompany the preparatory phase; the importance of certain relationships to give validity to knowledge transactions within and beyond ceremonial life; the sense of ritual which is passed on by the elder generation to descending generations, which in turn correlates with renewed respect accorded to the elders; a review of the knowledge embodied in the naming traditions; a review of the knowledge embodied in the songs, dances, and traditions which are uniquely Kayapó; a reenactment of community values often expressed in a broader-based system of reciprocity than is common in the everyday setting; the learning of ceremonial-specific tasks and roles; and the sharing of ecological knowledge, survival, and medicinal skills.

These features, which may be inferred from the following descriptions, will be further elaborated by the comments of the Kayapó themselves in the next section.

Preparation. Long before anyone knows there will be a festival, several of the name-giving grandmothers[18] secretly plan it out. These women will secretly go to the parents of the child or children they will name, telling the adults to plant bigger gardens so there will be plenty of produce, especially manioc with which to pay the festival performers. This might happen around August, when the new gardens are being cleared.

The grandmothers are the instigators of a festival (cf. Banner 1978:109; Lea 1986:162–164; T. Turner 1979a:206), but the onus of the preparations falls upon the parents of the children to be honored. The father will immediately marshall the support of his brothers, both real and extended, and the mother and her sisters, since these people stand in a parental relationship to the child being honored. Members of the real parents' societies or moieties will collaborate in many ways. In addition, all of the child(ren)'s grandmothers will eventually contribute with produce from their gardens. It is important for the festival sponsors to look after the people well, implying generosity. They become role models to exhibit the Kayapó ideals of highly social behavior. The grandmothers themselves are not sponsors. The sponsors are the parents of the child(ren) to be honored and those in the category of parents' siblings.

One elder, Bepnhô, had been honored as a child in the *Me Bijôk* festival, but had sponsored both a *Kôkô* festival and a *Kwỳrkangô* festival on behalf of his children. His mother, he said, told him far in advance so that he could plant bigger gardens. I asked him if he was happy to sponsor a festival or did he think about how much work it would be. He said he thought, "Oh, now I won't be able to eat!" referring to the dietary restrictions placed upon all participating sponsors. But he added, "when they

---

[18]The grandmothers may represent three ascending generations, including a child's (ego's) father's sister, mother's and father's mothers and grandmothers.

(sponsors) see their children in their beauty and the climax of the festival, then they are happy."

When the corn is ready (about March), the sponsoring father goes to the two men who will announce the festival and pays them meat for their services. These two then go to the men's house just as the men are about to disperse and officially announce the anticipated *Kôkô* festival out of earshot of the children. The role of announcer is an inherited festival right, which includes the onerous task of giving a dawn call for the duration of the festival to awaken people for the morning dance.

Within a few days, the announcers will appear, dancing around the village at dawn, saying *"kô kô kô kô,"* thus officially initiating the festival activities. That afternoon they will be wrapped loosely with some palm fibre in a make-shift anteater costume, foreshadowing the proper costumes which will now be prepared by some of the men, and the two do the dance of the anteaters. At this stage, the men who know how to weave will start making the monkey masks for themselves and others; these masks are a major part of the *Kôkô* ceremony. Meanwhile, two of the sponsoring fathers' ceremonial partners who have been chosen to accompany the child(ren) throughout the festival will be weaving the gigantic *kôkô* body masks which represent a mythological character, perhaps the big, striped catfish (Banner 1978:109), although I was unable to confirm this.

Two shelters, separated by distance, are constructed in the woods, one for the preparation of the anteater costumes and the other for the monkey costumes which represent the howler and capuchin monkeys, respectively. The palm fibre from which the costumes will be made is collected, heated, and dried, and each camp begins to fashion the masks, spying on each other like enemies to keep track of each other's progress. At regular intervals, the festival mother (sponsor) will bring food to each encampment in payment for the men's participation.

When the black fringes on the anteater costumes (representing the male and female and its child) are nearly done, the elders from the monkey encampment come openly to gauge the progress. When they see the completed fringe, they return to assemble all the monkeys—every available man in the village who is not part of the sponsoring family or dancing with the anteater costume. Each side gets ready to enter the village circle.

Commencement. A forerunner is sent to the village, announcing the impending arrival of the anteaters. This is a signal for mothers to gather their children to protect them from the fierce anteater, who might chase them with his big sharp claws. The songleader, shaking a gourd rattle, leads all the participants—the howler monkeys preceding the anteaters, followed by the capuchin monkeys.

The anteaters do their distinctive dance several times, beginning at their encampment, then nearby in a clearing, then behind the houses in the village, then in the village patio near the men's house. The imitative dance is said to represent the anteater tearing apart a termite's nest. The howler monkeys walk around, talking and joking in a laryngealized voice. They are followed by a long, impressive, silent file of swishing, swaying capuchin monkeys, walking two by two in their long grass skirts. The howler monkeys clown around with the anteaters prior to the dance in the village center to the amusement of all the women and children who have gathered in the men's house to watch the opening performance. The anteaters then do their main dance, followed by the song which will be sung each day, morning and evening, until the festival's climax.

Continuation. Once the ceremony begins, the monkeys and the anteaters circulate around the plaza for the whole day and into the evening, each and every day of the festival. The men, especially the young bachelors, take turns with the anteater costumes, doing the characteristic dance which resembles the actual behavior of the animal. When they are not enacting the anteater, they are in their monkey costumes going around the village. Some are always the howler monkey and others always the capuchin monkey. The howler monkeys are the ribald jokers, speaking in laryngealized voices to disguise their identity, entering the houses and teasing the women and children. The capuchin monkeys speak in a high falsetto voice and are allowed to go into the houses. If they spot meat, they can ask for it. They may also trade something for meat, but they must not eat the meat themselves. Their mother or wife will say, "So-and-so is selling meat. Go and buy some," and he will go and trade for it.

If the costumes are not receiving their due respect or the people are not doing the ritual correctly, the elders will give loud harangues in the evening, admonishing the adults to curb their teenagers (the apparent offenders), as happened several times during this ceremony.

Trek. The next phase of the ceremony is the communal trek, õtõmõr. The trek presents the Kayapó with a wonderful teaching and learning opportunity, concerning not only survival skills, but also traditional lore. (More will be said in this regard in the next chapter.)

One of the objects of the trek, in practical terms and as stated by the Kayapó themselves, is the collection of as many land tortoises *(Goechelene denticulata)* as possible. These can be kept alive for extended periods of time, without food or water, so are saved for freshly killed meat to be steamed in their shells in large stone ovens as part of the concluding ceremonies. When a sufficient number of tortoises has been collected, they are tied firmly between racks formed of two poles. The effect is a long ladder of tortoises, each rack holding up to sixteen reptiles. Eventually, the men carry these very heavy loads to the sponsor's house in the village. Their arrival signals the impending climax of the ceremony, and the women run to relieve the men of their baskets of cooked meat (from collective hunts and previously cooked by the men). These are exchanged for the garden produce of the women.

Those men carrying the tortoises file silently into the village and dispose of their burden. The racks of tortoises are laid down against the men's house and in the sponsors' house. Reciprocal obligations are fulfilled by all and sundry, and everyone eats well, except for the festival sponsors. They must now prepare for the final day of the ceremony, organizing themselves for the preparation and distribution of manioc pies,[19] the killing, cooking, and distribution of the tortoises, payment of corn and other garden produce in exchange for ritual roles being performed, and, above all, the elaborate painting and decoration of their children being named.

Climax. The women in the sponsors' household have been up nearly all night since the arrival of the men, grating and preparing an abundance of manioc to process into flour sufficient for many meat pies. They prepare one or more large stone ovens for the hapless tortoises. Various people come over to see the haul for themselves and begin picking and choosing which tortoise they want. The women sponsors kill some of the reptiles by hacking the undersides with an axe and removing the heart and entrails. Entombed in their hitherto protective shell, the creatures are thrown, with legs still flailing onto the hot stones.

In the late afternoon, the men, discarding their monkey costumes temporarily, become long-legged birds. They, with their young sons or grandsons, cover themselves with large palm leaves and dance to the sponsor's house in a manner imitating of the bird's behavior. They receive in exchange hunks of soft, well-cooked meat.

That same day, at dusk, representatives of those households with the right to perform the "useless songs" which are imitative of different

---

[19]This is not the flat bread *(beiju),* but a layer of home-processed manioc flour filled with meat or fish pieces, and covered over with more manioc flour, forming a large, thick, pie-like food.

useless animals or birds,[20] begin their performances. Each performance is done by a person or a group of people with the grandchild(ren) to whom the right to perform the role is being passed. In the name-giving ceremony we observed, there were seven such performances, each originating from the household whose occupants maintained the rights to the particular songs and dances involved and each danced with young household members learning the role.

The literal visual image from which the expressions "old head" and "new head" derive is that of the grandparents dancing with the tiny grandchild on their shoulders, the new head protruding just above the old. The significance of the grandchild dancing in front of or on the shoulders of the grandparent, often a grandmother, is that rights or a ritual role are symbolically being transferred by means of this action (Lea 1986:257). In addition, the children are being shown how to dance and generally participate in the ceremony. As one woman explained:

> The grandfathers tell their grandchildren their rights and their songs. They tell their grandchild, and so the younger generation go around with the songs and take their place next to the older ones in the singing.

Attitudes are apparently quickly learned, for two- or three-year-old children dance with the utmost gravity, as do their adult models.

Recording every aspect of the climax of the festival was totally chaotic for the ethnographer! Many events occurred simultaneously, and while I was one place taking a photograph, something equally interesting or important was happening somewhere else. Several household groups were performing their particular ritual role, their young members weighted down with bead decorations being shepherded here and positioned there. All the men from each society or moiety, including the bachelors from the sleep-new age set, danced in relays with the anteater costumes. Finally, the woman whose right it was to dance with the female anteater mask in this grand finale stepped into the costume, and she and her male counterpart knelt silently near the men's house. Then they began to dance and sing the familiar song one last time. Everyone listened for the more timorous female voice (they like the woman to sing out unabashedly) and snickered as she faltered over the words.

Then there was general bedlam as two men, lying in wait under a woven mat, leaped into action and chased after the anteaters, ripping the costumes off them. They raced with these toward two long poles (about fourteen feet in length) held by the men at about a twenty-degree angle from the ground.

---

[20]This may refer to common songs in the sense that ordinary people sing them, and not the songleader, or it may refer to less esteemed animals in terms of edibility.

The costumes were thrown onto the head of the poles even as these were being hoisted into the air. Then followed the spectacular scene of men and women, grouped at the foot of each pole, jump-dancing the pole towards the men's house. Two men with long forked sticks steadied the swaying poles upon which the costumes were precariously swinging. It was obviously a tense, anxious time, and later I learned that if the costumes had fallen off, it would have been a disastrous omen, jeopardizing the lives of the children about to receive their names.

Even as the poles were being danced toward the men's house, a dignified, beautifully decorated group of five people was standing quietly in a line, expressionlessly watching the exciting finale. They were the name-giving *Kôkô* grandmother, her two female grandchildren about to be named, and the girls' ceremonial partners. When the masks reached the men's house and were leaned against the roof, the songleader stood before the five and blessed them with the powerful words of the *bẽn* speech.[21] This is to ensure that the festival children will have a good forehead, good joints, be good looking, and so that females will have a good pubic area.

> The wisdom *(mana)* that is imparted...is not just an aggregation of words and sentences; it has ontological value, it refashions the very being of the neophyte. (V. Turner 1969:103)

Following this, the girls and their naming grandmothers filed silently to the house of the *Kôkô* grandmother and received their names in a lengthy rite which involved many elders making pronouncements, more blessings, and, not to be outdone by the visiting fieldworker, eight or more people tape-recording the event for posterity.

I have attempted, in this description, to illustrate and define the nature of the context we are considering as an educational setting. In addition to this ceremony, I also witnessed others—the people's painting ceremony, the stick-beating dance, and the *Kwỳrkangô* festival, to which I will refer as we consider the educational value of Kayapó ceremonial life and the knowledge transmission and learning which occur in this setting.

Underlying all the action and activity inherent to the process of ceremonial life, however, is a structure and organization which implies a community's mastery of traditional knowledge and practical skills. Ceremony, for the Kayapó, is knowledge performed in ritualized activity.

---

[21]The ritualized speech/chant *me'ã bẽno ku'êo mõ* 'doing the *bẽn*' is known as chief's speech although it can be performed by songleaders and others who are not chiefs, but have inherited the right to incant in this style. It is performed in ceremonies and is distinct from *bẽndji* or *bẽjadwry* 'placing the *bẽn*'. This latter refers to the chanting of a powerful ritual speech which, according to the elders, is not really performed anymore.

Ceremony as performed knowledge

Kayapó ceremony may be seen as PERFORMED KNOWLEDGE in the sense that its enactment represents the accumulated learning of its performers over time. In any given ceremony, many people will be performing some participatory action either for the first time or for the first time on their own. This latter category of participants will have observed the action many times previously. These actions include particular inherited ceremonial roles; costume making; dancing and/or singing; and the role of ceremony sponsors.

The knowledge of naming, i.e., onomastic knowledge, represented in ceremonial name-giving is incredibly complex. In spite of this, or perhaps because of this, only one empirical study of Kayapó naming practices has been undertaken (Lea 1986).[22] Knowledge of names and naming customs is stored in the minds of the female elders and implies, in part, a social memory of what names pertain to which household; who has temporarily borrowed some names which later have to be returned to a child in the household; which names have actually been conferred upon which person; and much more. In the village of Kretire alone, among 177 people, Lea (1986:174, 175) registered 1,477 names. Most people had between six and fifteen names apiece. Several had between sixteen and eighteen names and one child had thirty-two! Those who receive the names generally do not remember all of them. The name givers, especially the grandmothers, keep track of the names; and most mothers remember the names of their own children.

The ceremonial patrimony connected with households includes not only names, but ritual rights and ceremonial roles. Such rights are not primarily material goods, in the sense of something which is tangible and storable, although some things are. They include, for instance, the right to certain portions of particular animal meat, the right to raise certain pets, the right to perform particular roles in certain ceremonies, the right to special songs and dances, and the use of unique ceremonial paraphernalia, to name a few. These are all transmissible rights and are passed from grandparent to grandchild during naming and other ceremonies. One woman, explaining this to me, stressed the exclusivity of a particular right to a particular owner and household:

> They don't go around with another's rights. Just the actual owner of it. Just the actual owner goes around in it. Just the actual household where it is owned; that same household goes around in it.

---

[22]Other studies exist which focus primarily upon patterns of transmission (Bamberger 1974; Lave 1979; Verswijver 1983; Fisher 1989).

Rights, as well as names, may be loaned from one ceremonial partner to another, but must be returned to a grandchild of the original donor.

I asked a young man if he had ever passed any of his inherited rights to his ceremonial partners. He said he had not yet done so, but if he did he would "plan it out to him and he [the recipient] wouldn't give it to his own nephew or grandchild. He would give it back to my grandchild."

Rights are often passed on in this manner only after the death of the person from whom they were originally received, in which case this man may not have been in a position to pass anything along.

According to Lea (1986:181), the system of names and rights are a system of social classification. The people, especially male, whose names have been ceremonially confirmed, those with the truly beautiful or great names, are distinguished from the others (commoners) during rituals, by their decorations, particularly a certain type of shell earplug. They represent a Kayapó ideal of beauty which is socially produced.

> The name-giving ceremonies publicly articulate the knowledge which is divided among the various corporate entities. It is during the great name-giving ceremonies that the Kayapó come closest to achieving their esthetic ideal, in the sense that these constitute occasions when the entire social corpus is most completely composed. (Lea 1986:68)

For many participants, a ceremony is more like a test of past learning, than a lesson for present learning, since it provides the context for the individual to put into practice his or her own cumulative observations and bodily learning of past ritual performances. How a transfer of ceremonial knowledge occurs is the next consideration.

Learning within ceremony

It would seem that the learner of ritual is similar to an apprentice, learning both cognitively and bodily as he watches and immediately performs the actions observed. Expertise is not expected short of much repetition and many performances.

Many ritual activities included elements which the Kayapó themselves consider educational. In the men's and women's painting ceremonies, new songs were consciously and deliberately taught by the elders to their juniors, particularly to the newest members of the new adult group—male or female. The songs come to the elders in their dreams and are subsequently taught to others. In the men's version of this ceremony, one elder taught a song he had learned from another ethnic group in southern Brazil where he had spent some time undergoing treatment for tuberculosis. Later he asked me if the festival sponsors had commented on it, since teaching a song is a way of honoring the sponsors.

In the women's painting ceremony, in preparation for the climax of the singing and dancing, the women all went to a spot in the rainforest (but not too far from some gardens). I helped as we hastily cleared a dancing circle with machetes as well as a clearing for the whole group to be seated.

A red arnatto-seed dye was streaked across everyone's eyelids in a decorative fashion, and a headpiece of palm fibre crowned our heads in lieu of the men's headdresses, which would be worn in the final ceremony. We were all seated together with one or another of the elder women suggesting a song. Everyone joined in the repetitive phrases until the volume indicated we had all learned and were all singing. Then another song would begin. Often the music is the same to many songs, but the words change.

For the final night-long dance of the women's ceremony, each woman wore a man's headdress including the most prestigious, body-length headdress, *krokrànhti*. One woman had put hers on backwards, dancing around the circle twice before her husband stepped forward and placed it on her correctly. Surprisingly, no one laughed. Later, when I questioned her about this she replied, "Do I know about headdresses? Of course not!" Yet she would have danced with headdresses many times over the years, whenever that ceremony was performed. The implication was that it was not female knowledge, in spite of experience.

In the enemy dance described earlier, the male children danced at the end of the line of adults, learning as they performed. The dances in any ceremony are clearly arranged so that the young learners have elders before and behind them. The front ones set the example and those bringing up the rear shout directions and encouragement.

The stick-beating dance performed by the men is attractively colorful and catchingly rhythmic—energy in motion as the men dance and sing, each to the steady beating together of his pair of sticks. Just as the singing winds down with a loud, unanimous, collective sigh, they suddenly pick up the rhythm and start again. This continues from one dawn to another without interruption, although the men would spell each other off for brief rest periods. The goal is to show endurance with strength.

When this dance ended, I expected all the men would collapse into their hammocks to sleep the better part of the day away. But some went fishing and others went out to the clearing where they had prepared for the dance and coached all the boys of the *bôkti* age-grade to prepare for and perform the same dance in the village plaza. There was little doubt in my mind as I watched the boys preparing and practicing for this dance that they were being schooled by their elders in the many facets of performance. Not only had they just observed the men's stimulating performance but they were about to perform the same dance themselves. Several of the individual boys' true grandfathers functioned as teachers to the whole group, and the actual grandsons or the leader of the boys would question them when they were doubtful as to the correct procedure.

I was fortunately alerted to this learning event when someone came for me, wanting me to take pictures. I watched, fascinated, as the boys went through the same routine they had just witnessed in the men's performance. Although the above-mentioned elders were present, the leader of the boys basically organized the practice, and only when there was some confusion concerning the direction the dancing line should take did the elders intervene with instructions. Otherwise, they nodded and spoke their approval of the whole effort. Then one of the men indicated that the boys should dance to the village and perform in front of the houses. This they did with all the energy and voice they could muster, with several of the men bringing up the rear.

When they reached the village, all the women came to the doors of the houses to watch, and some grandmothers joined in the dance, dancing behind their grandson in their customary identification with him, but also giving the dance their prestige. The boys' dance was taken as seriously as the adults' dance, and everyone seemed satisfied with the result. Comments such as, "the boys really know well" were heard, particularly from proud grandparents.

In addition to experiential, bodily learning, there is the component of verbal instruction where talk plays a validating role, as much as, or more than a didactic role. "In tribal societies...speech is not merely communication but also power and wisdom" (V. Turner 1969:103). The verbal component signals the authority of the senior person over the junior and is expressed through particular kin and nonkin relationships which function in ritual to socialize individuals into the broader community.

The grandmothers discuss the whole strategy of naming: why this particular ceremony is being held, who is giving names to whom, or, in some cases, returning names to the correct household. The grandfathers use the occasion to recount stories to their grandchildren, stories of past festivals, past hunting experiences related to festivals, and other pieces of Kayapó history, much of which can be recalled by placing occasions in time in relation to what festivals were in progress and who was sponsoring them. The festivals are like a mnemonic device in that regard, aiding in a recollection of history.

In the ceremonies, there are the "inners," people who keep up the rhythm in the dances, who encourage the people, by word and example,

Ceremony as performed knowledge 121

to sing and dance. "They never let up," said Nhàktu. "They wake the people up in the morning and keep at them throughout the day to participate wholeheartedly."

The festival sponsor is meant to exemplify Kayapó ideals of good behavior and generosity. In order to encourage the people to dance all night (prior to the climax) a sponsor might say what one sponsor actually said, as he verbally expressed these ideals:

> Because the earth is hard and the night is long, you'll have to dance a long time before dawn. Would I take a club and hit any of you? [implicit: no]. I'm the sponsor. I'm kind. The ground is hard; sticking it out all night is hard. You want to quit. So continue on for your daughter, for your ceremonial partner [implicit: his child being honored]. I'm teaching you to go on and be good to each other.

As special ritual paraphernalia are being made by the senior partner in the presence of the junior partner, the semichant of "may my ritual partner see, may my partner see" is an example of the verbal component used almost magically, to validate the knowledge transfer—signifying that each is correctly fulfilling his role in relation to the other.

Many of the verbal harangues given by the elders serve as didactic monologues—a commentary on the ritual and a way of registering their input and thus stamping their authority on the ceremony. The ritualized blessings are unintelligible to the majority of people, yet occur as performative acts in and of themselves. When the blessing was performed over the girls being named, many people tape-recorded the speech. Later, in our house two of the junior women (no woman ever performs the blessing) played and replayed the speech, mimicking it until they had memorized it. They seemed to enjoy repeating it, but in Kayapó terms such learning was not valid—it was *kajgo* 'empty', not acquired through proper channels by reciprocal transactions, and could never officially be put to use. This fact did not seem to diminish their enthusiasm, however, and underlines a general point which should be emphasized with regard to Kayapó learning, i.e., learning does occur (and is considered by the Kayapo to occur) whether or not it is socially validated by being transmitted according to socially correct channels within their system of reciprocity.

Learning relationships. Several of the relationships which function to transmit knowledge within the ritual setting are more appropriately discussed in the next chapter since they are what I have termed intermediary relationships. These are social links which operate both in the everyday setting and in the ritual setting and which, in relation to ego, bridge the two settings. Such relationships are those of the grandparent to grandchildren, the relationship between ceremonial partners, and the role of the fictive parents of a child being named, especially that of a male child's substitute fathers.

One of the main channels for the transmission of ritual knowledge is to be found in the role of the songleaders. These men, and the knowledge they transmit, are indispensable to the continuation and continuity of Kayapó ceremonial life. The performance of any ceremony represents the accumulated knowledge of the community, but the people who are considered to know the most are the two songleaders, even though they are not the most elderly. These people inherited their knowledge from a grandfather who was a songleader before them, and they also manifested a desire to learn.

It may not be accidental that each songleader in Kubẽkàkre is from a different society or moiety. One of the songleaders told me that he was the only one chosen out of his grandfather's possible grandsons because he had been festivalized three times, implying that he would therefore be more "beautiful," meaning complete or socialized, and therefore, more qualified. He said that he was passing the role on to six of his grandsons, but that not all will follow it up. We see, then, that the knowledge possessed by the songleaders (most importantly the esoteric, verbal knowledge, such as songs and the blessing speech, but including also practical knowledge of the ceremonies' correct organizational features) is a form of instruction which enables ceremonies to be performed as they should be.

> Only the functions of chief, or ceremonial leader and of shaman require a specific instruction during youth. Other functions in question are acquired in consequence of personal qualities and the display of individual ambition. (Verswijver 1985:156)

I believe this to be the case, based upon more frequent reference in my data to the intent of teaching these roles.

Since the ceremonies given are those by which the name-giving grandmothers received their names, it follows that the male sponsor will not necessarily have the detailed knowledge required to sponsor a ceremony. For instance, one elder, as a child, had his names confirmed in the men's painting ceremony, but was required to sponsor two different ceremonies on behalf of his children. The sponsors must look after people well. They must provide adequate quantities of food from their gardens; they are "like the chiefs" during a ceremony; and they must pay the specialists, such as the spirit-knowers, to use their powers in ways that protect the participants against the dangers inherent in the ceremonies. But how do they know what to do? Who shows them?

One elder told me that since one of his (fictive) fathers had sponsored a *Kôkô* festival, he was the person whose advice he followed. Having sponsored such a festival, this man was known as a *Kôkô*-father and was, therefore, qualified to advise about that ceremony. The type of advice given was practical in nature, concerning how to handle the monkey men if they beg meat and how to make the most of the exchange of tortoises for valuable items. In his turn, this elder became advisor to the man who sponsored the *Kôkô* festival I witnessed. Again, we see the pattern of the senior advising the junior person, and every man who has sponsored a particular ceremony becomes a festival father of the ceremony they sponsored. As such they are now qualified to advise others, but preferably they will instruct a relative.

As the dances progress, many of the elders, unable to participate fully for very long, sit in the men's house and watch. From this vantage point they comment and give instructions, and if the younger men are in any doubt as to procedure, they will soon find out. If rules are broken, there will be harangues in the evening, given by one or two of the more prestigious elders pointing out what should have been done.

In point of fact, the elders are recalling the past participation of now-deceased people. They are watching the grandchildren of these people performing against the standard of the former participants and judging how well the younger person has learned and is performing. Does he remind them of the former performer? He should, for in a sense it is through the grandchild that the grandfather lives on. One man, recounting how his grandfather had performed a certain part, today sees his brother doing it, the role having been passed on to the brother. He reminisces nostalgically:

> Hmph. Why? Why is it all over? Why did he have to die? My grandfather, that one: his mussel-shell earrings glistened, his large armbands were red, and he lay in wait for the costume. And he was the real one who threw the costume onto the stick.

In relation to this, one of the important roles of the elder women in ceremonies is to stand in front of their houses and wail for the dead, often gashing their heads with machetes, until their daughters restrain them. In this way the ceremonies honor the dead, as well as the living, and the cyclical nature of life and death is recalled. In addition, the younger women are hearing and learning the special terminology and actions of ritualized keening, which they will later have to perform.

All of these things point to the authority of the elders. They alone can recall the past. They alone can say with assurance how the ancestors did things and how they should be done now. Thus, in terms of knowledge transmission, ceremonial knowledge, more than any other, gives the elders great prestige. As Werner suggests, "For [the] elders, knowledge is more important than the social ties they establish during their lifetimes" (1981b:25).

This raises the interesting question as to why ceremonial life should be so central to the Kayapó, that such a high percentage of the influence attributed to elders is correlated with their ceremonial knowledge. Is it for the geographical and ecological content? Is it because ceremonies build endurance, and thus physically prepare the group to withstand warfare? Is it because ceremonies regulate ecological and social relationships (Werner 1981b:24, 25)? Whatever may be the answers to these questions, the influence of the elders is apparent, and it would seem to be to their advantage to keep things this way. Certainly the elders make the effort to assert their authority, and this can result in some intergenerational learning tensions from time to time.

Learning tensions. During the *Kôkô* ceremony described earlier, I became aware that not all was going as the elders would have wished. The young girls being honored appeared under the huge *Kôkô* masks only two days of the daily appearance of the masks during the month-long ceremony: the first day and the last day. When I asked about this, Bepmotire reluctantly admitted that they should have been present every day, but "the younger one had refused, therefore it wasn't done correctly." The boy who took the role as the baby anteater, also did not perform every day as he was supposed to do. I thought perhaps he was sick, but was told by a disgruntled elder that the boy was "just fooling around, that's why he wasn't there!"

When the long lines of monkey-men appeared on the first day, I was told that they should have all come from the place where the anteater costumes were made, but instead,

> The young teens are all confused, so put their costumes on where they made them and started yelling and crying from there, and that wasn't right. They should start from the anteater place.

Towards the end of the ceremony, one woman gave a long harangue about how her son had been mistreated and his costume pulled off him violently. And the elders noted with irritation that the young children were peeking up inside the costumes and discovering the identities of the bearers, which was really wrong and not at all like they did it in the old days.

> The younger generation isn't doing it right. They don't know. They are supposed to be fierce and not reveal their true identities, instead of which they play around a lot and let people know who they are.

On one occasion there was a harangue about an even worse misdeed, and the whole village grew quiet following this one. Apparently, a girl had put on one of the costumes and had gone around the village as though she were a monkey (man).

There were also instances of older people refusing to participate for one reason or another. On the day before the climax, one role was not performed because, according to prevailing opinion, the festival sponsor had not offered enough pay, so the person had refused to appear. Another person became the defenseless victim of a taped session with me, as Bepmotire used the occasion (and the usual audience) to remonstrate about someone's lack of participation: "Who is going to be bold and fill old man Kôkôreti's place? No, differently, the grandson will get his wife and lie there with her in her mother's house night after night."

This tirade, directed at one of Kôkôreti's grandsons, implied that all the young man did was think about sex, and that he was not keen enough to perform his validated role in the ritual. The lecture included the contrasting ideal:

> But the ones who leave their wives, they fill their uncle/grandfather's place, then when the grandfathers are gone, the mothers and grandmothers tell them about their rights.

The rights thus become the possession of the new generation upon the death of the old, and the knowledge concerning these rights is stored with the elders including the elder women.

The problem is that the young people must signal their intent to receive, or better, confirm their inheritance by learning and performing the role, and apparently they are not always self-motivated in this regard. One evening my Kayapó "niece" was about half-decorated for her part in the dance that evening when she staunchly refused to put on any more beads! She sat in her hammock as her mother admonished in vain, then other adults joined in, including her father—all to no avail. The grandmothers came at the mother's request, but still the child refused to be moved. Finally, the adults desisted, and the girl (about 9) stayed wordless in her hammock. She never changed her mind.

Children in Kayapó society, especially the boys, are relatively free agents and are not always happy to subject themselves to the rigor and discipline required of them in the ceremonies. Achieving their cooperation in ritual or other events creates an underlying tension where the end result is not always predictable. Elders frequently give public harangues during ritual, exhorting the boys to join in the dances. After one lengthy harangue, I asked a gang of boys if they heard what the elder said.

"Yes."

"Will you go?"

"Oh, yes, tomorrow we'll go."

"I'll go to watch you," I said.

Later, when we saw the elder who had spoken, we told him of our conversation with the boys. "They lie!" he said, smiling.

That evening, the parents of the leader of the gang of boys admonished their son to be a leader and lead his followers to participate in the dance as the elders had exhorted. But, aside from some verbal pressure, no further measures were taken by the adults.

The boys did not join in the next day, and I waited with interest to see if any of the adults would comment. No one did. They seemed unconcerned. I asked the mother whether the boys would eventually come through. "Wait!" she said.

Sure enough, the following day they were there, participating in all seriousness, as though it had never occurred to them to do otherwise.

Participation, for the boys, then, is ideally required on a regular basis, but we see that the boys exercise a fair amount of freedom in this regard—a source of concern provoking comment by elders.

In addition to singing and dancing, novices should learn how to make ritual costumes or decorations. In an initiation rite, the young men watch as their adult ritual partner makes the thick, forearm-length bracelet for them. The adult says, "May my partner see, may my partner see," as he fashions the bracelet, thus indicating that the know-how is being officially, and willingly passed on in the correct manner from the elder to the younger partner. The boy will not actually make this bracelet himself until he attains adulthood and being the senior ritual partner instructs a junior. A common expression used in this regard is, "I, in my turn, will pass it on."

On one occasion, when the young men were said to be learning from their older ritual partners, I went to the location (away from the village) to observe how such learning actually took place. In spite of the accounts given me of the rapt attention of the young men to their solicitous elders, I found the junior ritual partners far from their senior teachers, apparently not watching at all. The senior men were busily fashioning the ornaments, chatting amiably among themselves, seemingly unconcerned that their young partners were not exactly their rapt students. As disappointed as I was, I realized this scenario tallied perfectly with the Kayapó philosophies of learner initiative and knowledge attribution, rather than acquisition.

Learner initiative is accepted and expected, yet the adults complain that the young people do not express interest often enough, and herein lies the source of tension between the elders and the young.

During the preparation phase of the *Kôkô* ceremony, the monkey masks were being woven for the young, unmarried men, by their grandfather. All the young fellows we talked to claimed to have been watching the weaving and decoration of the masks as they were being created, and thus learning how to make them.

In reality though, if any of them was truly intent upon learning how to weave the masks, they would already have demonstrated an interest at an earlier age, since a boy deliberately signals his intention to learn by experimenting with practice materials, when he is in a lower age-grade. When someone who knows how to make the masks sees him experimenting in this way, he will offer to teach the boy. Naturally, these experiments occur in the context of the ceremony, when everyone around is involved in the activities and materials are readily at hand. Not everyone has the ability to weave, and once a person is grown and married he will never learn; the opportunity has passed. It is something which is learned while young, yet not actually put into practice until after marriage. "They watch and practice first, then those who know teach them. When they become adults they use the real material," I was told.

Thus, when these young men claimed to be watching and learning, their claims were greeted with some skepticism by the elders, who had a fairly good idea concerning who was and who was not learning.

Not all of the knowledge relevant to the ritual setting is necessarily transmitted during ceremonial performances. Many activities related to a ceremony but not part of it, provide occasions for learning.

Learning related to ceremony

Learning in relation to ceremonies takes place in both work and play, but in contrast to the everyday living and learning, ceremonial events require participation in broader-based working groups where different rules of social interaction must be learned by the younger members submitted to this for the first time. This further reinforces the sociocultural values of the authority of the elders.

Learning in work. For the families sponsoring a festival, the women's work is constant,

> Every day the sponsors look after the people, give them food, distribute it correctly, set it out for the next day. They hardly see their children till after the climax of the festival. They just keep on baking meat...

complained one sponsor. If members of the sponsoring family do not become physically thinner during their sponsorship, people will think they have not worked very hard nor observed the dietary restrictions which accompany the role. Frequent trips to the gardens hauling supplies in baskets carried with a tumpline and long days and evenings of soaking and scraping manioc tubers in order to make the flour used for the meat pies which will be distributed to the dancers require as many hands as possible, and the young girls learn quickly.

The sponsors need larger gardens and must process a huge quantity of manioc tubers. Except for the clearing of gardens, most garden work on behalf of the festivals is performed by the women who work as part of an expanded network of parental kin in relation to the child being honored. This means that for any given festival a woman could be working with a different set of people.

Close to the climax of a festival, the village patio must be cleared of the weeds that have gradually overtaken it, and the women must collect bags full of stones for the stone ovens. This is performed by the women's societies working together, again, a new experience for some of the newly-adult women. Much of the work in relation to ceremonies is performed communally, ignoring moiety or society boundaries. My Kayapó sister, Nhàktu, said that during festivals, the sponsors tell everybody to prepare manioc flour or to gather stones or sweet potatoes or banana leaves, and everybody works together.

For girls who have recently attained puberty, working together with all the women, rather than helping with their younger siblings, will be a new experience. Different rules of social conduct apply between nonkin, and relationships seem a bit strained at times. It may be for this reason that the people frequently attribute kinship relationships to others, making a person like a sister, or like a brother. Whatever strategies are employed, working together communally definitely requires the learning of additional social skills, and mothers are generous with advice to their daughters.

The senior women often work the young girls hard. Good workers are not commended nearly as much as lazy ones are rebuked, and it is not uncommon to hear comments about someone being lazy. Naturally, the teenage girls prefer to work together, rather than with their older sisters or mother(s). Then they can escape some of the criticisms, and their conversations have much more to do with romantic exploits than the work at hand! Festivals provide one of the rare occasions for teenage girls to broaden their social relationships giving them the chance for peer interaction and learning beyond the confines of their own domestic circle.

For communal men's work, the boys who have recently become part of the puberty-level age-grade are subjected to many new experiences. They may have to help in clearing a chief's garden under the direction of more senior men. On treks they are required to go first, cutting paths through rainforest growth. In the company of their ceremonial companions or brothers, they are keen to impress others on the communal hunting expeditions.

Most ritual adornments are made by women, and the usual pattern is a daughter learning by watching her mother. Armbands, legbands, and waistbands are made from manufactured glass beads. The women, especially the elders, also grow and spin cotton from which many ritual decorations are made, although today cotton yarn is regularly purchased.

The men make the feather headdresses, however, and this is one of the few skills that a man may learn later in life, after he is already the father of many children. Headdress styles are said to belong to different households in conjunction with a ceremonial role. There are men whose right it is to specialize in making these styles and members of the user households could commission them to make them.

The butchering of game animals is the men's domain, performed by particular elders whose right it is. As they do the butchering they instruct their grandson concerning proper butchering techniques and concerning correct distribution patterns, i.e., which houses and which individuals have rights to which particular game animal and to which particular cut of meat. Knowledge of patterns of reciprocal obligations is shared by both sexes. Even small children learn by helping in the distribution. It is not all work, though. Much learning in ritual occurs as children play and mimic their elders.

Learning in play. It was a common sight during the festivals to see the little girls, arms around each other's waists, doing a dance in imitation of what they have seen the adults doing. "What dance are you doing?" I would ask, and invariably they would say, "We're climaxing a festival" (the most thrilling part!). My Kayapó sister, reminiscing about her own childhood, described how they used to reenact the entire festival, climax and everything.

The older boys would make very good imitations of the monkey costumes for their little brothers. The small boys would play in these for hours or sometimes just throw blankets over their heads, pretending they were the monkey men. Occasionally the boys would actually instruct their younger siblings in exactly how to perform a dance. In so doing they were confirming their own knowledge of the dance. Even as they play among themselves, there is deference on the part of a younger boy towards an older one. It is assumed that the older one automatically knows more.

Many times, as I watched the elders instructing the junior participants either in work or by commenting upon their play activities, it seemed as though they were schooling the youth in their traditions, which led me to consider ceremony as a form of schooling.

Ceremony as schooling

Initiation rites have commonly been considered as analogous to Western schooling due to the relative formality of instruction between elder and neophyte and to the obligatory and disciplinary nature of the rites, especially upon puberty-age males.

While there is certainly an element of instruction and formality in Kayapó initiation rites, especially for the males, we have seen that learning through ritual is by no means limited to the initiation rites nor to the initiates. Initiation, for the Kayapó male especially, is more analogous to enrollment in an ongoing education program, where nonkin are among his main tutors.

In thinking about learning within rituals, my focus has been upon the practical knowledge, rather than what meaning and message the ritual itself may communicate. That is to say, the concern is with how the subject matter is learned and conveyed within ritual when learning is intended; but not whether a ritual is, in fact, communication. The latter would require an emphasis on the exegesis of ritual, something in which the Kayapó show little interest. And while teaching and learning are not the main focus of Kayapó ritual, yet the Kayapó conscientiously show young members how they should dance and sing and generally comport themselves in Kayapó ritual activity. Each person is perceived as increasing in knowledge. Some knowledge is of the unearned variety, attributed to the recipient by virtue of the relationship through which it is received, and will only be appropriated later; some has already been learned, yet will be validated later. The ultimate end result and Kayapó ideal in terms of knowledge acquisition, is the elder, who literally "has it all together."

Ceremonies, in general, can be seen as occasions of learning for all the young, as well as many junior adults who may be playing a particular ceremonial role for the first time. The young performer is not only learning his particular ritual role by actually performing it, but by virtue of performing with a grandparent, he or she is actively taking on the right to perform the particular song or dance as a ritual role pertaining to his or her household. The ritual context legitimizes its actual transmission and thus symbolizes the closeness of the grandchild/grandparent relationship in this culture. In addition, any information, including medicinal knowledge, that passes from the elder to the younger through this relationship over time, will always be considered official and legitimate in part because the relationship was validated in ritual.

De facto learning does, however, occur in the measure that the child expresses an interest in his grandparent's expertise, but from the point of view of the public arena, what is relevant is that knowledge transmitted through this legitimized channel is considered attributed to the junior person by the senior, i.e., unearned. That is, the emphasis, from the Kayapó point of view, is on the validity of the relationship which, by extension, validates the knowledge transmission. What particular point in time the learner actually acquires the knowledge is of secondary concern. The only check as to whether real learning has taken place, will be far in the future, when the source is deceased and the replacement begins to practice the knowledge. There will always be those watching at that time, and the most senior members of the society comment upon the performance of the person who claims to be practicing the knowledge bequeathed him/her in this manner. The practitioners will earn respect and prestige to the measure that they can equal or surpass the performance of those (now deceased) from whom they received their knowledge.

Yet, there is a temporal element to knowledge acquisition, albeit, not linked to chronology. It is apparent, as we have seen, that not only do Kayapó adults overtly indicate their intent to instruct their grandchild during ritual performances since this is in the interest of every household, but the children themselves declare that they are learning the customs from their elders. Such activity-based learning has been shown to occur in a holistic, contextual mode, as compared to much school learning in Western culture where educational experiences are often fragmented and subject matter is specialized and noncontextualized.

Festival dances, songs, traditional stories, and other knowledge related to ritual, both esoteric and practical, comprise the subject matter for the

Kayapó and are presented in the actual framework of the activity. The children are not transported to a location far from the village. Rather, learning takes place during the performance itself, as well as in preliminary dry runs just prior to the enactment in the village plaza. The male elders take special responsibility for teaching dances to young male performers, usually their sister's child or child's child, and the female elders do the same for their male or female grandchildren (including brother's child).

Bodily learning is also a factor in Kayapó ritual. When children are still infants (eight months to two years), they feel the motions of their first dancing experience, seated upon the shoulders of their grandparent. Many dances are based upon imitating the behavior of birds or animals. Not only does this imply a close observation of the bodily behavior of these models but an ability to imitate such behavior and express it bodily.

In the *Kôkô* ceremony described earlier, the behavior of the anteater, two types of monkeys, and a large bird were incorporated into dances imitative of the animals and performed by essentially all the younger men and in some cases by children. In the ritual roles pertaining to households, the dances and songs performed at the climax were in imitation of animals and included a specific bird, a jaguar, a deer, two types of monkeys, the bush turkey, and a cow or horse.

Songs, like so much in Kayapó culture, could be a study in themselves. There are several categories of songs: *me ngrer djwỳnh* or *me ngrer kumrex* 'real/authentic songs', referring to the music and songs unique to each major ceremony and are led by the official songleader. In contrast, there are the *me ngrer kakrit* 'common songs' which are part of the ritual patrimony of households and are not led by the ceremonial songleader. These are sung in two name-giving ceremonies. In the *Kôkô*, seven songs, each representing a particular animal, are sung at the climax. These songs pertain to particular households and the singers and their grandchildren learners imitate some significant feature of the animal's behavior referred to in the song. In the *Kwyrkangô* ceremony there are the common songs performed by the people as they dance towards the sponsor's house.

Another category of songs is the persuasive or causative songs sung as performative acts to achieve some desired effect, i.e., to cause children to be conceived, or the contrary, to cause sickness to leave, etc. These songs are inherited. Everyone hears them and can benefit from the knowledge they represent, but only certain people have the right to perform them. They will be sung accompanying special ministrations of medicines, some of which may be referred to in the songs. Many of these songs and the accompanying medicines allude to a wealth of ecological information. One song which I recorded referred to four fish, four animals, and three plants known for their fertility. This was the song sung for a woman desiring to conceive. The counterpart referred to dry stream beds and vines that seemed like they would have water, but were false—no water, dry. In other words, ecological information is encoded in some Kayapó songs and many song texts provide a jumping off point, not only for the Kayapó learner, but also for the ethnobiologist towards a more detailed study of the ecological information to which they point.

Ritual activities for the Kayapó are a means for education. The young are learning their rights and the ritual roles pertinent to their households. They are learning ecological information, Kayapó values, and the social order of their world through their rituals, as will be seen. Yet ceremonial events are one of the first elements of Kayapó culture to come under attack from the outside—viewed by non-Kayapó as an idle pastime, as play, as dispensable entertainment, as a spiritist religion. The demands of ritual upon the time of the Kayapó are great and conflict with the Brazilian school year of one hundred eighty days. Frequently, the Kayapó are given the choice of cutting back on their name-giving ceremonies in favor of schooling.

We have seen that activities within ritual and related to ritual contain explicit teaching and learning situations, but much of what is communicated through ceremonies has more to do with the prevailing social structure of the entire group, as well as their deeply pervasive values—information that is basically implicit.

> ...what is actually being taught in the initiation schools is the whole value system of the culture, its myths, its religion, its philosophy, its justification of its own entity as a culture. (Hart 1963:419)

What is being communicated implicitly is often more significant than the overt, explicit information.

> ...I believe that the most interesting cultural knowledge is tacit, which is to say, unconscious for many participants, and implicit, that is, embodied, for a few. When knowledge becomes explicit...it can be learned by rote, but when it is tacit, it cannot; it must be reconstructed, improvised or reinvented in each new enactment. (Grimes 1991:10)

By looking at the sociocultural context of learning in Kayapó ritual activities, we discover that Kayapó ritual and Western schooling have much in common in terms of the tacit, implicit social messages each carries.

The sociocultural context of ceremonial schooling

Most studies which bring the concepts of schooling and ritual together do so by applying insights gained from ritual studies to education and schooling (see Ong 1963; Hart 1963; Lancy 1975; McLaren 1986).

Based upon the insight that ritual and schooling share some commonalities, I would like to look at ritual as schooling, rather than schooling as ritual, by comparing some of the sociocultural characteristics of schooling with sociocultural characteristics identified in Kayapó ceremonial activities. Some of these characteristics incorporate Kayapó values concerning status, roles, ritual wealth, much of which is communicated to its participants tacitly, as well as directly. In fact, it is possible to see many similarities between Western high schools and Kayapó ritual in terms of outcome, in spite of the difference in form, as I will attempt to illustrate.

Cusick says that the basic purpose of a high school is "to articulate a specific body of knowledge, skills and behavioral patterns in the form of a curriculum and then to pass this curriculum on to students" (1973:206). In order to do this, the school has some sociocultural characteristics which will be supportive of the process.

Ritual activity for the Kayapó is also designed to articulate a specific body of knowledge, skills, and behavioral patterns, and the curriculum through which this is achieved consists of patterned activities which follow specific rules and regulations passed along from generation to generation. There are many similarities between the goals of a school and the goals of a Kayapó ceremony, and some of the same sociocultural characteristics which operate in the school also operate in Kayapó ritual—characteristics which are supportive of the goals. But there is also at least one major difference. The overt, expressed purpose of school, as an institution, is to educate the young in an interventionist manner; whereas the expressed intent of a Kayapó ceremony, while including some educational intervention, is to pass along names and ritual wealth from one generation to another. This does not change the fact, however, that in Kayapó ritual, as in Western schooling, many things are taught implicitly and unconsciously, and these are the features I wish to discuss.

Cusick (1973:208), identifies nine sociocultural characteristics of the school's organization. The first four operate upon one another in a mutually supportive cycle:
    subject matter specialization
    vertical organization
    doctrine of adolescent inferiority
    downward communication flow

The compartmentalization of knowledge based upon teacher specialization reinforces the vertical organization in terms of authority, where the teacher is superior and the students inferior. This is fed by what Cusick calls the doctrine of adolescent inferiority, or the implicit notion that adults will know more than the students. This, in turn, justifies the downward flow of communications, where teacher talks and student listens.

Kayapó ritual organization, although differing in form and intent from schooling, nevertheless exhibits some of the same characteristics. For instance, the elders are specialists and transmit their particular speciality to the young on a one-to-one basis. Elders also address the entire village in their harangues. Definitely, the organization of knowledge transmission, in terms of authority, is vertical, where the elder transmits and the younger receives. There is also an expressed doctrine, among the Kayapó, not so much of adolescent inferiority as of the limited knowledge of youth and the unlimited knowledge of elders, but the effect is the same, since this doctrine is supported by a downward communication flow in terms of authority and knowledge transmission.

Cusick continues with the next five points:
    batch processing of students
    routinization of activity
    dependence on rules and regulations
    future-reward orientation
    supporting physical structure

Batch processing in schools refers to the one teacher to many students ratio, where the object is to reinforce the teacher's authority and promote conformity and lack of differentiation among the students. Routinization of activity helps to sustain this conformity and depends upon rules and regulations for its maintenance.

These three areas offer more contrast between schooling and Kayapó ritual, yet the outcome is not so different. The processing of the Kayapó student is not performed upon a group by only one person. Rather, there is some generalized learning as a result of participation in group activities, and there is the one-to-one knowledge transaction between an elder and his grandchild which more closely resembles the concept of tutoring. Yet, the end result is intended to achieve an ideal of cooperation and conformity to the whole. The routinization of activity in ritual events does occur, with the elders usually having the last say. Many rules and regulations are instilled during ritual. These include dietary restrictions and threats of supernatural dangers, which coerce cooperation to a large extent. The consequences of breaking certain taboos are feared as much for their effect upon the individual as for how that individual might affect the child being named.

Concerning the last two items: Cusick sees schools as being future-reward oriented in terms of the application of the learning accomplished, and in Kayapó ritual, this is also the case, since the motivation for most learning in ritual is so that one might become a social person and in turn pass along the rights and names to one's own grandchild in the future. With regard to the supporting physical structure, Cusick shows how even the spatial arrangement of a classroom supports the idea of a teacher's authority over the body of students. In a sense, the spatial organization of the men's house does the same, as authority is already inherent in the age-grade divisions, and people are seated in accordance with these divisions.

We see, then, that the very structure of Kayapó ceremonies, relying as it does upon the expertise of the elders, emphasizes a vertical organization in terms of authority and a downward communications flow, where the wisdom of the elders is unquestioned, as is the limited knowledge of the young. This tends to exercise a conservative pull on the young, thereby revalidating the authority of the elders and Kayapó tradition (see table 1).

But just as there is "noise" (Henry 1975:34) and a hidden curriculum in Western schools (Cusick 1973:206–216), which is learned, rather than explicitly taught, so there is in ritual performances. In Kayapó ceremonies, many ideals may be expressed, but not all may be achieved: someone refuses to participate for some reason, and tensions arise; the hunt is unsuccessful, so a sponsor's obligations remain unfulfilled; a dispute breaks out and threatens group cohesion. Both the strengths and weaknesses of a society may become apparent in the organization of ritual pursuits, and participants will learn as much from failure as success, and from the descriptive, as from the smooth and intentional outcome.

Table 2. Comparison of Kayapó ceremony and Western secondary schooling

	Kayapó ceremony	Western high school
Sociocultural characteristics		
	Learning set in context; dance and song exclusive to ritual; remade at each performance not rigid.	Specialized curriculum is divided from extracurricular activities; rigid rules and regulations.
	Vertical organization is built upon relationships determined by birth. Teachers have kin, nonkin, and affinal relationships to learners.	Vertical organization is built upon relationships determined by teacher's professional status; learner is often not even from teacher's community.
	"Doctrine" of limited knowledge of youth; unlimited knowledge of elders.	"Doctrine" of adolescent inferiority.
	Instruction is learner initiated.	Instruction is teacher initiated.
	Teaching is one on one.	Batch processing of students.
	No time pressure on learning.	Time pressure on learning.
	Future reward: to become a social person (place in social world).	Future reward: place in economic world.

	Kayapó ceremony	Western high school
Effects of above characteristics	Spatial organization reinforces age hierarchy. Ordinary space temporarily transformed into ritual space; draws teacher and learner together.	Spatial organization supports teacher/student hierarchy. Special space for school. Sets teacher apart from students.
	Learners are honored (differentiated) by transmission of names (individuality).	Students are undifferentiated; denied freedom; students are massed.
	Knowledge and status are unearned.	Knowledge and status are earned.
	Knowledge validated by relationships that give rights to specific knowledge.	Knowledge validated by testing.
	Initiation = identity change.	Graduation = identity change.
	Maximum compliance elicited from participants.	Students learn minimum compliance.
	Learners learn to expect close teacher/student interaction.	Students learn to expect little teacher/student interaction.
	Educational experience holistic.	Educational experience fragmented.

	Kayapó ceremony	Western high school
Results	Ritual structure exerts conservative pull on young, validating authority of elders and Kayapó tradition while providing activity, involvement, and participation of learner.	School structure provides students few opportunities to gain the rewards of activity, involvement, and participation.
Outside reinforcement	Influx of outside goods makes possible more ritual performances (providing social rewards).	Extracurricular group identities provide students with social rewards in school.
Effects of outside reinforcement	More ritual validates knowledge base of elders and tradition.	Students have a strong, active, and involving extra-school group structure.

Cusick (1973:217) shows both the intended and unintended effects of the school's sociocultural characteristics upon the students and suggests that they reflect broader societal values and thus help to maintain a societal status quo. For the Kayapó, some of the intended effects of ritual, which help to maintain the status quo in their society, are: the legitimization and transmission of names and ritual rights, thus ensuring the continuation of households as ritual entities whose members are responsible for special ceremonial roles; the attribution of knowledge and ritual status to individuals as household members; the practice of reciprocity as a strategy for achieving certain goals; and the achievement of group cohesion and cooperation on a village-wide level.

There are several unintended effects of learning upon the young in Kayapó ceremonies which may not be of any consequence unless they are carried over into the Western-style schooling they so much desire. For instance, there is no time pressure upon the young to learn. There is the expectation of one-to-one, context-oriented, holistic teaching involving most of the senses. There is learner-initiated rather than teacher-directed interaction with a knowledge base according to the learner's timetable. There is the built-in idea that expertise and its accompanying status comes mainly with age and experience, unearned, rather than earned.

In many ways, the performance of ritual would seem to limit the freedom, potential, and ambitions of young Kayapó; yet temporary status, earned by exhibiting generosity in reciprocal transactions, display of ritual wealth and perpetuation of the ritual role of households, and the desirability of celebrating the parent/grandparent opposition for the children's sake continue to be powerful incentives for the continuation of ritual. This, in turn, promotes the status quo, especially the authority of the elders. Implicitly, the knowledge of the Kayapó elders and the authority of Kayapó traditions is legitimized in ritual performances in the measure that the success of the ceremonial performances lends support to the status of each.

The truth of this is demonstrated by the continuing vitality of the Kayapó ceremonies, even in the face of great changes, particularly access to material wealth in the form of revenue from their land concessions to lumber and gold extraction. In fact, rather than exerting pressure against the performance of ritual, wealth may do the opposite, in the measure that the availability of more goods increases the chances of parents, at a younger age, to gain support in sponsoring rituals for their children. Their aim may be to gain prestige earlier in an effort to overcome some of the limitations placed upon them by their system (Verswijver 1985:157). Yet the successful performance of ritual only feeds back into the system by supporting the sociocultural characteristics of ritual, especially the authority (not control) of the elders.

> Ritualized practices, of necessity, require the external consent of participants while simultaneously tolerating a fair degree of internal resistance. As such they do not function as an instrument of heavy-handed social control....Ritualization as any form of social control, however indirectly defined, will be effective only when this control can afford to be rather loose. Ritualization will not work as social control if it is perceived as not amenable to some degree of individual appropriation. (Bell 1992:221–222)

Kayapó ceremonial practices allow for this flexibility to a greater degree, no doubt, than does most Western secondary schooling. Interestingly enough, there have been attempts to recapture some of the benefits of ritual in Western schooling, with workshops in experiential education designed to show the value and application of rituals in the classroom environment (Horwood 1983). Perhaps something can be learned from the Kayapó.

Summary

Kayapó learning and teaching of the skills related to ritualized activity are, "directly and intimately related to the structure of the event in which the knowledge is publicly performed, especially to the act of performance" (Sherzer 1983:224). Children, in the process of inheriting ritual rights and wealth, participate in ceremonies even as infants carried by their dancing, singing grandparents. Young children often participate formally as objects of a name-giving ceremony or in order to learn a ritual role.

All of Kayapó social space is transformed by ritual, shifting the focus of daily activity from the domestic units to larger productive units in which cooperation is required between extended kin as well as between nonkin. In these broader-based social interactions, young people's place in the larger group is confirmed, defined in terms of expanded social interactions beyond the limits of their household.

The exciting, most colorful events of any ceremony are endlessly enacted by the small children in play activities, with older siblings providing costumes and sometimes direction. Adults acknowledge that children are learning through play by foreshadowing what they will do as adults.

While scholars argue whether the acquisition of new knowledge occurs in ritual activities, the Kayapó say it does. Learning, they say, takes place as you practice what you are learning. You see it, then you do it. Both body and mind are considered to be involved as a sense of ritual is developed in the individual through participation in ritual over time. For this reason, the oftentimes recalcitrant teenagers are strongly encouraged to participate, and they usually do, capitulating eventually to their mildly coercive elders.

Women play a central role, especially in Kayapó name-giving ceremonies, as rights, names, and ceremonial roles connected to matrilocal households are being transmitted from generation to generation. Women are the custodians of an elaborate system of name-transmission, and name-giving ceremonies could not be held without their expertise and their material contributions. Nevertheless, women's participation in dances are confined to only two festivals—the women's painted *(me ni pi'ôk)*, and the *Kwỳrkangô* festival (borrowed from the Jurúna)—plus individual ceremonial roles within the men's dances, giving the impression that women's involvement is mainly domestic and spectatorial in nature.

Further, Kayapó ritual activity and name-giving ceremonies are a way of setting up and fulfilling reciprocal obligations incurred by networks comprised of both sexes. In this respect, women are fully involved, especially in their role as name-giving grandmothers. In fact, the scale of the reciprocity being practiced, especially by the ritual sponsors and their siblings, both real and fictive, is a major strategic function of ritual activity of consummate importance to the Kayapó. Children learn the intricacies of reciprocity and payment as they help in the distribution of food. The men provide the meat, and the women, the garden produce, especially manioc flour. The interdependence and propagative power of the sexes[23] is symbolized by a joint product in the form of large, moist, manioc pies filled with meat, which are given as payment to all who cooperate in the festivities.

The provision of such large quantities of food requires cooperative hunting or gathering—an opportunity for young teens to work with people beyond their domestic group. This, in turn, reinforces Kayapó structures of authority (as distinct from control).

A significant aspect of ritual activity, in terms of knowledge transmission, is the resemblance it bears to Western schooling with regard to specific sociocultural characteristics. Kayapó ceremonies and Western schooling reinforce a vertical, top-down authority structure and communication pattern, where the young person is considered to have limited knowledge resources in comparison to the unlimited knowledge of the elders. This implicitly validates the knowledge of the elders, be they the teachers in Western schools or the grandparents among the Kayapó, thus exerting a conservative pull on society. Yet, changes occur as tensions between the elder and younger arise and are subsequently resolved by compromise.

Much tacit learning occurs both in schools and in Kayapó ritual. For the Kayapó, there is an implicit understanding that some knowledge is unearned and legitimized by virtue of the source, but over time there is the expectation that this will be backed up with real learning—always at the initiative of the learner.

How this occurs will be the topic of the following chapter as we look more closely at the particular teaching/learning relationships involved.

---

[23]Many interpretations of this symbolic exchange are possible, such as wild meat symbolizing nature and tame garden produce symbolizing culture, or the raw and cooked dichotomy outlined by Levi-Strauss (1969)—all fascinating, but beyond the scope of this study.

Summary

We will consider especially, the relationship of the grandparent category to the grandchild category as these function in ritual. The contribution to the child's knowledge base by members of the grandparent category is indispensable.

6

Onward and Upward
Education and Identity Building

The education of a Kayapó person through time takes place in family-oriented daily activities which occur mainly within a circle of parental kin and particular segments of the community and in the ritual activities involving grandparental kin and the entire public community. In this chapter we will consider three sets of relationships which play a specific instructional role with regard to children in their accumulation of the customs and specialized, sometimes secret, knowledge which contributes to their social state. These are the grandparents/grandchildren, substitute parents/substitute children, and ceremonial partners.[24]

The Kayapó organization of knowledge transmission by means of certain relationships provides individuals with a network unique unto themselves. This network is a resource pool, both in the social and instructional sense, and it is up to an individual, given particular ambitions, to maximize access to his or her unique knowledge base. There is some inequality built into this system, and individuals must develop strategies to deal with these.

A focus upon cases of intended instruction should not obscure the fact that learning is occurring all the time everywhere, and some occasions provide special opportunities for individuals to acquire knowledge which might not normally be available to them. The trek associated with ceremonial events is such an opportunity.

---

[24]Turner refers to this relationship *(kràmdjwy)* as "ceremonial companions" and "ritual kin" (1987b:11).

A foot in both camps

The relationships of grandparent/grandchild, substitute parent/child, and ceremonial partners have many social functions, but the focus in this study is upon the educational role these relationships might play in an individual's life in both the everyday and the ritual settings. In relation to the child, the counterpart has a foot in both camps, instructing the child both in everyday events as well as in ritual events. For this reason I use the term INTERMEDIARY to refer to the relationships, but not in a structuralist sense. Of the three, the grandparent/grandchild dyad is the most significant in transmitting traditional knowledge to the child.

One characteristic of these relationships is a factor they share in common. As people in the preparenthood or postparenthood[25] category, neither the youth nor the elder is presently in a relationship of substance with his or her own children, with the possible exception of mother's brother (MB) or father's sister (FZ). For this reason, each can deal with the knowledge which would normally be considered dangerous to younger children, without actually endangering children. This characteristic could possibly be one of the reasons the postparenthood people are those considered socially responsible to teach the preparenthood people, but there are also other important reasons (see table 2).

The grandparent/grandchild[26] dyad is of prime importance in Kayapó culture. It is a legitimized channel for traditional knowledge that is being transmitted in socially defined ways. This relationship functions in the two principal educational settings: everyday and ritual, and in this sense, the role of the grandparent category is a mediating role. Not only are these grandparents mediators between these two worlds, but they also mediate between the child's elementary family and various domestic groups or households.

---

[25]Postparenthood is meant in the sense that parenting is not the primary responsibilty.

[26]The term *ingêt* includes: MB, FF, MF, MBS, MBSS, FZH, FMH, MMH, so 'grandfather' or 'uncle' is a loose translation, referring to the primary terms.

The term *kwatỳj* includes: FZ, MM, FM, MFW, FFW, so 'grandmother' or 'aunt' is a loose translation, referring to the primary terms.

The term *tàmdjwy* refers to the reciprocal relationship of the above terms. For the *ingêt*, this includes: CC, ZC, FZC. For the *kwatỳj*, this includes: CC, BC, HZC, so grandchild, niece or nephew refer basically to the primary terms.

Table 3. Education of a Kayapo person through time

Knowledge transmission factors	Educational settings and links*		
	Everyday	(Intermediate)	Ritual
Resource/receptor relationships	domestic	(intermediary)	ceremonial
Knowledge resource	parent category	grandparent and nonkin categories	grandparent and nonkin categories
Knowledge receptor	child to young adult	child [+adult]	child to young adult and beyond
Knowledge focus	natural	cultural + ceremonial	social
Goal of education is the formation of...	physical person	"beautiful" person	social person

*( ) = links

The main responsibility of those in a child's grandparent set is to pass on specific names and ceremonial rights to the child as well as information which he or she acquired as a child from the elders of that day. As one woman commented: "The older adults thoroughly tell the younger generation, tell them all about the names of their grandfathers and relatives, so the younger generation will know the names thoroughly."

The grandparent category is responsible for the formation of the social aspect of the child, just as the parent category is responsible for the formation of the physical aspect. Without these two elements being properly developed, the child would not be a complete person.

> The teleology of Kayapó kinship takes each individual as the center and orients ego towards participation in surrounding

society. The individual passes from a state of pure undifferentiated biology to become a person who is both natural and cultural in make up. (Fisher 1991:343)

During festivals, the special, almost isomorphic nature of the grandparent/grandchild bond is emphasized when the two dance as though one, and as rights, ritual roles, and in some cases, names are being transferred from the senior to the junior person.

In the everyday setting, people in the grandparent set are responsible to tell their grandchildren the type of knowledge not officially learned from parents—knowledge related to the customs, traditions, and history of the Kayapó people, as well as concerning the specific cultural wealth (names and ritual decorations and roles) the child will inherit from them personally in an act of identity sharing. Fisher, who refers to the grandparent set as "mentors," comments,

> Moreover, this instruction is a means, along with name transmission and ceremonial role playing, that a junior can approximate the ideal of a social identification with his or her mentor. This ideal of identification is played out in a number of different ways. (1991:357)

Theoretically, every child could have a minimum of seven *ingêt*—people in the grandfather/uncle/cross-cousin kinship slot—and five *kwatỳj*—those in the grandmother/aunt slot. This number is invariably increased by reason of marriages and other social alliances to include the wife of ego's mother's brother(s) and the husband of the father's sister(s), and, for a male ego especially, the parents of his false parents. Both male and female children are considered to be the *tàmdjwy* 'grandchild' of these people.[27] I use the terms inheritor, possessor, right or legitimate, with caution—more to convey a general idea than to state a literal fact. Knowledge transfers obey the rule of senior to junior person in spite of terminology. I have records showing that a grandson taught something to his grandfather, but upon checking it out, I discovered that the grandson was older than the grandfather. In fact, the adults laughed at me for even imagining a young grandson or nephew would instruct an older grandfather or uncle. The primary relationships in the grandparent category, however, are the cross siblings of a child's parents and the parent's parents.

Another important relationship for a child is that of substitute parents, which he or she will gain upon moving up an age-grade near puberty. The

---

[27]The grandparents may represent a person in ego's generation (MBS), as well as one descending generation (MBSS) and two ascending generations, (parent's cross siblings, parent's parents).

girls move into the thigh-blackened grade and the boys into the painted grade. At this stage, one of their fictive parents—a false mother, in the case of the girl, and a false father in the case of the boy—becomes a substitute mother or father to their charge, accompanying them in an initiation rite which may be part of or follow one of the name-giving ceremonies.

The person in this relationship is sometimes called the painting mother or painting father, because they paint the initiate's body with the black genipapo paint. The girls' thighs are painted by the substitute mother, a recent female initiate herself, and the substitute father does a rough hand-painting on his son's body, painting over the design freshly painted by the boy's mother. In both cases, the substitute parents remove what ritual ornaments the child is wearing—red cotton leg bands, waist belts, and arm bands and keeps them as payment for taking them on. The substitute parents will now look after the child, a bond signified by the sharing of food. According to one woman, the girls' ceremony is just like the boys', although the men would never say so. She claimed:

> The older thigh-blackened girls paint the young girl for themselves and look after her. They just keep on being partners. Do they call them "mother" and do they make them their children? Yes, its just like when they call the real mothers "mom" and the husbands "dad."

In the boy's case, the relationship is more significant, perhaps, because the boy is removed from his natal home by the substitute father and moves into the men's house. This removal is not a strict severance. It is more a symbolic release of parental ties accompanied by a gradual decrease of his presence in his house of birth. A boy may go through a big initiation ceremony in one of two important festivals, or he may just move into the age-grade without it, but in either case, the substitute father is a key person in the boy's transition.

In initiation the boy is said to become a person, as he becomes, at least symbolically, a son-in-law through a symbolic betrothal, thus entering into an affinal relationship and becoming in a sense, socially viable, a potential provider. He receives goods, i.e., ritual decorations and rights from his set of grandparents, which further enhance his social viability. Some of these goods go to the substitute father, so that some parents actually tell the substitute father not to take their son away yet. They advise him to wait until their son is initiated in the big ceremony so that he will be lying in goods, that is, so the substitute father can gain more. If the boy does not go through the initiation ceremony, but gets a substitute father anyway, the man is said to be a substitute father *kajgo,* i.e., without receiving goods normally bestowed in the initiation process.

One of the functions of the substitute father is to help the son kill game so that the symbolic mother-in-law can be presented with meat, foreshadowing the boy's real obligations later in marriage. If the boy is not betrothed, the father and son just go hunting *kajgo*, i.e., not in fulfillment of the customary obligation.

I inquired whether those boys who went through the prestigious initiation ceremony were any better than the others. "Yes," I was told, "they are, because they have substitute fathers and besides, it's a big ceremony with lots of ornaments/goods." The goods seem to add to a person's social value in an almost material sense.

In the daily routine, the substitute father, a man who might be the age of the boys' real father or younger, provides food for the boy, takes him hunting, fishing, and is generally meant to nurture the child in place of the true father. They will go around together as though they were father and son, eating together and slinging hammocks together in the men's house, where they will sleep. For the boy, the substitute father is a link between customary activities in the everyday setting and political and communal activities in the area of the men's house. The parents of the substitute father become another set of grandparents to the boy with all the role obligations that relationship entails.

The third important dyad, which has an instructional as well as social component is *kràmdjwy* 'male and female ceremonial partners'. This relationship, also, is inherited from a child's father(s), both real and fictive. Every one of the fathers has several ceremonial partners, and at the time of a couple's first baby rite, the ceremonial partners of all of these men, i.e., the child's fathers' brothers, become potential ceremonial partners for each other's children. This process continues from generation to generation. Whenever there is a name-giving ceremony, for instance, each child being honored will be accompanied during the ceremony by someone from the collective pool of the fathers' ceremonial partners. One partnership does not replace another, i.e., a person may have lots of partners. The act of dancing together in a ceremony, as well as sharing food, means the partners "make each other partners really well," a relationship that lasts over time.

Ceremonial partnerships may link members of one household with another for the duration of a ceremony and beyond, links which might ordinarily be limited by kinship rules. The two partners dance together "so they may be happy together" and often exchange the usufruct of ritual body ornamentation, which each is responsible to transmit to the grandchild of the other. When one partner dies, the other may nevertheless participate in his customary role as that person's ritual partner, when it is the deceased's name-giving ceremony. He does this in memory of his deceased partner, especially if the ritual role was prestigious and even if another person is now performing it.

In the everyday realm, ceremonial partners of the same gender, especially male, may hunt or fish together, and exchange knowledge about medicinal plants. Male/female partners, however, are not supposed to speak to one another, having an avoidance relationship marked by respect/shame. The spouses and children of ceremonial partners enter into a joking relationship with the ceremonial partner of their spouse/parent, and insults may be exchanged which would normally become the basis for a feud. It is common, though not always successful, for intentional insults to be passed off as *kràmdjwy* talk.

These networks of relationships, which play a part both in the everyday and the ritual settings, provide a dynamic framework for the education and socialization of the Kayapó child. The network provides a potential bank of traditional knowledge and specialties available to the child. Some relationships are latent for a time period, but are activated by a ritual event. Some are potential resources which may never be tapped, depending in part upon a child's interest and ambition, parental influence, and other factors. If some of these people die or move to another village, there will nearly always be at least one person to fill a particular slot on the child's behalf, a built-in back-up system ensuring that knowledge and information will be saved and re-transmitted from generation to generation.

It seems evident that the men, as fathers and grandfathers, are strengthening alliances between each other by their appointment of ceremonial partners to their children. By their choices they are also having a direct influence upon the educational resources which will be available to their child(ren), although this may not be a factor in their choice. For the child, especially a male child, the choices made by these men help to set the stage for his own strategy of knowledge accumulation.

Bridges and backups

This section looks more closely at actual situations of teaching and learning, inside and outside of the ritual context, which occur between members of the grandparent/grandchild category, the substitute parent/child relationship, and the ceremonial partnerships. We will note the influence of factors such as setting, teaching methods, gender, and age and their relationship to knowledge distribution.

The grandparent set

Of all acknowledged teaching/learning relationships, the grandparent/grandchild is the most celebrated. Knowledge passed along through this strongly legitimized channel includes both the practical and esoteric: the special information that will contribute to the social viability of the child by providing for him or her the socially-validated knowledge which can be used as an asset in future reciprocal relationships. Medicinal knowledge is considered especially important.

When a boy in the painted age-grade goes to a grandfather to learn medicines, he will present the grandfather with food gifts, *o djuw mex,* a formal transaction in which knowledge is exchanged for food. As I was told by many elders,

> They [learners] get honey for them [specialists], kill meat for them and carry the meat; and they set it up behind the house for them. Then they [specialists] carry it and bring it to their wife.

The boy's mother may make a meat pie for her son to present to his grandfather. He may also bring him honey or meat. Sometimes this food is left at the feet of the grandfather right inside his house.

> The content of such instruction is reinforced by its being made part of a paid transaction. The mentor [grandparent] is always paid a price agreed on between him and ego's parents. Ego enters into this transaction only indirectly; being a pupil does not imply indebtedness to one's mentor but a sharing with him or her. (Fisher 1991:357)

Since I did not observe many of these purported knowledge exchanges in action, I wondered if my data was becoming biased in the direction of the elders' notions of the ideal, as opposed to the real. One day I asked a group of boys whether they were really learning anything from their grandparents. Did they actually go to them anymore? After some mumbling they began to tell me they were going, but no one would say directly that he was going; rather, they would each tell on the other. Later, one of the boys returned alone and offered to tell me what he, himself was learning from one of his grandfathers.

He told how he goes to 'Êkêtti's house and how 'Êkêtti tells him the various medicines. He cited a long list, including even the medicine to make a thief sick from the field produce he has stolen from another's field, then make him well again. After hearing about the medicines in the house, he said 'Êkêtti would take him to the rainforest and point out the plants from which to make the medicines.

The boy volunteered that he also intends to learn from a "spirit-knower" (another of his grandfathers) and be "introduced to the spirits." I asked if those who learn from their grandfathers come back and tell their friends what they have learned? "No," he replied, "he just learns it for himself."

The normal teaching method is for the young person to lie in the same hammock as his grandfather (or a nearby hammock) and listen to the elder man tell him the songs or whatever it is he is teaching. I had, in fact, observed this telling/listening pattern several times without even realizing what I was witnessing, for the old man talks, and no specific person appears to be listening. It is not apparent (to the outside observer) that a particular child is the main object of the lesson, as the elder talks loudly enough for the whole household to hear. Yet the knowledge is being officially transmitted to the man's grandchild even though others are listening.

Medicinal knowledge includes the concept of negative magic, for which plants, birds and animals, or parts thereof are used as agents of control over the natural and the supernatural forces inherent in the environment. In selecting appropriate agents, the Kayapó manifest a detailed knowledge of the surrounding ecology: a bird that warns of a snake; an ant that smells like the wild pig; a bird whose flight is direct and whose call says, "Take me across, take me across." They believe that properties such as odor, sound, shape, behavioral attributes, and color are transferrable from a given agent to a given patient. "Magic" in this sense, may be defined as a worldview:

> The magical world has a rigorous causal scheme of a pragmatic and retroactive character. Success demonstrates the presence of Power; failure its absence. Life is not an accidental succession of chance occurrences, but exhibits the presence of varying kinds and extents of Power as affected by relationships among beings. (Wax and Wax 1962:184)

Many negative uses have to do with the age-old battle of the sexes. For example, if a woman refuses a man, and he becomes angry, he can cause a sickness to attack her by wrapping certain things into a small packet, calling her name, and throwing the packet at her. When she becomes ill, she must request the services of this person to cure her, because only he will have the antidote. He, in turn, will get his payment after all. (This probably explains the absolutely horrified reaction I received when I tossed an eraser to a young fellow who was searching for one!)

Other forms of control by means of medicines are practiced. There is medicine to be used against thieves who steal garden produce; medicine to cause good crops, or an abundance of sweet potatoes; medicine to make hunting dogs fierce and able to follow prey; medicine, in the form of talismans, to protect one while hunting or to aid specifically in killing prey.

There are many facets and stages in the acquisition of the various categories of medicinal knowledge and both positive and negative magic. The boy must accompany his grandfather to where the plants are and learn to recognize them, not by name so much as by location and function. Some of these plants may be cultivated in secret in a section of the man's garden. There is not much agreement between people on the plant names, but a teacher will say, "Look at this plant, see where it grows, here's what it does, and how you use it." If a learner is having trouble mastering the knowledge, the teacher might motivate him a little. "Hey! Be smart! Be smart and see something. You won't be able to doctor your grandchild, won't be able to get the medicine and doctor him with it." An added incentive is the fact that the person who really masters medicinal knowledge can go ahead and eat all the meat he wants when his baby is newborn, because he trusts in his own medicines! Normally there are many prohibitions upon the parents in order to safeguard the child (see appendix B).

There are several ways in which herbal medications may be administered, and the learner must be familiar with these and the details of preparation. They may be applied externally as poultices or prepared as baths. Some element of the plant may be rubbed on the affected place or worn as a headband or loosely wrapped around affected areas. Odoriferous plants may be inhaled, or the leaves may be chewed, or its juices drunk. Some plants are used as emetics, others as irritants, others as prophylaxis.

Medicinal herbs are often perceived to have an analogous quality to some characteristic of the disease or the animal believed to be causing the disease. For example, if a man kills a hawk for its feathers, his child may become ill with diarrhea. The bark of a particular plant looks like the leg skin of the hawk, so this is used to cure the illness. One particular plant's leaf looks like the head of the poisonous snake against which it is said to be effective. This plant was among the samples one of the elders brought to show me, and it began to wither quickly. "Hmm," the elder muttered with interest, "maybe this would also be a good contraceptive. You see how fast it dries up?"

To the Western mind, the rationale of analogical relationships between a plant's qualities and the characteristics of a disease often obscures the fact that Kayapó herbal remedies have more than an analogous relationship with curing power. In fact, the ethnopharmacological knowledge of Amerindian cultures is the subject of scientific inquiry which should inspire a wiser use of plant resources in the Amazon rainforest (see Elisabetsky 1986:136–148).

When a person has learned all the medicines the instructor can teach him or her, then the apprentice is presented to the animal or to the leader of the animals, so that he is known by them by name. For this encounter, they rub themselves with their own medicines, strengthening their outer shell/skin, against the penetration of negative forces or the departure of their own insides/spirit, which could happen if they become afraid.

Many people told me they had learned the medicines, but had not been presented to the animal. This seemed to imply a sense of incompleteness: either the guarantee of power was missing, because the animal did not know the person, or the course simply was not considered finished. In spite of this lack of closure, however, it seemed that the knowledge gained was useful and could be practiced.

At the end of the training, the specialist warns the learner to really doctor people well and to keep on at it and not give up on anybody or use his medicine to kill anyone, because if he does, the medicine will turn against him or a non-Kayapó person will kill him.

A nonrelative may also learn from a specialist if he desires, and he too will be presented to the animals' leader upon completion of his training. He would also look after, or feed the specialist throughout the course, as do relatives of the specialist.

Men are believed to possess the more powerful knowledge, particularly medicinal remedies many of which are secret. I remember the day I asked an elder to tell me all he knew about the common-knowledge medicines. I could not understand why he was giving me his life story, or a traditional story, or anything else, rather than the information I wanted. I asked again with my colleague's help emphasizing I was not after his secret knowledge, just the medicines everyone knew for headache or toothache or things of that nature. "Ohhhh!" he sighed with relief. He thought I had meant his own private store of secret information.

Women never officially learn the songs which empower the ministration of many remedies yet they hear them all the time and certainly retain them cognitively. Socially, however, they do not know them, i.e., have not received them as part of their negotiable assets and, therefore, cannot officially use or transmit such knowledge.

The persuasive nature of Kayapó medicines and doctoring practices illustrates the Kayapó ideal of themselves, i.e., masters in charge of their world, and this implicit philosophy is being learned along with the practical knowledge.

One elder assured me they still tell about medicines, but in reality there is great ambivalence on this point.

> They still go around telling each other about the medicines. They still deal with it; they'll still be telling each other, still, still, forever. They'll still deal with it on and on [forever].
>
> The uncles, grandfathers, and grandmothers who know about medicine and witchcraft keep on telling their grandchildren, and the outsiders hear and tell other people's children.

I understand outsiders to be a reference to affines in the household, who may pass along some of this information to their own grandchild (other people's children) at some point. This is legitimate since the father-in-law may teach his son-in-law by such indirect methods.

The distinction between official and unofficial *(kajgo)* knowledge again seems apparent. Many people will learn the facts and will teach/tell others, but when the transaction is between the possessor of the knowledge and the one whose right it is to receive it, the transaction is socially validated due in part to the reciprocal nature of the relationship. Further, when a mother's brother (in the grandparent category) is passing along knowledge to his sister's son, he returns to the sister's house, his own growing-up place, to teach. Thus, he is fulfilling, in the presence of his own natal family and in the place of his household of birth, his obligation to teach his sister's son knowledge concerning the ritual rights which are the patrimony of the household as a ritual entity. In this way some specific rights are being passed on, and the boy's knowledge is considered official, not *kajgo,* because it has been transmitted in lieu of the reciprocal obligations operating between the parent and the parent's cross-sibling (MB, FZ) or parent's parents.

Another type of knowledge transmitted through the grandparents is skill-related knowledge, and predictably, this is gender-based, i.e., a grandmother teaches things to a granddaughter, and a grandfather to a grandson. The grandmothers are the official teachers of the making of ritual ornaments such as arm bands and leg bands, and they may also show the girl how to do body painting. Grandmothers traditionally teach granddaughters the female skill of spinning cotton, while the grandfathers teach the male skill of weaving. Both of these arts are in decline now, as the elders fervently complain, yet there are those still interested. Each skill can potentially convert into currency as men need cotton (owned by women) to finish off some of their weaving and for ritual decorations, and the women need the baskets and mats which are provided only by men.

When a boy wants to learn weaving skills, he may go to one of his grandfathers and learn from him. He is at the age where he has moved to the men's house (around eight or nine), so he will be exposed to the elders' daily gatherings where they weave and chat in a leisurely manner.

The boy, if he desires to learn, stands watching his grandfather. "Do you want to know?" asks the elder.

"Yes, I want to understand."

"I'll show you."

So the weaver stands weaving the fibres to make a sleeping mat or a baby carrier or a basket, while the boy watches closely. He watches for weeks, maybe months. During this time he tries it out and privately practices with green palm fibre, not the regular material. Later, when he reaches the age of initiation in the painted age-grade, he is ready to really learn.

I asked if it was difficult for the teenagers to learn, and the elders would all answer in a similar vein. Some are smart, they would say. They have a good eye and will learn. Others are stupid, no eye, things swim before their eyes, so they say they just cannot see it. When this happens, the elder might actually poke his fingers in the learner's eyes, saying, "You don't have eyes; you don't have a sense of pattern! I'll squeeze your eyes." Or he may actually pull on the joints of the learner's fingers to make them more agile! If things do not improve he might say, "Hey! Be smart! Be smart and see to your ability. You won't be able to make your wife a sleeping mat or your child a baby sling!"

If a stupid person persists in learning, the old ones just stop showing him. At first, the teacher will try to correct the person. They will say, "No, you've got two strands together, you do it this way...," and the teacher sets it right. If the learner shows prowess, the teacher will say, "Yes, your weaving is good. Now you'll be able to make a bag for your mother-in-law so she can dry her manioc in it." Or he might say, "That's good, do it like that. Make my handwork ability your own," or "You have a good hand; you've made my ability your own."

The teacher may also say, "Come here, sit here, and let's see you weaving; I'll watch you." So the teacher watches, as the other weaves for him. Then, in addition to the teaching of the skill, the elder also addresses the question of ideal behavior and a generous attitude in the use of the skill.

> There, it's really good. You know how to make it now. You just make them nicely for people. Don't refuse to do it. If people say to you, make me one, you just make it nicely for them. That's what you should say to them, and show them how to do it. Make it nicely for them. Don't refuse anybody. That's how you should speak to them.

By the time the youth learns, he has reached the sleep-new age-grade of young bachelors and should be able to weave baby slings, manioc baskets, other baskets, and the sleeping mat. This is the ideal. In point of fact, few of the men ever master the sleeping mat, especially at that age. It is considered the apex of achievement, and often men have several children before they master the skill.

Substitute parents

The knowledge that might be passed between substitute parents and their charges would seem to classify as general knowledge and routine subsistence skills. In the case of boys these would include tracking and killing animals, everyday uses of medicinal plants, and other things a father would normally teach a son. Yet, part of the goal of these relationships is to contribute to the social side of the child's person by symbolically moving him away from his or her own household and towards the broader community.

The elders say the institution of substitute father/son is not functioning today as it once did in the past. The old men remember when their substitute father took them over. Subsequently, they would go off together, raiding an enemy faction or non-Kayapó, and be gone perhaps for months from the village. The boys were useful to the young men, serving as spies and scouts, helping in gathering food, fruit, firewood, etc., and other servile tasks. It seems as though the raid was the real initiation in the classic sense of some hardship training, and invariably the boys would return to the village already having acquired their penis sheaths, marking the next stage of the age-grade ladder.

Bẽpnho, now an old man, remembered his substitute father being advised by other men not to tease him or speak harshly to him, wanting him to do something. He said his substitute father showed him how to follow animal tracks, find tortoises and armadillos, and hunt and kill animals. He became an adult in his substitute father's care, but when he moved into the bachelor age-grade, ties with his substitute father were terminated.

Another elder recalled that as boys they went along with their substitute fathers, learning medicines: for headache, for curing people from being yellow (anemia). "That's what they painted them for,"[28] he concluded, i.e., in order to show (teach) them things.

Now, he complained, since contact with the majority society,

> The new adults don't want to learn; they have no understanding; the thoughts of their ancestors are not their thoughts....Now, they just don't care—don't want to know the medicine of the forest, have no interest in it. When the old ones die, and a snake bites one of the young ones (new generation), they won't know how to doctor them.

---

[28]Indicating the ceremony whereby the relationship of substitute "father/son" is formalized.

Of course, according to many of the young boys, they are learning from their substitute fathers, and not just showing off their tape-recorders as the elders frequently accuse.

While there are exceptions to the pessimistic views of the elders, there is no doubt that things have drastically changed. The institution of substitute father may continue, but gradually the content of the knowledge will shift, according to the interests of the young and according to what is becoming relevant to their changing lives. In this sense the dynamic is not so different from that of North American school systems where the elders are prone to lag behind their juniors in presenting a relevant curriculum in keeping with the changes in society.

Ceremonial partners

As long as ceremonies are a vital part of Kayapó culture, the system of ceremonial partners should continue to thrive. This ensures that the real (though limited) educational transactions which occur in many of these partnerships will also continue.

Knowledge exchanges between ceremonial partners *(kràmdjwy)* are constrained by two factors: gender and age. Gender rules out exchanges between partners of the opposite sex, and age defines either peer exchanges or senior to junior exchanges.

The primary role of a ceremonial partner is to be like a bodyguard, accompanying and protecting an initiate during what is perceived to be a dangerous transition. In the boys' initiation, the partner does everything with the initiate. They eat, bathe, sit, get oiled and painted, dance, and sleep together for the duration of the ceremony. The answer to why, is "for them to be happy with each other; so they'll be happy in their dance." Different ceremonies have varying ceremonial roles for the partners to enact.

The type of teaching during ceremonial events which occurs between the partners includes the senior partner showing the boy how to make the special bracelets used in initiation, as well as other skills connected with the ceremonies. They do things together, like killing small birds in order to appropriate the decorative feathers for a costume or killing fish in waterways using the juices of vines and bark which affect the supply of oxygen in the water. But the relationship between male partners continues far beyond ceremonial occasions.

Ceremonial partners are meant to defend one another in disputes as would siblings. The men, especially, use the relationship to gain new knowledge. They say to each other, "Hey, show me how to weave," and the one who knows will teach the other. Or they will discuss medicinal knowledge, "Hey, this is medicine" (pointing out a plant), and one of them may introduce the other to something, "They tell each other things and present them to something—the fish, the leader of the animals, the spirits...then the other [learner] already knows something [has learned]."

The ceremonial partners are all appointed by the child's fathers from the collective pool of these men's own ceremonial partners, so the mothers' partners or the grandmothers' partners have no connection with the children, except in one interesting, but negative way.

When a child is misbehaving, its mother will say, "I'll tell your *angêti* [title of grandmother's ceremonial partner] to come here and frighten you." Usually, just the threat stops the child's misdemeanor. If the threat is ineffective, often the grandmother's or mother's ceremonial partner will really come, and the tot is paralyzed with terror. The adults all laugh hilariously as the child runs screeching into its mother's arms (the intended effect), and the problem is solved. I saw more tiny children being frightened by this method than by any other. A father explained:

> The children, because they don't know any better, get scared, but when they're older they don't pay any attention. When they're little, they fear the *angêti;* when they're older, they don't.

Another social effect of the system of ceremonial partners is the license it gives to relatives of the partners to speak negatively with one another. "Because of the joking, relatives of the ceremonial partners are just fierce with each other," one person told me happily.

I can only speculate that in a face-to-face society, this outlet helps to protect nonkinsmen from getting into serious disputes, since they have a safety valve for negative feelings which may be passed off as joking or *kràmdjwy* talk, although it can, and often does, backfire.

Education and transformation

One of the outstanding features of the knowledge transmission effected by the grandparents, substitute parents, and ceremonial partners concerns the work this knowledge is meant to accomplish in the life of the receptor. The everyday educational setting is commonplace—the grandparent's hammock, the forest, the gardens—but the source of the knowledge distinguishes it from the common, general knowledge of the type transmitted by those in the child's parent category. The source ensures that the knowledge communicated is related to the culture, customs, traditions, and social nature of Kayapó society, and thus educates the child socially.

It is not possible to identify and classify every skill taught, every item of information told, every song shared, as pertaining strictly to the everyday versus ritual, natural versus social, general versus traditional categories. The focus is not only upon the content; it is also upon the relationships. It is a question of the Kayapó perception that knowledge transmitted through certain relationships, especially via the grandparent set, transforms the child from the biological to the social state of being. Perhaps this is due to the perception that culture and traditions are seen as defining humanness in contrast to animals. In addition, such knowledge must be transmitted by telling, by language/word where speech is the essence of humanness, and the most highly socialized person in Kayapó society is the elder who has good or big speech (see table 3). This transformation is the broadest goal of Kayapo educational endeavors. Part of the symbolism in the exchanges of food in payment for the grandparent's dancing with the grandchild and teaching is the stamp of validity it places on the transaction in that relationship.

Table 4. Production of the Kayapó person

	Natural producers: Parent category	Social producers: Intermediary category
Where	private arena	public arena
Who	kin	grandparents and nonkin (community)
	junior producers	senior producers
What	general knowledge in biological sphere; practical, concrete biological focus	traditional knowledge in social sphere; practical, esoteric cultural focus
Goal	physical growth: garden, medicines, child's health beauty of natural body	social growth: names, rights, medicines beauty of social body (rights)
	Child ⟶ Person	

The power of analogy so common in Kayapo thinking possibly underlies this transformation. Just as analogical physical attributes of animals eaten by the parents are believed to be transmissible to a child via the parent's physical substance, so social qualities may be conveyed by grandparents to their literal counterparts, or from a teacher to a learner. This is because the learner is perceived to actually take on the qualities and abilities of the teacher—becoming like him in social qualities and eventually replacing him in terms of abilities.

Although I was very much the naive learner, I began to see ways in which the Kayapó person, especially male, could manipulate the systems of relationships on his own behalf or that of his children, given certain conditions. I also observed that the "dice were loaded" against people who by accident of birth did not have large enough networks or people of prestige within their network. This subject deserves more study, but my purpose is to illustrate how the accumulation of knowledge involves ambitions, goals, and strategies, and not all have equal access to opportunities.

Accumulating knowledge: The strategies of learning

As Kayapó children move from childhood to adulthood, they become aware of their potential access to an enormous pool of knowledge stored in the heads of people with whom they have special social connections. Initiative for knowledge and skill acquisition is expected from the learner, and the onus is upon the one acquiring the information, not upon the one imparting it.

Knowledge and knowledge transactions are legitimized by the status of ego's relationship to a resource person and the status of the resource person, as much as, or more than by the nature of the knowledge. Children are informed that it is basically up to them to tap into these resources. Doing so becomes an individualized strategy of learning motivated by the learner's interest and ambition. The pool of resources is not equal for every person, either limiting or enhancing social mobility, and various strategies are pursued in an effort to overcome perceived deficits.

Knowledge gained through mediating relationships represents wealth in and of itself. It becomes a form of currency which can later be exchanged in important relationships of reciprocity the child will have in relation to other members of society. This special patrimony of rights, names, and social knowledge makes a child unique in society, since no two people will receive exactly the same set of names, the same rights, or identical knowledge. This combination of assets not only creates a unique individual according to the Kayapó, but gives that individual social viability in the sense that he now has social currency that can be used in future

Accumulating knowledge: The strategies of learning

social contracts. In this sense, though abstract in nature, knowledge is regarded as something tangible, as are rights and names.

For the Kayapó, social knowledge has many qualities. It has status, some knowledge being ranked as superior to other knowledge. Some knowledge—medicines, for instance—is perceived as powerful and potentially life-threatening or life-saving. Knowing something has a socializing or civilizing (social value) potential. Social knowledge, as mentioned above, is regarded as a material possession (to be passed along); as property, as unique, and some of it secretive. This means that no individual's knowledge base is an exact replica of any other's. The mathematical possibilities of different combinations of knowledge and skills are many—and parents and elders guide and motivate the learners to make the most of their particular resources.

The Kayapó constantly make statements which are meant to account for their lack of knowledge in a certain area.

> My mother died when I was young so she didn't tell me about my names (middle-aged female speaker).

> I was just about to be introduced to the fish [spirit] when the non-Kayapó killed my grandfather. So I was never introduced (middle-aged male speaker).

> My grandfather would have taught me about the good crying [ritual wailing], but he died before he could tell me (middle-aged male speaker).

> If I had been older my uncle could have told me and I would have understood fish medicine, but no, I wasn't yet born. Tawe told my other uncles who were born first, all the knowledge, and then when I was born, Tawe was dead and he hadn't told me. But he had told the others. So I was really sorry I missed Tawe telling me (elder male speaker).

In each case, the people were describing their sources and the reasons why they had not had an opportunity to learn particular information to which they potentially had access.

Another man explained that he had learned a little of the ritual speech (an important requisite for leadership), but that his brothers had been told really well. He explained that he would only perform the ritual speech if his father or brothers were not present. This powerful ritual speech is prestigious knowledge. People may know and practice it without being leaders, but one cannot be a totally legitimized leader without having received the knowledge from a publicly-acknowledged resource person.

When one aspiring political leader wanted to prepare himself for a leadership role, he lacked the qualification of knowing ritual speech, so he asked the old principal leader of Mekràknõti, now Kubẽkàkre to tell him, in return for considerable payment. The old man never did—perhaps because it would have set the younger man up as a rival to his own sons—and to this day, although a leader in a neighboring village, the man is not considered a real chief, partly because of a lack of this knowledge.

Since virtually everyone hears the ritualized speeches and has been tape recording them for some time, it could not have been due to ignorance of the actual words or lack of virtual access to the knowledge that caused the knowledge deficit. Rather, the young man had no legitimate claim on the ritual speech, since no person (alive) in his network was an inheritor or possessor of this knowledge.[29] The above examples and countless others point to the importance for the Kayapó of the sources of social knowledge. The question then becomes, does the accident of birth determine the destiny of a Kayapó person?

While the Kayapó do give all of the above reasons and more for not attaining to certain knowledge, they also do not appear to be weighed down by this situation in a fatalistic way. Why not? Are there other factors influencing access to knowledge?

Referring to the above case of the aspiring young leader asking the old leader to teach him the all-important ritual speech, the old man could have consented, and the political fortunes of the young man might have been different. In other words, there is room in the system for politicking, and the Kayapó are masters at this, whether within their system or on the national scene.

It would be difficult to pinpoint when politicking begins. When the adults tell their children to learn something from the old ones, they are, in effect, telling them to be aware of their resources. Among their network of grandparents, fathers, substitute fathers, and ceremonial partners, there are people with particular specialties. The child, especially the male, is encouraged to pick and choose from the skills represented in his particular group, so that he can accumulate the knowledge necessary to care for his own children and grandchildren.

As suggested above, fathers especially have some influence in providing such a network for their children by the choices they make concerning their child's ceremonial partners.

---

[29]I use the terms inheritor, possessor, right or legitimate, with caution—more to convey a general idea than to state a literal fact.

In addition, parents and grandparents try to achieve a better position for their child or grandchild. The grandmother who tried to gain the anteater role in the *Kôkô* ceremony for her grandchild and the mother who claims to be the youngest, but illegitimate daughter of the old leader are examples. If he acknowledged her, which he does not, she would have claim on him and all his relatives. She keeps on agitating, ostensibly for the sake of her child, since her present state does not offer the child many benefits.

Parents watch the development of their children to see if they will be like, i.e., take on the features or identity of one of their grandfathers. The leader of the boy's gang (*me bôkti* age-grade) was being scrutinized in this respect. Several times his mother—and occasionally other adults—reminded me that this boy had three leaders in his family, and one elderly lady said perhaps the boy would be a leader after the old leader died. Strange, I thought, since several other leaders would presumably be ready to step into the position immediately. Principal among the necessary qualities—perhaps above heritage—was the leader's capacity to gather others around him, lead them, and look after them. So, qualifications other than access to knowledge and heritage are also considered necessary.

If ceremonial knowledge, rights, prestige, honor, and knowledge of ritual speech were sufficient to qualify a person for a prestigious role in society, then one of the songleaders would be the greatest. He told how his grandfather had chosen him from among several potential grandchildren candidates for the position of songleader, because as a child he had been honored in three naming ceremonies (implying wealth of knowledge, roles, rights, and goods). Yet he and his brother, the latter with fewer qualifications, had a bitter dispute for a leadership position. The brother was chosen because the people liked him better. The rivalry still exists with the brothers rarely speaking to one another. The most qualified was apparently not the best politician, and a people's mandate is necessary for leadership.

The brother, explaining how he achieved this mandate, attributed his success to people liking his speech. He said that he started haranguing in the men's house, and that people responded favorably:

> The people recognized me, gave me recognition. When I moved here to the village, the people kept their eyes on me. "That one should do like that [speak, lead]. That one's speech is good." So I went around telling them good things. I prevented people from fighting by my speech and encouraged them to be

peaceful so we can be many...And so I made a leader of myself, and people recognize me.

In fact, he had other qualifications, although fewer than his rival brother. Knowledge, wealth, ritual roles, and goods, therefore, are not everything. Yet, there is obviously some ranking, and people do try to improve their positions if possible. The chiefs, or leaders, are said to be important because they have big speech, i.e., they can influence others. Several leadership positions exist, including leadership of the men's and women's societies. Men undoubtedly have more political prestige in general, although women are important and have influence within the matrilocal household. Children are greatly esteemed—above wives and single women—yet children of single mothers and orphaned children have fewer chances socially. In a quantitative study of the same group, Werner (1981a:370) illustrates that there is lack of equal opportunity among the Kayapó, but distinguishes between "absolute inequality" and "inequality of opportunity." He suggests that they have few absolute differences in power, but they have a great deal of inequality in the opportunity to acquire it, due to the "accidents of birth." From my own observations, this would appear to be partly the case, yet not entirely, since even members of the same family do not have identical networks nor identical rights or knowledge.

While this whole subject merits closer study, in particular the concept of knowledge under the rubric of *kajgo* versus not *kajgo,* the social position of the individual would not seem to be entirely determined by forces beyond his control. Although individuals are limited or benefited by the potential of their network, they are not determined by it in any absolute sense. There are strategies available by which people may gain support, if leadership is sought. But not everyone is trying to be a leader. Other resources of knowledge contribute to the welfare of one's own children and grandchildren, either in the present or in the future. When people perceive their own networks to be deficient in some knowledge desired, they have the option to negotiate with someone outside their network for that knowledge, but they must be ready to pay a price.

The knowledge available to a person through his or her particular network or beyond it is social currency. For the male, it ensures him the potential success of being able to protect and care for his children and please a mother-in-law and wife. Knowledge, in other words, can be accumulated by one person, negotiated and renegotiated in order to benefit others, thus enabling the person to fulfil social contracts. For this reason, parents encourage their children to get the most out of their networks, whatever they may be, for the benefit of their children of the future and society as a whole.

The option to negotiate access to knowledge is a potential levelling device. Another is the communal trek which occurs prior to the climax of most ceremonies.

The educational value of trekking expeditions

The trek, especially the trekking associated with ceremonial events, õtõmõr, is a form of general education, especially for the young men and women. The ceremonially-related trek is a communal event which may last from several weeks to several months. The size of the group on trek and the communal nature of many activities provides contrasts with the normal methods of hunting individually or in pairs.

During a trekking event, teaching relationships from both the domestic and the ritual spheres are brought together geographically for the young person within one neutral setting. Socially, politically, and economically, the trek is the male counterpart to the female contribution to a ceremony. The brothers, i.e., fathers of the honored child, organize the trek and provide the meat necessary to complement the female (sister/mother) contribution of garden produce which is emphasized in the village.

It was once thought the produce collected on treks was wild, but there is now ample evidence that the Kayapó travel over territory trekked long ago by their forefathers, and that the produce is actually semicultivated, i.e., seeds are pushed into the ground and allowed to grow, but the plants are not cultivated (Posey et al 1984; 1990:51).

The trek, therefore, as a vehicle for Kayapó knowledge transmission, is a subject in itself, a survival school *in loco* (Werner 1983, 1990; Stout and Txucahamãe 1990), where learning and experimenting in context is emphasized. Stout and Txucahamãe (1990) observed that the education on trek complements that received in the village. The oral tradition is dominant in the village, but on trek the history and geography of the local group is recounted as the elders actually teach the old, nearly invisible paths, by pointing them out to the young men responsible for clearing them. The paths are thus reclaimed as Kayapó territory, confirming their historical occupancy of the land.

Stories of other expeditions are recounted within the hearing of everyone, citing the actions of past Kayapó warriors. Observations concerning changes in the environment are instructional, as comparisons are made concerning whether there are fewer macaws than usual or fewer tortoises, or more tapirs, and the people discuss whether they should hunt less in the area, or worry that the roadbuilding is too near and affecting the distribution of game. These discussions, heard by all and commented upon freely by both women and men, may help to explain the high political involvement of Kayapó women, as well as men, as they defend their land in national forums.

Often the young men grumble that the elders do not hunt anymore. How would they know if certain paths existed? The elders calmly reply with predictions of fruit trees or other rainforest wealth, if the young men continue clearing in a certain direction, and their authority is constantly affirmed as predictions come true.

Each day, individual family groups organize themselves spatially around a central clearing where the young men have placed palm leaves marking the men's house. The groupings may or may not replicate village organization, though in my experience, they did not. Nevertheless, everyone was in close proximity, and in the evenings each could easily eavesdrop upon the conversations of other families. Most importantly, everyone, including women and children, had access to the traditional war stories, myths, and other oral tradition told by the prominent elders recognized for their story-telling abilities. In the village setting, such access was limited to the occupants of the men's house or people of the storyteller's household. In this way, certain important oral tradition becomes everyone's patrimony. It is knowledge which unifies the people as a whole and is made available to a wide audience.

It is important to note that the Kayapó do not distinguish between myths and historical accounts in their categorizations of oral communications. Instead they have three distinct terms for genres which include both mythical and historical information. They are aware, in other words, of their history and do not think of it only in mythical terms as has often been supposed. They speak of *kukràdja* 'the customs', an abstract term which covers a variety of knowledge, including ceremonial songs or, T. Turner says, "directions for starting an outboard motor" (1988:198). They also speak about stories the old ones tell; these include tales of a mythical or folklorical genre and are usually told to children. In addition, there is the haranague, or instructing ad-lib, which is reserved mostly for the adult population and includes historical tales of the speaker's or a group's past exploits, or good speech which is often prescriptive. Turner (1988:208–213) shows how a good Kayapó speaker is able to interweave a mythical consciousness and historical consciousness of Kayapó past to make arguments about what they should do today, especially in relation to contact with Brazilians.

Trek is the occasion for the budding orator to test his skills. If people confirm his skills, he will be encouraged to carry on with oratory in the village, but if he is shamed, as often happens, he will not embarrass himself further in the village. Other skills are tested on a trial basis also.

Each afternoon, on the trek in which I participated, the young men would return from hunting activities, grab some palm fronds, and begin to practice weaving. When a senior person arrived, they would show their efforts to him with comments like, "I don't know how" or "it isn't right" or "I only know a little," and that person would relate to each of them, correcting their work, as children of both sexes and various ages stood around watching.

The trek associated with ceremonies, then, provides a way for the Kayapó to expand their horizons in terms of learning opportunities. Young men with an eye to improving their status may discover some treasure of knowledge which would be outside of his relationship network, but which could, through negotiating some transaction, become part of his repertoire. It is not that relationships change on trek. Brothers still act together, ceremonial partners go around together, family groupings remain intact, but everyone is cooperating in closer proximity geographically, and this intimacy and unity of endeavor creates favorable conditions for more knowledge sharing and makes the trek valuable educationally.

Summary

Focusing upon individualized and intentional knowledge transmission may obscure the obvious fact that learning is occurring everywhere, all the time, by people of all ages. According to the Kayapó, the die is cast by the time a person has children of one's own. Official instruction time is over.

It is imperative, therefore, for the young person to avail himself or herself quickly of these opportunities, which may explain the parents' and grandparents' constant goading of the youth to ask their grandfathers something, to learn something quickly. At a young age, these children will become parents themselves, so must be prepared to look after their children and later their grandchildren. In this sense, the goal of Kayapó learning, in addition to being directed towards the formation of a person, is directed towards the preservation and maintenance of the nuclear family.

Dyadic relationships between preparenthood and postparenthood people circumvents the difficulty parents might have in teaching their children medicinal knowledge which would be dangerous to their own infant children, given their belief in shared physical substance. The fact that people in the grandparent category are mainly responsible for transmitting social knowledge to children further contributes to the hierarchical opposition between grandparents.

> The two categories of kin place ego in the center of two distinct circles of sociality and social action. There is the world of subsistence and work where an individual's diligence and energy produces and allows him or her to fulfill ongoing needs through cooperation and exchange with other producers. Contrasting with this is the realm where one's own effort does not create anything new but concentrates on receiving what already exists—here one can only assimilate what is passed down. (Fisher 1991:359)

Yet the assimilation is not passive and involves some form of transaction, either between a child's parents and grandparents on the child's behalf, or between the child and teacher. The exchange of food for knowledge, puts knowledge on the level of something symbolically material. It becomes a form of wealth or currency and something which can be exchanged for something else in the child's future. In addition, the child is now in a position to, in turn, pass on knowledge to a future grandchild, thus fulfilling an important social contract. The possession of knowledge makes the child socially viable, and, thus, contributes to the linking of the physical component of the child nurtured by parents and the social, nurtured by grandparents—fulfilling, thereby, the Kayapó concept of personhood.

Each person has a network of relationships which represent a knowledge resource base to be tapped. Yet one individual's potential does not equal another's since knowledge is ranked to some degree. This means that there is not equal opportunity by birth, but there is room for negotiation and tapping into another's resources, so that strategy becomes a significant part of learning as a learner attempts to choose what he or she wants or needs. This attitude of manipulating or controlling one's destiny has a bearing upon Kayapó attitudes to life in general, particularly their relationships with the surrounding national culture—the subject of the next chapter.

7

Changes and Chances
Education Outside of the System

The previous chapters have progressively documented a model of Kayapó knowledge transmission as an internally integrated system. Taken at face value, it would appear as if the model in its apparent cohesiveness is a closed system.

What there is of new knowledge seems to be internally generated coming from dreams and revelations through the channel of the elders. Otherwise, traditional knowledge is just that—traditional; and general knowledge, too, represents the status quo—the-way-we've-always-done-it kind of knowledge.

If the people of Kubēkàkre were content to live at a subsistence level, they would do very well. There is adequate game, good fishing, flourishing crops, all sufficient to sustain daily life as well as ceremonial events. But they desire more.

Other Kayapó villages have acquired a Pandora's box of manufactured goods by granting concessions for lumbering or gold-mining on their land. A spirit of materialistic competitiveness exists between villages as well as an innate distaste for being perceived as poor. The village of Gorotire, especially, has acquired cement houses, airplanes, clothes, electricity, tape recorders, video cameras, television sets, and other symbols of modern affluence, and few are the Kayapó villages which do not desire the same.

The young leadership of Kubēkàkre, as well as the younger men and women, are willing to forfeit their present sufficiency for all that glitters. This, of course, creates tensions between generations and between those who hold to traditional values and the many enticed by new values. These values are not only materialistic, but are also manifested by a reevaluation of what is considered worth learning.

So the village of Kubẽkàkre is in a state of flux, as are so many Kayapó villages and Brazilian ethnic groups in general.

The inclusion of this chapter on how outside knowledge is incorporated is necessary to counterbalance the idea of the Kayapó system of knowledge transmission as a closed system. The Kayapó, in fact, have a term for the leader who deals with outsiders, and consider his knowledge of outsider's ways a valid speciality in its own right.

A useful way to approach the topic of culture change is to apply a model of LIFE CHANCES (Dahrendorf 1979; Levine and White 1986) to Kayapó society.

The Life Chance model

The Life Chance model is developed around the interplay of people's LIGATURES or social networks and role options available. It is suggested that human life is the product of the balance between choices and social networks. The good life would be the optimal balance: choosing satisfying options and maintaining satisfying social networks.

When relationships are seen as functioning to transmit traditional knowledge, as is seen among the Kayapó, we may well wonder what will be the effect upon these traditional channels of knowledge transmission when new knowledge and new channels of transmission present themselves in consequence of contact with outside influences.

Life Chance is the joint product of choices (options) and social attachments (networks and relationships) made available in any given society (Levine and White 1986:18). It is a concept which provides a means of recognizing flexibility within a system by pointing to an individual's possibility of choice as conditioned by his social network.

Modernization and development have often implied the expansion of options at the expense of social networks. This can lead to isolation and loneliness for individuals. Where relationships are rigorously maintained at the expense of new options, stagnation may set in. Either extreme may lead to cultural decay.

The Kayapó seem to be involved in a process of reorganizing and expanding networks in nontraditional ways as new options present themselves, many emanating from the surrounding Brazilian society. In this chapter, we will consider this process and its relationship to the Kayapó system of knowledge transmission.

Life Chances and the Kayapó

Kayapó patterns of knowledge transmission clearly show the importance of certain relationships to the acquisition of traditional knowledge. The elders are the repositories of the social knowledge so crucial to the formation of the Kayapó person and character. Traditional Life Chances, as outlined in the Kayapó model, would be the product of maximizing one's access to the traditional specialists, acquiring secret knowledge and other valued information by utilizing one's own personal network, and creating relationships with other specialists based upon payment as necessary. Historically, the acquisition of new knowledge from the outside involved high risk.

Traditionally, young men, middle-aged men, and boy initiates were the seekers of new knowledge. On their raids of other ethnic groups and rural nonindigenous settlers, they would bring back cultural items, children, and even women to enrich Kayapó society with new information and new blood. Following a successful raid, they would reenact the excitement of it in the village plaza so that all the women and children could appreciate their exploits.

Today, the Kayapó forays into Brazilian towns and cities is in some ways reminiscent of the old-time raids. The male teenagers to middle-aged men are the most frequent travellers. Often they visit cities to stage an attention-getting war dance for Brazilian officials, in order to achieve concessions with regard to the use of Kayapó territory. Then upon their return to the village, they will often reenact their city exploits in the village plaza, or a leader at least will harangue about it.

The youth are increasingly leaving the village and spending large amounts of time in or near the Kayapó beacon of change, the village of Gorotire. Or they will be in the dusty, interior town of Redenção buying goods with money belonging to Gorotire, but made available to the young men of other villages in exchange for their political alliance with Gorotire leaders. What options are the young men seeking and at what price?

New options

The encroachment of the majority society upon their villages and traditional territory is the reason that the Kayapó, in general, are seeking new options and new knowledge.

After a long history of relatively little contact with the dominant society, the Kayapó have had new opportunities within the past thirty-five years and have had to deal with many challenges requiring new understanding.

Increasing encroachment upon their territory in the form of gold mining and lumber extraction has introduced powerful influences into the Kayapó culture, including money, marketing, and divergent lifestyles.

The Brazilian government has entered several Kayapó villages through FUNAI (Fundação Nacional do Índio), the national government Indian foundation, to set up medical clinics and schools. Missionaries and anthropologists have lived in several Kayapó villages since 1935.

Rather than becoming overwhelmed by such momentous change, the Kayapó self-esteem comes to their aid. In addition, the Kayapó are pragmatists and access oriented. Just as the Kayapó learner seeks access by one means or another to the traditional knowledge he desires within his system, so the Kayapó politician seeks access to the secrets and sources of outside influence. He is thereby seeking to control the unbridled flux of outside influence upon the internal system with knowledge gained from the alien society. In the same way, traditional Kayapó knowledge could be said to be aimed at controlling unbridled natural flux within the system.

When the outside influences were no longer avoidable, the Kayapó began to figure out how to gain access to their goods and manipulate the outsiders to their own advantage. When gold and lumber were discovered on Kayapó land and understood as valuable assets because of outsider's desires, the Kayapó found a way to maintain control of the resources. This caused many interchanges with outsiders, as well as trips to the city, the purchase of several small airplanes, hiring pilots, starting charge accounts, hiring accountants, and meanwhile trying to get the education necessary to lead to independence in this regard.

When questioned as to why they particularly wanted a national school in Kubẽkàkre village, one chief replied candidly, "because of the outsiders" or, literally, "outsiders, for the purpose of." The outsiders "know paper" and use legal documents which are meant, according to Kayapó perception, to outwit the Kayapó in land settlements. So they in turn must learn to fight with the outsider's own ammunition. Outside knowledge is seen as strategy, even a weapon, and they are not slow to learn.

When I first arrived in the village, one of the new leaders paid a cordial call, asking what I intended to do for them while I was there. What did they have in mind, I inquired. The men need to know writing, he answered. Fine, I replied, with a measure of relief, since it was something I could handle with limited language ability. When did they want to begin? That evening! Consensus had been reached even before consulting me.

The men came faithfully for many weeks, happily learning to master the alphabet. Then one day, before learning all the letters, they all asked to learn how to write their names. Thinking this would be a good motivating factor to get them to the end of the alphabet, I assured them they would be able to write their names at the end. Then one of the older leaders, not a class participant, entered. He wanted to know how to write his name!

It transpired that they were being asked to vote for one of the Gorotire Kayapó as a local representative for a political office in the interior town of Redenção. Under Brazilian law, a list of signatures was required to nominate the candidate, and in response, the Kayapó leadership had marshalled an intervillage campaign for signatures. Needless to say, they all learned to write their names that evening!

For the above reasons and more, schooling is seen as an important option and is actively being sought. Many Kayapó villages have had schools run by the government or missionary schools, but they are unhappy with their lack of control over these resources. New options are becoming available, however, as commercial companies are providing schooling in some Kayapó villages in exchange for the extraction of gold and lumber. A British cosmetic company with a positive environmental philosophy, has "adopted" two Kayapó villages. The company is willing to provide a school and teacher for each village in exchange for the extraction and processing of rainforest resources which provide the oil for their products.

New leaders and new networks

The need to communicate with members of the dominant culture has created a new role for village leaders. In fact, another kind of leadership seems to have become necessary.

> The man who, with the support of his village can negotiate forcefully with Brazilian officials is more important today than the old style of (chief) whose mannered harangues and exhortations served to safeguard village traditions. (Bamberger 1979:145)

Of eighteen people questioned in Kubẽkàkre village, eleven agreed that Bepkũm, one of the headman's younger sons, was the best haranguer. Next was the headman, and third, another of his sons. These three all belong to one society or moiety.

The leader of the other society, Kôkôreti, had only three votes concerning the quality of his orations, but when asked whose advice they followed regarding outside contacts, the people's opinion divided along party lines, each voting for the leader of his/her society. These results mark a shift in the Kayapó perspective regarding leadership qualities, for usually only the traditional, most elderly or most pugnacious man would be most esteemed, not one of the younger leaders.

Bepkūm is one of the most successful in Kubēkàkre village to exert this new type of leadership. Although Kôkôrêti is older, they both join an increasing number of Kayapó men who are becoming involved in the larger political process which involves attending meetings with pro-Indian groups and government officials to discuss land rights, schooling, and other new options suddenly within their grasp.

The old-style leadership and orations are still in vogue, but with increasing pressures from the outside upon their system, these new-style chiefs are breaking new ground, while still attempting to conserve tradition. They harangue in the old style, but the content is now directed towards problems and adaptations foisted upon them because of the increasing encroachment of outsiders and the consequent desire on the part of their young people to move away from village interests towards the larger, beckoning Brazilian society.

Young men, especially, have begun to follow the new younger leaders, rather than the traditional elder(s). They are creating new peer networks across village boundaries, rather than the in-village networks common traditionally. They are thinking in terms of new strategies for achieving goods, but not the traditional wealth symbolized by ritual rights, names, and traditional knowledge. The prized possessions are now manufactured goods, and the new leaders are constantly vying for access to these resources. The political strategies they use are their tried-and-true traditional networks, constructed of young followers, but driven now by new motivations.

The new leaders are creating new personal networks, as well as working on behalf of their respective villages to create sources of outside wealth. When the new leaders of Kubēkàkre go to the town of Redenção, they seek out specialists in outsiders' customs, leaders from other Kayapó villages, much as the sponsor of a ceremony seeks counsel from a former sponsor. New alliances are being sought.

One of Kubēkàkre's new leaders was receiving advice from one of the other village leaders concerning renting a house in Redenção for the use of Kubēkàkre villagers when they go to the town for medical treatment and other ventures. In addition, he was seeking advice from this person concerning the negotiation of a contract with a lumber company so that Kubēkàkre would not lag behind other villages in modernization projects such as electricity and new housing.

More than mere vestiges remain of traditional competitiveness between villages and between the leaders, however, as each tries to achieve great things for his own village. But on many occasions, the various Kayapó leaders are attempting to put differences behind them in order to present a united front to Brazilian society when necessary.

Beyond even this, is the pan-Indian unity, promoted in part by interested outsiders, but responded to with aplomb by the Kayapó leaders. True to form, they do not show signs of following; but they are ready to lead.

A conference of Brazilian Amerindians, international journalists, environmentalists of all stripes, and Sting, the British rock-star, was promoted by a young Kayapó leader. This attracted world-wide attention, as the conference sought to challenge Brazilian government and hydroelectric authorities to abandon the proposal to construct a huge hydroelectric dam which would effectively have flooded 400 square miles of traditional Kayapó land, displacing most of their villages and gardens. The result was the withdrawal of a World Bank loan which had been earmarked for that purpose.

New knowledge

The new Kayapó leaders, through their exposure to pro-Indian group meetings, were the objects of well-defined consciousness-raising tactics (Murphy 1991). These represented, not only knowledge new to them, but knowledge they would be sharing in the village through discussions and harangues. The pedagogical tactics to which the Kayapó were subjected were one-on-one encounters between themselves and pro-Indian activists. At these consciousness-raising meetings the Kayapó learned about politics on a national and international scale and became aware of the competing ideologies and practices of the various pro-Indian organizations. They heard expositions and denunciations about FUNAI, the government Indian agency, and began to understand the national power structure. They also began to learn about their own ethnic identity.

The Kayapó traditionally considered themselves essentially human beings while all other Amerindian groups were considered explicitly subhuman. But increased contact with many such groups has caused a (slight) shift in their opinions. They hear other indigenous languages and then watch other Amerindian leaders and spokesmen from other indigenous cultures conduct themselves in the Portuguese language in order to communicate effectively with nonindigenous people. They have met indigenous leaders of the indigenous movements in Ecuador and Peru.

With the development of these broad societal relationships, a new world view has emerged. The Kayapó have now come to see themselves "as one 'Indian people' among others, with similar problems and a similar culture."

> From seeing themselves simply as the paradigm of humanity...the Kayapó now see themselves as an ethnic group, sharing their ethnicity on a more or less equal footing with other indigenous people in their common confrontation with the national society. (T. Turner 1987b:127)

Now, as the national community is learning to appreciate indigenous people as humans, the Kayapó are learning to appreciate their ethnicity and beginning to see their relationship with the national society as something over which they can exercise some control and influence. One manifestation of this is a change in the power relationships with outsiders living in their villages, especially with the personnel of the government organization FUNAI.

Channels of outside knowledge in Kubēkàkre

At the time of my research there were two external influences in the village: personnel of FUNAI and the Summer Institute of Linguistics (SIL) (my colleague and myself).

Over the years, the personnel of FUNAI constantly shift and change. The supervisor of the station at the time of my research had set a record with seven years among the same group, but left shortly after I did in 1988. School teachers and medical personnel come and go with even greater frequency so that continuity has never occurred in Brazilian-style schooling in Kubēkàkre village. The desire of the Kayapó to control the school is something most FUNAI schoolteachers are not prepared to deal with.

During the final month of my study, a new schoolteacher was hired, and there was great excitement among the young men and boys. The supervisor invited two of the Kayapó leaders in Brazilian affairs and my colleague and me to be present at the first planning session with the teacher. From the beginning there were tensions as both the teacher and the Kayapó leaders tried to establish the ground rules for the school. My colleague, who had been requested to translate, was immediately suspect—the Kayapó wondering if she was agreeing with the teacher, and the teacher thinking she was taking the Kayapó part. Everyone contributed ideas and the meeting ended cordially.

The next day I asked the school-age boys if they were planning to start school when it opened. Most said they were going, although a few said they did not wish to attend.

"Why not?" I inquired.

"Because I already know Portuguese," said one, to my surprise.

"But there'll be counting and other things," I countered.

"We already know money!" chimed the group.

The boys were assessing their knowledge of Brazilian cultural skills according to what the adults in their life knew, and no doubt they did know as much as the adults. But they had no way of knowing how limited such knowledge really was.

The girls were not planning to attend at first, believing the classes would be coeducational. But when they learned the boys would go in the morning and the girls in the afternoon, some wanted to go. The mothers, however, were not so keen, since that was the time they needed their daughters to help with baby-sitting and other chores. Would the morning be better? No, they needed them then, too!

SIL personnel have lived among the Kayapó since 1967,[30] moving between several villages, sometimes living with Kayapó families in their homes, and sometimes having the use of an unoccupied house. They moved with the Kayapó from Mekrãknõti to Kubẽkàkre and had a Kayapó-style study house built, which could double as a school, since the FUNAI had not built a school at that point. They lived with the family of the head man.

The SIL team specializes in language-related work, including linguistic analysis, partnering with and training the Kayapó in the teaching and production of literacy materials in the Kayapó language, and translating the Christian Scriptures. The literacy materials are culturally relevant, including processes, hunting stories, and traditional knowledge to which all would have free access.

While I was there, the Kayapó leaders asked me to supplement Ruth Thomson's classes by teaching writing and typing. Thomson, in addition to translation work and cooperating with me, was preparing several young teens to attend Brazilian school in the village of Gorotire. The Brazilian teachers there all claimed that the students who had learned initially in their own language made the best transition into Portuguese and were ultimately the best students.

---

[30]Ruth Thomson and Mickey [Miriam] Stout, were the first team with Katherine Jefferson joining later. Mickey died in 1986, a few weeks after I had begun my research. The Kayapó of two villages honored her memory with a moving performance of the *myr kati* 'death dance' which I witnessed. Rarely is this performed for an outsider.

Although neither the FUNAI nor the SIL personnel were aware of the fact, it appears that the Kayapó were following their traditional methods of learner-initiated knowledge-seeking in their relationships with both these sources of outside knowledge. The young men, the traditional seekers of outside knowledge, were the regular students, and women learned second-hand through them.

Women's literacy classes have been held over the years with limited success due in part to the difficulty they have in concentrating, as their attention is divided between learning and tending the babies. Husbands do teach wives, however, and many women know how to read.

Literacy in the Kayapó language and schooling in the Portuguese language are options theoretically available to all, as far as the outside agents are concerned, but in fact, they are available mainly to young male adults due to Kayapó patterns of knowledge acquisition. The information learned by the young men through outside schooling presents many challenges to their traditional knowledge system. Teaching and learning styles are different. Much of the knowledge is totally irrelevant to them, and some conflicts with traditional knowledge on the level of worldview assumptions, specifically, all that is termed "science" (Murphy 2000).

In seeking a deeper commitment to schooling the Kayapó are opening the door to a variety of challenges, which, given their traditional patterns, could have many unforeseen consequences.

Traditional versus new attitudes to knowledge

One of the first potential consequences of a school run according to standard Brazilian guidelines is that a school curriculum implicitly underwrites a society's major values and contributes to the manitenance of a social status quo. In this case, the values and status quo of the majority society are in focus.

Another consequence will be the effect schooling may have upon traditional Kayapó society, as production networks and social networks are rearranged according to the time demands of a classroom and curriculum, possibly even undercutting the demands of Kayapó ceremonial life—an important channel of traditional learning and authority.

It is worth considering also what effect the introduction of new specialists (teachers) and school might have upon traditional authority patterns, since traditional Kayapó knowledge is associated with the prestige of Kayapó elders. Werner suggests, "perhaps an emphasis on new knowledge may also dampen the importance of what older people know. Obsolete knowledge would not be so highly valued as more relevant, recent information" (1981b:25).

It remains to be seen how well old-style options and networks will be balanced with the new, forming new life chances for the young without completely destroying everything life offered to the old. LeVine and White (1986) mention that for Westerners, an improvement in life chances is often taken at a cost in the linkages and attachments that make choice and success most meaningful and satisfying. This is not so common, they suggest, among non-Western people, who are more likely to strike a better balance between options and social networks.

School, as a source of outside knowledge, may never be a place where Kayapó traditional knowledge can be included in any idealistic attempt to reconcile the two systems or cultures. A bilingual program could run into difficulties, because of the Kayapó idea that new knowledge is introduced from outside of the culture. In fact, the idea of innovative knowledge from within seems to be unheard of. Anything culturally significant is traced to some source which legitimizes it; it is introduced, but not invented.

> The Xikrin-Kayapó are nothing if not pragmatic in adapting themselves to new situations or inventing new ideas and solutions to problems. But novelty is always seen to enter society from the outside as in the case of new songs, beautiful names, shamanistic cures, technology and even rituals derived from other tribes rather than as a cultural improvisation of Xikrin-Kayapó culture. (Fisher 1991:283)

All songs, names, rights, and roles were traceable, at least in theory, to an ancestor or some person or event in Kayapó history. One of the elders, disgruntled with the introduction by another storyteller of a certain song into a version of a story he usually told, said, "That song isn't part of it. Nikà'iti got that song from the village of Gorotire." Even songs taught by the elders in several of the song festivals are received in dreams and not attributed to the elder's authorship.

While questioning a man about the names of the different patterns used in the woven sleeping mats, I asked if someone would weave anything different, i.e., make up his own pattern. He looked astonished, but surmised that maybe these new ones (meaning the youth of today) could do something like that. No one ever had, though.

The fact that new or innovative knowledge is traditionally viewed as something which is centered outside of Kayapó society may mean that the school as a channel of new knowledge will never really become indigenous—and perhaps will never need to. Outsiders working with schooling would need to understand this possible source of conflict.

Another potential conflict between Kayapó ideas of learning and Western ideas of education is the teaching versus learning focus—and the possible consequences of learner-initiative upon school attendance.

When the young men asked my colleague and me to explain the eclipse of the moon, it had to be couched in the familiar framework of received knowledge. "This is what our ancestors told us..." we began, as, with flashlight, orange, and globe, we proceeded to present an alternative view of an event which still fills them with fear. The next evening the women came to hear our story of the eclipse and seemed greatly amused. While we saw their explanation and our explanation of an eclipse as polar opposites, they saw it as an interesting variation—an alternative view.

This is in keeping with attitudes to knowledge within the group, also. Was one shaman's knowledge superior to another's, I wondered? Did they feel competitive with one another when several were called to the hammock of a sick person? If the person improved, would one of them claim credit over another? Such questions seemed imponderable to them. Surely, if one cure was good, two were better, and all knowledge was useful.

I was reminded of an observation made by Margaret Mead:

> There are several striking differences between our concept of education today and that of any contemporary primitive society, but perhaps the most important one is the shift from the need for an individual to learn something which everyone agrees he would wish to know, to the will of some individual to teach something which it is not agreed that anyone has any desire to know. (1978:98)

Mead continued by observing, also, how in traditional societies, customs are imported, but at the initiative and desire of the importing group, rather than the desire of an exporting group. In other words, the emphasis in societies like the Kayapó is upon the desirability of learning as against the desirability of teaching.

Further, there is no hierarchical notion of one truth being superior to another. When the notion of a superior view is held, then education, she suggests, becomes the concern of the teacher, and not of the learner. I venture to suggest that the Kayapó may experience this assault upon their pragmatic philosophy of knowledge and their learner-initiative patterns to an even greater degree—even though it is they who are seeking schooling.

The introduction of new knowledge is not new, but schools among the Kayapó have had limited success. This suggests that there has never been a well-defined contract negotiated between the Kayapó and those responsible for the administration of the school, where the agendas, hidden and otherwise, of each side have been clarified and mutually understood.

Summary

We see that Kayapó Life Chances are changing dramatically. One of the keys to whether change is destructive is whether it is out of control. If change can be controlled and moderated, then it may even be positive, if viewed as such by the subjects rather than the agents of change. One way to control change is by balancing new options with old and new social networks in a way that is satisfying to an individual and a community.

The contribution of social linkages such as kin, associations, and neighbors provides a quality of life which must not be underestimated. Linkages provide support to the individual by providing ties upon which he can rely for goods, services, and emotionally significant symbols of personal security (Levine and White 1986:21). The importance of Kayapó relationships has been demonstrated, not only as social ties, but as channels of Kayapó traditional knowledge. Yet Kayapó society is not a closed system; new knowledge, new options for education, and new options for acquiring wealth all challenge the traditional system with a new definition of what is available to the Kayapó individual as a life chance.

Life Chances are the product of a balance between options and social networks. If new options are taken at the expense of social linkages, the individual may be impoverished and frustrated. An application of this model to the Kayapó identifies areas in which the Kayapó are actively balancing new options with old linkages, as well as creatively pursuing ways to broaden and strengthen intratribe linkages. In addition, helpful and strategic links with the Brazilian society are being sought.

Traditional Kayapó knowledge, as highly valued and necessary as it is to the Kayapó way of life, is threatened, not so much by new knowledge, as by rejection on the part of the young—an observation constantly reiterated by the Kayapó elders. In rejecting the content, the source is also being rejected, and new options are being taken at the expense of traditional relationships.

Schooling, coming from outside the culture and representing a contrasting set of values and assumptions to those of Kayapó society, may need to be renegotiated and reevaluated by the Kayapó leaders, together with the outside teacher or administrator in order to minimize potential conflicts.

This simple model of Life Chances as the function of options and networks clarifies the dynamics of culture change by providing an essentially realistic and human focus. It reveals the Kayapó as active participants in their own change process, not the passive victims of fate. As long as the Kayapó can continue to assert some political control over their declining social environment, they have an excellent chance of flourishing—changed, perhaps, but essentially Kayapó.

8

The Research Questions and Conclusions

The overall objective of this study, as indicated in the introductory chapter, was to identify how the Kayapó of central Brazil transmit their knowledge between one another and from generation to generation. An emerging data base (following Hansen's 1979 set of questions) lead to the following six research questions:

1. What relationship is there between cultural constructions of spatial organization and knowledge transmisstion events?
2. How do the Kayapó categorize and conceptualize their cultural knowledge? What factors influence knowledge distribution among the Kayapó people?
3. What social relationships function to transmit general, everyday knowledge between people and between generations? What methods are employed?
4. What is the pedagogical value of ceremonial activity within the Kayapó?
5. What social relationships function to transmit traditional knowledge between people and between generations? What methods are employed?
6 How will the introduction of new knowledge affect the Kayapó traditional patterns of knowledge transmission?

The following section gives a brief summary of the research results.

Summary

Spatial organization and knowledge transmissions events

Spatial orientation is an essential part of traditional Kayapó life. A typical village can be diagrammed as a series of concentric circles, beginning in the center with the men's house in the central plaza (often the focus of political and ceremonial activity), then (mostly for everyday activities) the dwellings with their yards, beyond them rough clearings, then gardens, and finally the forest. Who uses what space, when, and how, is relevant to Kayapó education. Knowledge transmission can take place in either an everyday or a ritual setting. Village space provides these settings through its transformation as effected by the focus and goal of a specific social activity. Everyday space is thus transformed into ritual space at given points of time.

Neither the space itself nor the spatial location is the exclusive factor in learning transactions; knowledge is conveyed through the relationships which are ascendant during either a ritual or everyday activity.

Categorization, conceptualization, and distribution of knowledge

The Kayapó have three categories of knowledge: general knowledge (what everyone knows), ceremonially-related knowledge (ritual), and specialist knowledge (tradition, sometimes secret). Specifying what type of information is appropriate at a given time, as well as from whom it should be learned, facilitates control of the transmission of knowledge.

General knowledge is transmitted mainly through the parent/child (including fictive parents) dyad and deals with subsistence and survival knowledge—the physical formation of a child. Transmission of this type of knowledge occurs in the everyday setting. Learning occurs through participation and practice and from following role models. Much of the knowledge transmitted in the daily routine is gender-specific, related to male and female domestic activities. The parents are considered responsible for the child's physical formation in the measure that they obey food regulations. Other activities of parents in relation to their children—body painting, nurturing, teaching survival skills—contribute to the physical aspect of the child's being.

Ceremonially-related knowledge consists of many aspects of Kayapó life, such as customs and traditions, ceremonial life, naming customs, ritual, songs, dances, and traditional lore. It is transmitted to the learner in the midst of ceremonial events, and includes both bodily and cognitive learning styles. Elders direct ceremonial events both actively and passively, reaffirming their authority in ritual events. Kayapó ritual follows a sociocultural model of learning and demonstrates the transmission of both implicit and explicit knowledge of values.

Specialist knowledge is transmitted in either everyday or ritual settings and concerns special and sometimes secret knowledge, which is transmitted in exchange for some paymant. This formalized exchange ensures that the knowledge will be considered properly transmitted in a socially valid way and that it can be exchanged later as part of a social contract. Members of the grandparent category are mainly responsible for the transmission of traditional knowledge, which is perceived by the Kayapó as contributing to the social formation of the individual (complementing the parents' contribution to the physical formation of the child).

The function of social relationships in transmitting general, everyday knowledge

Activities in the everyday setting provide the milieu for the education of Kayapó children and young adults. They learn general, everyday knowledge according to top-down social categories such as age, experience, and gender. For example, the social category of age includes teaching/learning relationships such as older and younger siblings, the parent category and children or youth, and the grandparent set and children. On the village level elder males have the most authority, elder women on the household level. Learning in the everyday setting is gender related, with girls learning from female role models and verbal instructors, while boys learn from older males and from playing with their age mates.

The three groupings of relationships for knowledge transfer are the nuclear family, the domestic group, and interhousholds. Children's education begins with modeling the behavior of adults in the nuclear family, an important social unit since the Kayapó believe that common substance is shared between parents and their offspring. The nuclear family is part of a larger domestic group consisting primarily of the mother's parents, sisters, and especially the grandmother. Interhousehold relationships include sisters-in-law and their children (as well as fictive parents and siblings), giving opportunity for broader social horizons and increased learning opportunities.

The pedagogical value of ceremonial activity

Kayapó ceremonial activities are the performance of traditional knowledge. As learning events, they are both cerebral and corporal, involving both mind and body, and contribute to the formation of the sociocultural and spiritual aspects of a child's being. Information learned in ritual is holistic, integrated, and experiential, providing an emotive context to facilitate and confirm the transmission of knowledge.

Ceremony is perceived as performed knowledge; people learn and perform actions such as inherited ceremonial roles, costume making, dancing, and singing. They are like apprentices, learning cognitively and bodily as they watch, then immediately performing what they have observed. Verbal instruction is also included in ceremonial teaching, with talk playing a validating role as much or more than a didactic one.

The function of social relationships in transmitting traditional knowledge

The Kayapó use three intermediary relationships to transmit traditional knowledge to children: grandparent/child, substitute parent/child, and ceremonial partners. The grandparent/child dyad is of prime importance; involving the transmission of traditional knowledge in socially defined ways. The grandparent category mediates between the everyday and ceremonial educational settings and also between the child's nuclear family and other domestic groups or households. The grandparent set is responsible for the formation of the social aspect of the child, passing on specific names, ceremonial rights, and other specialized knowledge such as preparation and use of herbal medications, ecology, positive and negative magic, and a personal store of secret information.

As children near puberty, one of their fictive parents becomes a substitute parent, accompanying them in an initiation rite. The substitute parents take on the role and responsibilities of natal parents, providing for and teaching the child, as well as providing another set of grandparents with all the role obligations of that relationship. Fictive parents contribute to the social aspect of children's being by symbolically moving them from their own household towards the wider community.

The third instructional and social relationship is that of male and female ceremonial partners. Their primary responsibility is to accompany and protect initiates during their transition period. Ceremonial partners may link households together, broadening the social and educational opportunities for the child and, especially for a boy, helping him develop his own strategy for knowledge acquisition.

The effect of new knowledge on traditional patterns of knowledge transmission

Outside knowledge contrasts with Kayapó knowledge not only in terms of content, but also in terms of the relationships by which it is transmitted. Potential conflicts may be introduced by formal schooling, which represents a contrasting philisophy of knowledge, contrasting ideas of knowledge transmission, and contrasting ideologies concerning notions of the truth value of information.

Younger Kayapó leaders are considered specialists in the ways of the outsiders. An application of the Life Chances model shows that the new options available to the Kayapó in terms of new knowledge and applications of that knowledge are being chosen at the expense of traditional relationships. Yet, new social networks are being formed across village and cultural boundaries. All in all, the Kayapó are active participants in their own change process and continue to assert some control in acquiring and transmitting new knowledge.

Importance of this Study

The methodology used in this study of Kayapó knowledge transmission contributes to the field of educational anthropology in two important ways: first, as a research tool for in-depth analysis and description of one society's educational system, and second, as a model for studying the educational and socialization patterns of other societies.

The Kayapó study

In the present study I first determined the major categories of knowledge classification and second the channel of transmission to which each category connects. My data sources included observation, participation, interviews (in the Kayapó language), tape recordings, and photographs. My interpretation of the data was mostly inductive, based on Kayapó comments, opinions, insights, and explanations in their own words.

The application of this methodology among the Kayapó shows definite connections between the type of knowledge transmitted, the relationship existing between the person transmitting the knowledge and the one receiving it, and the context in which the transmission takes place.

Future Research

The application of this research model to other societies will facilitate the discovery of their patterns of knowledge transfer. By this means we can ascertain the educational goals of a given community, as well as what the people consider to be appropriate knowledge categories, educational settings, and transmittor/receiver relationships.

A comparative study is beyond the scope of the present study. Nevertheless, the model presented here could be profitably employed to compare and contrast the educational goals and methodology not only of other indigenous communities, but also those of national or regional societies.

Epilogue

The New Knowledge Transmission Ritual

Mydjêre, at 17, has turned into a handsome young man. Raised as a traditional Kayapó, he had received so many names he claimed he could not remember them all. "My grandmothers know them all," he laughed. He had learned many ritual roles so well that he could perform them flawlessly. This was a source of great pride both to him and his father and all his family. This ritual knowledge gave Mydjêre prestige and status among his fellows. It gave him the confidence so characteristic of most Kayapó.

In January, 2001, Mydjêre was in the city of Cuiabá, MT, sitting in a classroom discussing and comparing cultural traditions with ten men from six different ethnic groups. They discussed similarities and differences in their oral traditions, beliefs, rituals, and each one had a chance to describe something from his group's traditions. Mydjêre volunteered to tell about the Kayapó naming ceremonies. The common language among these groups is Portuguese, which he does not completely master. Nevertheless, he started his speech with great enthusiasm. He told them how he had learned the Kayapó ceremonies to the point that he, himself, had been a sponsor on more than one occasion. He stated with pride how he had led the two- or three-month festivals without making a single mistake. He mentioned how the grandmothers and grandfathers were watching him, and that he had not disappointed them. Mydjêre's father was listening to him tell this, and even joined in a few times to emphasize a point, his eyes shining with pride. But as Mydjêre looked at his audience, he realized that the only ones who really understood what he was talking about were his father and I. His enthusiasm began to wane. Finally, he stopped abruptly. "That's all," he said, and sat down. I could tell he felt deflated. What did it matter, among these people, and in this place, what he knew about his traditions? It wasn't relevant. Outside of the Kayapó villages, the major part of his life's learning did not seem to be appropriate. What was important for him and for the others now was the common goal they all shared of becoming educated within the Brazilian school system.

So it is that Mydjêre, and so many Kayapó youth, feel the pressure to become masters of a different corpus of knowledge, a corpus foreign to them, but suddenly relevant and important—more important and relevant, they think, than everything they have learned till now. They are ready, although the educational system is not quite ready for them. In spite of many significant advances in the area of education for Brazil's indigenous people, the offering and quality has varied from state to state, with minimal federal guidance concerning uniform standards. Mydjêre began school in a regular Brazilian school in Colíder, the city closest to his village of Baú, but he complained that the teachers were always on strike, and that the other Kayapó students "just wanted to fool around all the time." Drinking was a regular pastime, in which Mydjêre had little interest. Eventually, he found a place which would prepare him for a special examination aimed at qualifying students for secondary education. His father backed him unconditionally.

The above case is just one of many similar dramas taking place among the Kayapó today, as parents seek ways and means for their children, sons especially, to have access to Brazilian education. All over Brazil the indigenous people are clamoring for equal rights to education, while those who could facilitate this, vacillate, anxious to avoid past errors committed in other countries and their own in the area of education for ethnic minorities. While a multitude of conferences, meetings, legislation and books, projects and experiments are produced, and seem to be a necessary part of the process to provide schooling for indigenous people, the ethnic groups are becoming impatient.

> Things are difficult and slow because nobody understands indigenous education. The non-Indians don't know anything. They say, "leave the Indians to themselves; their teachers don't know how to teach a class." The non-Indians don't know about our knowledge...On the other hand, I am happy, because I feel things are improving. Today everybody talks

about indigenous education. (Gilda Kuitá, Kaingáng 2001:23)[31]

Traditionally, as we saw in chapter 4, Kayapó parents are responsible for teaching their children all that pertains to their physical development, including survival skills. The knowledge the parents hope their children will accrue from Brazilian schooling is definitely categorized by the Kayapó as a survival skill, providing protection and a semblance of control in today's frequent interaction with the dominant society. This may help to explain the dedication and sacrifice on the part of fathers, especially, in accompanying their sons to the cities and towns where schooling is available, if it is not provided in their village.

The provision of a school in the villages presents a great challenge to the government or to any agency attempting to sustain a school. Few are the non-Kayapó teachers who can adapt to life in the village, at the beck and call of the people. In the eyes of the Kayapó, non-Kayapó in the village are their "workers," their servants. Consequently, the teachers either leave shortly, of their own volition, or are asked to leave, which leads to a constant, unsatisfactory turnover. Due to this, there is a risk of eventually inoculating the students against schooling, a phenomenon I have observed in the village of Pykany.

The Kayapó try to solve the problem by attempting to control their access to (western-style) schooling. If they are unable to negotiate a teacher for a village school, those who are able will send their sons to a city school. Outside knowledge, therefore, whether channeled through schools within the village, or outside the village, comes to the people on their own terms. Parents strongly encourage their children—sons, especially—to attend school but the rule of learner-initiative still applies. A child will not be forced against its will. When they do attend city schools, the fathers accompany them and seek to influence and regulate and even pressure them to do well. Mothers admonish them via the two-way radio system to "stick with i persevere, to learn the talk" (Portuguese). The difficulties of maintaining teachers in villages is pressuring the Kayapó of Kubẽkàkre to send their children to schools in Redenção. During the 1980s, this strategy was increasingly pursued, especially by the Kayapó of Gorotire village, nearest to Redenção. In 1998, Redenção schools had 120 Kayapó students—some from Kubẽkàkre (de Sousa 2001:261). Not all families have the resources to do this, which will cause inequalities within

---

[31] "As coisas são difíceis e demoradas porque ninguém sabe da educação indígena. Os não-índios não entendem nada. Eles dizem assim: 'ah, os índios que se viram lá, esses professores aí não sabem dar aula'. Os não-índios não sabem do nosso conhecimento...Por outro lado, eu me sinto muito feliz, eu sinto que as coisas estão melhorando. Hoje todos falam em educação indígena."

the system beyond any the society has previously tolerated (cf. de Sousa 2001:264).

The schools and teaching staff in these contact towns have not received any special preparation for receiving students culturally different from themselves. Thus the whole onus of adaptation is upon the Kayapó pupils. The school curriculum is not adapted in any way to Kayapó reality or worldview—indeed, the teaching staff have little awareness of the Kayapó students' special needs. Although the Brazilian Constitution[32] guarantees the indigenous populations schooling which respects their language, culture and learning styles—thus creating an obvious role for indigenous teachers—many teachers in Kayapó areas are not indigenous, do not speak the language or understand the culture, and know little about Kayapó learning styles.

Schooling, when pursued away from the village, removes both a father and his son(s) from village life for extended periods of time—periods over which the Kayapó have no control, since the schedule conforms to state and federal education regulations. This has begun to undermine traditional commitments to their gardens and to their participation in the elaborate Kayapó naming ceremonies. As a result, ceremonies which require a two- or three-month time span are being substituted in many villages by the *Kwyrkangô* ceremony (traditionally non-Kayapó) which is a shorter festival. Other ethnic groups are experiencing similar changes. Darlene Yaminalo Taukane, of the Kurâ-Bakairi indigenous society, in her article, "Kurâ-Bakairi Education in Traditional Context," observed:

> The time a girl stayed in seclusion was up to the grandparents, but today, one month would be a lot. Our ancestors used to stay in seclusion up to a year. We realize that this has changed because we are living in another era, in another situation which no longer permits us to spend so much time in seclusion. (1997:115)[33]

The traditional education Mydjêre and other young Kayapó men (especially) have received imbues them with many characteristics which are helpful to them in the uphill struggle within Brazil's educational system. The highly-prized stamina gained from lengthy, all-night ceremonial activities and other physical endurance tests means that they do not easily

---

[32]Brazilian Federal Constitution, 1988, Article 210.

[33]"A determinação do tempo de duração da reclusão é tarefa que cabe aos avós, mas hoje dura um mês, quando muito. Nossos antepassados chegavam a permanecer até um ano reclusos. Entendemos que isso ocorra em virtude de estarmos vivendo em uma outra época e em uma outra situação que não mais nos permite guardar demoradamente o tempo *wanke*."

give up. Having many relatives who watch their progress is a powerful incentive for them to keep trying in this new educational milieu, just as it was in the traditional format, back in the village. Oral skills, so well developed by their exposure to the teachings of those in the grandparent category, now facilitate their second-language acquisition abilities, as well as their capacity to absorb new information without necessarily comprehending it immediately.

The embedded educational events in Kayapó ritual, discussed and illustrated in chapter 5, have conditioned them to place great value on the form and less on the information load of the educational event. This is true of many traditional societies, but not true, in general, of Western education. Thus, for the Kayapó, schooling is interpreted as a type of ritual—where transformation is expected to occur. As such, it is extremely important to them that their students be exposed to the "ritual" space of a Brazilian school; participate in and endure the "ritual" of the teaching and learning activities, preferably with a Brazilian specialist (teacher); participate in repetitive activities such as copying, memorizing, and performing what is being passed on, including writing, reading, Portuguese, arithmetic, etc., with the emphasis being on performance over comprehension.

Whether the Kayapó student actually passes into another grade is less important than their continuing presence in the school. Repetition is not redundant in the Kayapó view—rather, it is basic to learning. Yet there is satisfaction in advancement and achievement and the Kayapó parents are becoming increasingly aware that annual promotion from one grade to another is important and that schooling is a long-term investment, if indeed their children are to attend school from the first to the eighth grades or more.

> The "ritual" paraphernalia is also significant: textbooks, notebooks, pencils, erasers, folders, paper, and the productive use of the same. There are increments of importance in school materials as students are promoted, just as there are in Kayapó learning events, such as weaving. Brazilian schooling norms (ritualized behavior) are carefully observed and followed, such as hand-raising, answering questions, obeying the teacher.

Traditional Kayapó ritual events are agents of the transmission of Kayapó customs (kukràdja), a distinctly socializing process. The knowledge-transmission relationships are more formal in nature, opposite to the category of substance relationships. The learning takes place in ritual space, and many transactions require payment for legitimization. So it is with Brazilian schooling. The schooling "ritual" is believed to be a secure agent for the transmission of Brazilian customs (which the Kayapó desire to master). The relationship between teacher and pupil is relatively formal, and the teacher is nonkin. Payment is often involved, at least in the acquisition of materials. There are many parallels which, interpreted through a Kayapó grid, make the process of schooling understandable and desirable, and hopefully transformational and effective according to Kayapó expectations.

At the same time, these facts present Brazilian educators concerned with the indigenous question with a paradox. They are trying to find creative and constructive ways to provide culturally appropriate and differentiated education to indigenous populations, while many or most ethnic groups desire formal, traditional Brazilian schooling, as inappropriate and passé as it may seem to the Brazilian educators.

> We are faced with a paradox: there have been times when indigenous teachers in training have expressed their desire for traditional Brazilian schooling, defined by them as "the white man's school," while Brazilian staff, responsible for indigenous teacher training courses, want to present a new model of school education, based upon the construction of knowledge. (Peggion 1997:152)[34]

Given the Kayapó view of tradition (revered), knowledge (received, not constructed), and customs (socializing, civilizing) and how these are transmitted by ritual means, it is not at all surprising that the Kayapó feel that their appropriation of "the white man's" customs should conform to specific rules, regulations, and rituals traditionally used by the "white man" to pass his knowledge on. The ritual of school is one of the more obvious ways. Furthermore, it is accessible to the Kayapó and their expectation is that their children, through this process, will demystify the inscrutable customs of the *kubẽ* (Brazilians). The elders in the village testify to the success of this method as they complain regularly that the young boys who attend school are *kubẽ*, and not really Kayapó. Thus their complaints, voiced in chapter 6, that "they don't like us any more" because they no longer learn from them. Life, for the school attendee, caught between two worlds, is not easy either at home or abroad.

The Kayapó student "abroad" is aware that he starts schooling with a disadvantage. The older student (teen) has spent his formative years becoming educated as a Kayapó, within a supportive and familiar environment. Now he must begin again, in another system, away from family and

---

[34]"Temos, de fato, um paradoxo: em determinados momentos, os cursistas têm reivindicado um ensino tradicional, definido por eles como 'escola de branco', enquanto os consultores do projeto [de preparo] têm-lhes apresentado um novo modelo de educação escolar, baseado na construção do conhecimento."

friends, often with only one parent present to show interest. For the first time, he must learn to negotiate with teachers who are not relatives, in a culture unfamiliar to him. The younger student, starting on a par with non-Kayapó students, is more likely to succeed, in spite of language[35] and cultural barriers. But the younger student will be acquiring schooling at the expense of traditional Kayapó education, since time demands alone will not permit him to have the best of both worlds.

As the Kayapó students successfully master literacy in Portuguese, numeracy, and other skills, they become a valuable resource to their community. They will be employed in the buffer zone, mediating between the Kayapó domain and the dominant society's domain. So far, the purpose of schooling from a Kayapó perspective is for the student to serve his village, "to help his relatives" in the difficult negotiations between the village and those in a wider perimeter. Those who have proven themselves capable will be at the service of the village leaders to mediate between the village and lumber companies or gold miners, the commercial entities, FUNAI, and other relevant agencies. The youth were traditionally at the beck and call of their elders within the age-grade hierarchy, and this system continues to function, thus providing some control over those whose schooling sets them apart from the others. Parents gain prestige and benefits also, if their sons become politically useful to the village leaders and/or village elite—those who command prestige and power through personal gain from lumber and gold, especially.

If schooling within the villages is difficult to provide, and more Kayapó youth are effectively exiled from their villages in the pursuit of non-Kayapó knowledge and customs in nearby towns and cities, a dependency situation is created which threatens Kayapó autonomy. One strategy to avoid this could be the training of Kayapó teachers, and in fact, some Kayapó men have participated in teacher-training courses run by university students and professors and a few are actually involved in teaching in village schools.

In general, however, the Kayapó have not proven to be good candidates for teacher training, nor have they shown much desire to become teachers, except for personal political benefits (cf. Silva and Salanova 2001:341). I believe there are many reasons for this:

- The source of outside (Brazilian school system) knowledge resides in a non-Kayapó domain.
- The Kayapó do not master this knowledge. It is not "theirs" to teach. They have not inherited it.

---

[35]Ideally, Portuguese should be taught to non-Portuguese speakers as a second language, which, of course, the average school is not equipped to do.

- The Kayapó are interested in learning the outsiders' customs, customs which are innate to Brazilians, but not to Kayapó; therefore, a non-Kayapó is considered to be a more qualified source of transmission.
- The Kayapó are unhappy with schooling which diverges in any way from the norms they observe within Brazilian schools. In their view, the way it is done in the city is the way it ought to be done (cf. de Sousa 2001). In spite of conflicts engendered by divergent worldviews, the Kayapó insist that the content of schooling—the knowledge content—be identical to that offered to non-Kayapó. The Kayapó may not control the content (and others may question the appropriateness of the content to the Kayapó needs), but they do control their exposure to it (cf. Silva and Salanova 2001:337).
- The indigenous teachers' interest is highly pragmatic, basically taking advantage of the job offer as one more source of coveted personal revenue.
- There is no clear precedent within the Kayapó community for this type of specialist. If a person accepts the role it is more likely to be for his personal benefit than for the good of the community (Silva and Salanova 2001:340).
- Even if a young man becomes a teacher and engages in teaching, the window of opportunity for such a career is short, interrupted by marriage and fatherhood, service to his father-in-law, and increasing involvement in the internal politics of the village, as he moves along in the age-grade system.
- Due to the relatively short career of an indigenous teacher, it would be necessary to prepare a constant supply of teachers on a regular basis, in order to fit into the rhythm of the age-grade system—something which could happen if both the Kayapó leaders and outside providers of teacher training were to appropriate the cultural base (age-grades) which already exists within the system.
- Teacher-training programs have limited success, due to the conflicting agendas of those offering training and those being trained (cf. Silva and Salanova 2001). The outside agent sees the pupil as a potential teacher. The pupil sees himself as a learner. He is aware that his community may or may not validate him as a teacher, i.e., a "specialist" of outside knowledge.
- Many times the intent of teacher training courses is not entirely clear to the Kayapó participants, especially those who are relatively monolingual.

The above points pertain to the Kayapó and are related to their specific cultural traits. Teacher training among other ethnic groups in Brazil is having a measure of success, even though handled with some ambivalence by the Federal and State educators. Says one Kaingáng teacher, Pedro Seg-Seg:

> Education, in the future, for me, will be a constant dispute [positioning oneself to contend] with State and Municipal agencies, the FUNAI, NGOs or other Government agencies.... (*Paraná Indígena* 2001:22)[36]

Marcolino da Silva, a Guaraní teacher, recognizes both the positive and negative side of the pursuit of schooling:

> In many Guaraní and Kaingáng villages, to tell the truth, they have lost their culture and language. This is why I say that studies are good, but there is a negative side. Many Indians who have studied, when they graduate from university, don't want to be Indians any more; they don't want to speak their language, or they are ashamed to speak our language here in the city. I was born an Indian and I am going to be an Indian, because I speak my language. (*Paraná Indígena* 2001:20)[37]

Marcolino goes on to say that he considers the Guaraní, the Xavante, and the Kayapó to be the most resistant ethnic groups because they have not lost their language. Pedro Seg-Seg, a Kaingáng teacher also makes a comment along these lines: "And how will we win respect? It will be speaking our language and writing our language. What good is it to say I am an Indian, but I don't speak my language? You will lose a lot if you lose your language" (*Paraná Indígena* 2001:22). Possible language loss due to educational experiences which do not value the indigenous languages is an ongoing concern of many educators and linguists. Thomas D. Peacock and Donald R. Day discuss a number of practical recommendations aimed at dealing with "Native language loss, maintenance, and restoration in American Indian and Alaska Native communities, focusing on successful efforts of schools and communities" (*ERIC Digest* 1999).

---

[36]"A educação no futuro, para mim, será uma constante disputa de postura, no Estado, no Município, na Funai, em qualquer organismo governamental ou não-governamental."

[37]"Em muitas aldeias dos guaranis e dos caingangues, para falar a verdade, eles já perderam a cultura e a língua. É por isso que eu digo que o estudo é muito bom, mas tem um lado negativo. Pois muitos índios quando têm estudo, quando terminam a faculdade, não querem mais ser índios, não querem mais falar em sua língua, ou têm vergonha de falar na nossa língua aqui na cidade. Eu nasci como índio e vou ser índio, porque falo a minha língua."

The fact that the Kayapó fathers accompany their children in their experience with outside schooling should not be underestimated. This ensures that the child keeps his Kayapó language ability active and may even enable him to transfer some of the concepts learned in Portuguese into the Kayapó language, as he discusses what he is learning with his father. As in the case of the rural Brazilians, studied by Brandão, a child whose parents had attended school was more likely to succeed in school (1990:68), and in only a short time, this Kayapó child will be accompanying his own child as he himself was accompanied. This is part of the Kayapó ethos of passing things along—"and I, in my turn, will pass it on."

Concluding Remarks

The purpose of this study was to provide a systematic probe into one knowledge transmission system in both its traditional and contemporary forms. It can serve as a model for studies of cultural and knowledge transmission and acquisition, as well as adding to studies in educational anthropology that focus upon culturally-specific nonschool patterns of education. One supporting factor for this study was the optimistic provision, in the Brazilian Constitution, Article 210, which secures the right of indigenous communities to their own language and learning styles in educational endeavors.

As with most legislation, it is easier to legislate than implement, as Nietta Lindenberg Monte's article, "Problemas de um Currículo para a Educação Intercultural e Bilíngüe," testifies (1997:129). While others debate, the Kayapó, at least, do not wait. This study of their internal educational system gives many clues to their cultural persistence. They have a strong and functional social organization, clear societal roles for their participants, an innate pride in their language and culture, and a strong sense of their own superiority over non-Kayapó. They are a "take charge" people—active, never passive. This sense of control is foundational to their survival.

A study of the knowledge transmission system reveals that the Kayapó have a clear and operating agenda concerning the transfer of knowledge and customs, names and other cultural goods, both tangible and intangible. The contribution to a child's formation, both by those in the parent category and in the grandparent category, provides for the construction of the whole person, complete and socialized. Kayapó education is a transformational process and project and Kayapó ritual provides ways and means of legitimizing all "official" knowledge transmission, ensuring that the Kayapó natural child becomes (is transformed into) a social being—a person.

As a system of traditional education (knowledge transmission), that of the Kayapó shares many characteristics with most traditional systems. For example, their social organization including age-grades provides a functioning hierarchy through which knowledge passes in a controlled way. The content of their knowledge is specific to their physical survival in a specific ecological environment. Their ethnohistory and ethnoscience, explanatory myths, legends, and other stories are cultural-specific and told in patterned ways by qualified agents of transmission. Their ritual practices, in their case, naming ceremonies, are fundamentally important to the transmission of knowledge, and if these break down, the Kayapó society will suffer as have so many other traditional societies in the world, with the disintegration of their physical environment and the rituals tied to it.

In Brazil, within another Gê society, the Xavante, a counsel of elders must approve the school curriculum and ensure that the schedule allows time for the young to also participate in the traditional rites of their society. In other societies, such as the Kurâ-Bakairi, traditional education continues, of course, but in a reduced form. The old ways are spoken of with some nostalgia today (Taukane 1997:109–128), as the life-cycle rituals so fundamental to their system of knowledge transmission have undergone great changes, most practiced only rarely today. Nevertheless, Taukane identifies strong cultural values still being transmitted currently, values which contribute to a cultural sense of personhood, differentiating the Kurâ-Bakairí from other ethnicities. The Kaingáng also feel they have lost many of their traditions. Nevertheless, there are many cultural revitalization efforts occurring as ethnic groups try to recapture their traditions, their sense of unique identity, and, if possible, their language.

The Kayapó differ from the majority of Brazil's groups, in that their traditions are still strong, are being practiced, and they have many elders who champion this cause, even as there are many young leaders who would lead the tribe in the opposite direction. Ropni (Rauni) is an elderly Kayapó warrior whose efforts to defend the Kayapó culture and land will become legendary. He states, "We must resist and continue to divulge our indigenous traditions so that the white man will see, hear, believe, and have respect." *That one sentence succinctly summarizes the Kayapó ideal of education: to see, to hear, to believe, and to learn respect.* The Kayapó feel the need to learn from others, but they strongly believe they have much to teach others. Ropni decries the negative influence of the white man on indigenous peoples. He describes his efforts to educate the white man.

> I fought with the FUNAI. I fought with the Minister (government official). I fought with the President of the Republic. At one time I fought for land. I fought for our rights. They spoke badly, they argued, but I continued my fight. I was courageous, I tugged at their earlobes, tugged at their noses so they would hear and understand the reality of my struggle, of my struggles on behalf of all of us [indigenous peoples].
> (*Paraná Indígena* 2001:13)[38]

The Kayapó and other indigenous people around the world have much to teach, and increasingly, nontraditional societies are recognizing this. The work of Posey and others has contributed to an appreciation of Kayapó traditional knowledge and its role in environmental management, but in general, the greater burden is upon the indigenous peoples to adapt to the ways of majority societies and learn the knowledge, skills, and ways of thinking which make such societies tick. The Kayapó would, "in their turn," pass their knowledge on to us, if we had the wisdom to receive it. If their knowledge is lost, it is not only their loss; it is ours, as well.

---

[38]"Eu brigava com a Funai. Brigava com o ministro. Brigava com o presidente da República. Na época, brigava por terra. Brigava por todos os nossos direitos. Eles falavam mal, respondiam, mas eu continuei a minha luta. Chegava, falava e eles respondiam mal. Mas eu criava coragem, puxava a orelha, puxava o nariz para escutar e conhecer a realidade da minha luta por todos nós."

Appendix A
Replication of Werner's Questionnaire

The following peer rating questionnaire was administered to twenty men and twenty women during house visits. Adults were asked to name up to five people they thought of in response to the questions. While I did not do a statistical analysis of the ratings, I was able to compare them with Werner's findings and found that there was high agreement with Werner's results as well as agreement among respondents (see Werner 1981a:372, except for 4 and 5).

1. Whose advice (orders, suggestions) do you (Kayapó) follow in doing traditional things? (general influence)
2. Whose advice (orders, suggestions) do you (Kayapó) follow in doing things for outsiders (nonindigenous people/others *civilizados*)? (culture mediator)
3. Who is generous? (generosity)
4. Who is a fierce man? Who is a fierce woman? (negative characteristic)
5. Who is a kind/tame man? Who is a kind/tame woman? (positive characteristic)
6. Who kills (has killed) enemies well? (warrior)
7. Who kills game well? (hunter)
8. Who makes things well? (craftsman)
9. Who paints people well? (painter)
10. Who knows Kayapó things well? (knowledge of tradition)
11. Who knows "civilized" things well? (knowledge of outsiders)
12. Who knows ceremonies well? (knowledge of ceremonies)

13. Who knows the ancestors well? (knowledge of ancestors)
14. Who has many paramours? (extramarital affairs)

Appendix B
Kayapó Dietary Regulations

Pregnancy and during child's illness	Observed by	If kept, child will	If broken, child will
Animal: meat of forbidden hairy animal not to be eaten (to insure health and proper physical development of child)	pregnant woman and husband until child is strong, especially for first child	be large with tough skin; grow to adulthood; and be happy and strong	
anteater	as above	as above	
deer (leg)	as above	as above	walk poorly
monkey (head)	as above	as above	have a round head
pig (breast bone and stomach)	as above	as above	
(general)	as above	as above	have diarrhea
wild pigs (*queixado* and *caitutu*)	as above	as above	have a protruding forehead and a narrow, flat head
raccoon	as above	as above	

Kayapó Dietary Regulations

Pregnancy and during child's illness	Observed by	If kept, child will	If broken, child will
tapir (hump, base of skull, tail, head, eye)	as above	as above	grow hair to long point at base of neck or have a cowlick
(scruff, liver, flesh from leg bones, lower part and strip surrounding intestines)	as above	as above	have diarrhea
armadillo	parents of sick child	become well	have diarrhea; become crazy
Honey not to be eaten, if from: black-skinned, round-headed bee or bee that makes white honey or is weak	pregnant woman and husband		have black skin and a round head; won't be strong or walk well; will be pale (weak)
kakranhti honey	as above		pant hard
bees that compartmentalize hives with lots of wax clogged at bottom of hive	as above		be constipated; can die
ydjy bee's honey	as above		be short of breath
blind bee whose sting blisters and leaves a scab	pregnant woman		be blind and have a scabby head

Kayapó Dietary Regulations

Pregnancy and during child's illness	Observed by	If kept, child will	If broken, child will
mnumkure bee, who lives with an ant; bees that have dangly legs	as above		have weak legs and won't walk soon
Birds: flesh of following forbidden:			
krwytkanbrek bird	newly pregnant		have soft skin, like dandruff; be small with small, round (bird-like) head
mutum	as above		as above
turkey-like birds	as above		as above
macaw types	as above		as above
azulão bird	as above		have dandruff
Fish– forbidden types:			
krwyti-re fish (bad)	pregnant woman and husband; parents until child is well	become well	
surubim fish	as above	as above	
tucunaré	as above	as above	
matrixão fish (angry)	as above	as above	
kripite fish	as above		
Tortoise liver forbidden	as above	as above	have diarrhea

Kayapó Dietary Regulations

Pregnancy and during child's illness	Observed by	If kept, child will	If broken, child will
Sprouting part of palm-heart forbidden	pregnant woman and husband		have a little of hair at base of skull
Sting of stingray			
The injured shouldn't eat foods classified as wet; boiled meat, boiled fish, papaya, squash, watermelon, bananas	person stung	injured area will not go pulpy	injured area will get pulpy; pain will return
Shouldn't use soap on body over long time period	as above	injured area will not become soft	injured area will get soft
Pregnancy positives			
Small armadillo—when killing it, they wipe their hands on their backs	husband of pregnant wife when hunting	walk and be born quickly	
When eating *tepakax-tykere* fish they wipe their hands on the back	as above	come quickly when born	
Stays with wife until baby moves in the womb, after which he goes to the men's house	pregnant woman's husband		

Kayapó Dietary Regulations

Pregnancy positives	Observed by	If kept, child will	If broken, child will
Medicine to make it safe to eat *menhokane* honey	as above	husband can eat honey, but must take medicine first	honey can kill eater
When eating *paca* they rub themselves with the fat (with their hands on their backs)	pregnant woman and husband	have wide, flat forehead	
When hunting must carry club instead of bow and arrow or gun	husband during first pregnancy	be smart	be blinded if gun is used; wife may hemorrhage if arrow is used
Eat *noroti* honey—then woman wipes hands on back; man wipes hands on thighs (bee is small, but tall/long; hive is located in stump)	pregnant woman and husband	be tall	

Medical positives	Observed by	If kept	If broken
Sting of stingray			
Victim should eat only foods classified as dry: sweet potato, rice, parched corn, manioc flour, meat that has been well baked over the fire, green banana paste, thin bread (well-baked), *açai*	person stung	injured area will not go pulpy	injured area will go pulpy

References

Agar, Michael H. 1980. *The professional stranger: An informal introduction to ethnography.* New York: Academic Press.

Bamberger, Joan. 1967. *Environment and cultural classification: A study of the northern Kayapo.* Ph.D. dissertation. Harvard University.

Bamberger, Joan. 1979. Exit and voice in central Brazil: The politics of flight in Kayapo Society. In David Maybury-Lewis (ed.), 130–146.

Banner, Horace. 1978. Uma cerimônia de nominação entre os Kayapó. *Revista da Antropologia* 23(1a parte):109–115.

Bell, Catherine. 1992. *Ritual theory, ritual practice.* New York: Oxford University Press.

Boster, James and Carolyn Mervis. 1987. Toward an information economy theory of culture. Ms.

Bourdier, Jean-Paul, and Nezar Alsayyad, eds. 1989. *Dwellings, settlements and tradition: Cross-cultural perspectives.* Lanham, Md.: University Press of America.

Brandão, Carlos Rodrigues. 1990. *O trabalho de saber: Cultura camponesa e escola rural.* São Paulo: Global.

Caraveli, Anna. 1985. The symbolic village: Community born in performance. *Journal of American Folklore* 98:259–286.

Connerton, Paul. 1989. *How societies remember.* Cambridge: Cambridge University Press.

Coy, Michael W., ed. 1989. *Apprenticeship.* Albany: State University of New York Press.

Crocker, Jon Christopher. 1979. Selves and alters among the eastern Bororo. In David Maybury-Lewis (ed.), 249–300.

Cusick, Philip A. 1973. *Inside high school: The students' world.* New York: Holt, Rinehart and Winston.
Dahrendorf, Ralf. 1979. *Life chances.* Chicago: University of Chicago Press.
Elisabetsky, Elaine. 1986. Etnofarmacologia de algumas tribos brasileiras. In *Etnobiologia,* Berta G. Ribeiro (coordenação), 135–150. *Suma,* Vol 1. Darcy Ribeiro (gen. ed.). Petropolis: Vozes.
Da Silva, Aracy Lopes, and Mariana K. L. Ferreira (Org.). 2001. *Antropologia, história e educação: A questão indígena e a escola.* São Paulo: Global.
Da Silva, Marcolino. O apelo do arroz, dos refrigerantes e do frango asado. In *Paraná Indígena,* 19–20.
De Sousa, Cássio Noronha Inglez. Aprendendo a viver junto: reflexões sobre a experiência escolar Kayapó-Gorotire. In *Antropologia, História e Educação.* SP. Global, 238–274.
Dobbert, Marion Lundy, and Betty Cooke. 1987. Primate biology and behavior: A stimulus to educational thought and policy. In G. D. Spindler (ed.), *Education and cultural process.* 2nd ed., 97–116. Prospect Heights: Waveland Press.
Fernandes, Florestan. 1975. Notas sobre a educacão na sociedade Tupinamba, Capitulo II. In *A investigação etnológica no Brasil e outros ensaios,* 33–83. Petropolis: Vozes.
Fisher, William. 1989. Personal names, shifting boundries and conflict among the Xikrín (Para, Brazil). ms.
Fisher, William. 1991. Dualism and its discontents: Social process and village fissioning among the Xikrin Kayapó of central Brazil. Ph. D. dissertation. Cornell University.
Goody, Jack. 1961. Religion and ritual: The definitional problem. *British Journal of Sociology* 12:142–164.
Governo do Paraná, Secretária de Cultura. 2003. Paraná indígena: Memória da terra. Proceedings from a Conference attended by Indigenous leaders from eighteen Indigenous areas in Paraná state, 20 to 22 of May 2002.
Grimes, Ronald L. 1986. Appendices for a sense of ritual. ms.
Grimes, Ronald L. 1991. Inventing ritual. ms.
Hansen, Judith Friedman. 1979. *Sociocultural perspectives on human learning.* Englewood Cliffs, N.J.: Prentice Hall.
Hansen, Judith Friedman. 1982. From background to foreground: Toward an anthropology of learning. *Anthropology and Education Quarterly* 13(2):189–202.
Harris, Stephen. 1977. Milingimbi aboriginal learning. Ph.D. dissertation. University of New Mexico.

Hart, C. W. M. 1963[1955]. Contrasts between prepubertal and postpubertal education. In G. D. Spindler (ed.), 359–377.
Hecht, Susanna B., and Darrell A. Posey. 1990. Indigenous soil management in the Latin American tropics: Some implications for the Amazon Basin. *Proceedings of the First International Congress of Ethnobiology, Belem, 1988.* Vol. 1:227–241. Belem: Museu Paraense Emílio Goeldi.
Henry, Jules. 1975[1963]. Golden rule days: American schoolrooms. In James P. Spradley and Michael A. Rynkiewiah (eds.), *The Nacirema,* 30–42. Boston: Little, Brown and Company.
Horwood, Bert. 1983. Rituals and ceremonies for teachers: A demonstration workshop. Paper presented at the Annual Conference of the Association for Experiential Education, Williams Bay, WI, 1983. ERIC Digests file ed241207.
Hugh-Jones, Christine. 1979. *From the Milk River: Spatial and temporal processes in northwest Amazonia.* Cambridge: Cambridge University Press.
Ireland, Emilienne. 1990. Neither warriors nor victims, the Wauja peacefully organize to defend their land. *The Latin American Anthropology Review* 2(1):3–12.
Jefferson, Kathleen. 1980. *Kayapo pedagogical grammar: Kayapo-English version.* 3 volumes. ms. Brasilia: Summer Institute of Linguistics.
Jennings, Theodore W. 1982. On ritual knowledge. *The Journal of Religion* 62(2):111–127.
Jensen, Allen A. 1990. Biological information transmitted through festival. *Proceedings of the First International Congress of Ethnobiology, Belem,* Brazil, 1988. 1:113–123. Belem: Museu Paraense Emílio Goeldi.
Jordan, Brigitte. 1987. *Modes of teaching and learning: Questions raised by the training of traditional birth attendants.* California: Institute for Research on Learning. IRL87-0004.
Kuitá, Gilda. 2003. A dura conquista da educação diferenciada. In Paraná Indígena, 23–24.
La Fontaine, J. S. 1977. The power of rights. *Man* 5(12):421–437.
Lancy, David F. 1975. The social organization of learning: Initiation rituals and public schools. *Human Organization* 34(4):371–380.
Lave, Jean Elizabeth Carter. 1979. Cycles and trends in Krĩkatí naming practices. In David Maybury-Lewis (ed.), 16–45.
Lave, Jean Elizabeth Carter. 1988. *Cognition in practice: Mind, mathematics, and culture in everyday life.* Cambridge: Cambridge University Press.
Lave, Jean, and Etienne Wenger. 1991. *Situated learning.* Cambridge: Cambridge University Press.

Lawrence, Denise L., and Seth Low. 1990. The built environment and spacial form. *Annual Review of Anthropology* 19:453–505.

Lea, Vanessa Rosemary. 1986. Nomes e nekrets Kayapó—uma concepção de riqueza. Volumes 1, 2, and 3. Ph.D. thesis submitted to the Federal University of Rio de Janeiro.

Levine, Robert, and Merry I. White. 1986. *Human conditions.* New York: Routledge and Kegan Paul.

Levi-Strauss, Claude. 1969. *The raw and the cooked. Introduction to a science of mythology, 1.* Chicago: University of Chicago Press.

Loos, Eugene E., Patricia Davis, and Mary Ruth Wise. 1977. El cambio cultural y el desarrollo de la persona: Exposición de la filosofía y los métodos del Instituto Lingüístico de Verano en el Perú. *Actos du XLIIe Congrés International de Américanistes.* Paris 1976. 2:499–525. Paris: Fondation Singer-Polignac.

Mato Grosso. Secretaria de Estado de Educação. Conselho de Educação Escolar Indígena de Mato Grosso. 1997. *Urucum, jenipapo e giz: Educação escolar indígena em debate.* Conselho de Educação Escolar Indígena de Mato Grosso—CEI/MT.

da Matta, Roberto. 1982. *A divided world: Apinaye social structure.* Cambridge, Mass.: Harvard University Press.

Maybury-Lewis, David, ed. 1974. *Akwe-Shavante society.* London: Oxford University Press.

Maybury-Lewis, David, ed. 1979. *Dialectical societies.* Cambridge, Mass.: Harvard University Press.

Maybury-Lewis, David. 1990. The Indian question. *Wilson Quarterly* (Summer):38–42.

Maybury-Lewis, David, and Uri Almagor, eds. 1989. *The attraction of opposites: Thought and society in the dualistic mode.* Ann Arbor: University of Michigan Press.

McLaren, Peter. 1986. *Schooling as a ritual performance: Towards a political economy of educational symbols and gestures.* Boston: Routledge and Kegan Paul.

Mead, Margaret. 1978. Our educational emphases in primitive perspective. In N. Keddie and Tinker Tailor (eds.), 96–107. New York: Penguin Education.

Melatti, Julio Cesar. 1978. *Ritos de uma tribo Timbira.* São Paulo: Editora Atica.

Meliá, Bartomeu. 1979. *Educação indígena e alfabetização.* São Paulo: Edições Loyola.

Monte, Nietta Lindenberg. 1997. Problemas de um curriculo para a educação intercultural e bilígue. In *Urucum Jenipapo e Giz,* 129–136.

Murphy, Isabel I. 1991. Liberating the oppressor: Consciousness-raising education in the Brazilian indigenous movement. Proceedings of the Comparative and International Education Society's Annual Meeting, Pittsburgh, 1991. ms.

Murphy, Isabel I. 1992. "And I, in my turn, will pass it on": Indigenous education among the Kayapó Amerindians of central Brazil. Ph.D. dissertation. University of Pittsburgh.

Murphy, Isabel I. 1998. Educação indígena Kayapó: Orientação para professores não-Kayapó. In Secchi, 195–207.

Murphy, Isabel I. 2000. Conflitos de Cosmovisão no Ensino: Educação Escolar Indigena. *Capacitando* March 2000.

Ong, Walter J. 1963[1959]. Latin language study as a renaissance puberty rite. In George D. Spindler (ed.), *Education and Culture*, 444–466. New York: Holt, Rinehart and Winston.

Paulston, Rolland G. 1977. Social and educational change: Conceptual frameworks. *Comparative Education Review* 21:370–395.

Peggion, Edmundo Antônio. 1997. Notas sobre o papel do professor na educação escolar indígena. In *Urucum Jenipapo e Gis*, 149–158.

Posey, Darrell Addison. 1979. Ethnoentomology of the Gorotire Kayapo of central Brazil. Ph.D. dissertation. University of Georgia.

Posey, Darrell Addison. 1989. *Resource management in Amazonia: Indigenous and folk strategies*. Advances in Economic Botany, 7. Bronx: New York Botanical Garden.

Posey, Darrell Addison. 1990. The application of ethnobiology in the conservation of dwindling resources: Lost knowledge or options for the survival of the planet. *Proceedings of the First International Congress of Ethnobiology, Belem, 1988*, 73–86. Belem: Museu Paraense Emílio Goeldi.

Posey, Darrell A., John Frechione, John Eddins, and Luiz Francelina da Silva. 1984. Ethnoecology as applied anthropology in Amazonian development. *Human Organization* 43(2):95–107.

Posey, Darrell A. and William Leslie Overal, org. 1990. Ethnobiology: Implications and applications. *Proceedings of the First International Congress of Ethnobiology, Belem, 1988*. Vol. 1 and Vol. 2. Belem: Museu Paraense Emílio Goeldi.

Raoni, Kayapo Leader. 2003. *Coração chora, mas não abandona o combate*. In Paraná Indígena, 12–14.

dos Santos, Silvio Coelho. 1975. *Educação e sociedades tribais*. Porto Alegre: Editora Movimento.

dos Santos, Silvio Coelho, Dennis Werner, Neusa Sens Bloemer, and Analiese Nacke, organizers. 1985. *Sociedades indígenas e o direito: Ensaios*. Florianapolis: Editora da UFSC.

Schieffelin, Bambi B. 1990. *The give and take of everyday life*. Cambridge: Cambridge University Press.
Schieffelin, Edward L. 1976. *The sorrow of the lonely and the burning of the dancers*. New York: St. Martin's Press.
Schieffelin, Edward L. 1985. Performance and the cultural construction of reality. *American Ethnologist* 12(4):707–724.
Secchi, Darci (Org.). 1998. *Ameríndia: Tecendo os caminhos da educação escolar*. Anais da Conferência Amerindia de Educa. Secretaria de Estado de Educação. Cuiabá. MT.
Seeger, Anthony. 1989. Duelism: Fuzzy thinking or fuzzy sets? In David Maybury-Lewis and Uri Almagor (eds.), *The attraction of opposites*, 191–208. Ann Arbor: University of Michigan Press.
Seg-Seg, Pedro. 2003. A longa jornada até a universidade. In *Paraná Indígena*, 21–14.
Senado Federal. 1988. *Constituição da Republica Federativa do Brasil*. Brasília: Senado Federal Centro Grafico.
Sherzer, Joel. 1983. *Kuna ways of speaking. An ethnographic perspective*. Arlington: University of Texas Press.
Shreve, Anita. 1989. *Women together, women alone: The legacy of the consciousness-raising movement*. New York: Viking Penguin.
Siegel, Bernard J. 1963. Social structure, social change, and education in rural Japan: A case Study. In *Education and culture*, George D. Spindler (ed.), 530–560. New York: Holt, Rinehart and Winston.
Silva, Maria Amélia Reis, and André Pablo Salanova. 2001. A assessoria lingüistica nos projetos escolares indígenas: o caso da formação de professores mẽbêngôkre. In *Antropologia, História e Educação. SP. Global*, 331–359.
Singleton, John, comp. 1985. Syllabus and reference notes for educational anthropology. ms.
Smith, Frank. 1985. A metaphor for literacy: Creating worlds or shunting information? In David R. Olson, Nancy Torrance, and Angela Hildyard (eds.), *Literacy, language and learning: The nature and consequences of reading and writing*, 195–213. Cambridge: Cambridge University Press.
Smith, Jonathan Z. 1987. *To take place: Toward theory in ritual*. Chicago: Chicago University Press.
Spindler, George D. 1963. *Education and cultural process: Anthropological approaches*. New York: Holt, Rinehart and Winston.
Spradley, James P. 1980. *Participant observation*. New York: Holt, Rinehart and Winston.
Stipe, Claude E. 1980. Anthropologists versus missionaries: The influence of presuppositions. *Current Anthropology* 21(2):165–180.

Stout, Miriam [Mickey] and Megaron Txucahamãe. 1990. A expedição venatória dos Kayapó. *Proceedings of the First International Congress of Ethnobiology, Belem, 1988.* 1:227–241. Belem: Museu Paraense Emílio Goeldi.

Stout, Mickey and Ruth Thomson. 1974. Fonêmica Txukuhamei (Kayapó). *Série Lingüística* 3:153–176. Brasília: Summer Institute of Linguistics.

Survival International. 1989. 'Stop the Destruction!' Brazil's Indians Unite to Save Forest. *News* 24:1.

Taukane, Darlene Yaminalo. 1997. A educação Kurâ-Bakairi no contexto tradicional. In *Urucum Jenipapo e Giz*, 109–128.

Thomson, Ruth, trans. 1981. *Lendas Kayapó (Me Bakukamã-re'ã Ujarẽnh-neja)*. Brasília, DF: Summer Institute of Linguistics.

Turner, Terence. 1966. Social structure and political organization among the northern Cayapo. Ph.D. dissertation. Harvard University.

Turner, Terence. 1979a. Kinship, household, and community among the Kayapó. In David Maybury-Lewis (ed.), 179–217.

Turner, Terence. 1979b. The social skin: Bodily adornment, social meaning and personal identity. In Jeremy Cherfas and Roger Lewin (eds.), *Not work alone: A cross cultural survey of activities superfluous to survival.* London: Temple Smith.

Turner, Terence. 1987a. From cosmology to ideology: Resistance, adaptation and social consciousness among the Kayapo. ms.

Turner, Terence. 1987b. The Kayapo of southeastern Para. ms.

Turner, Terence. 1988. History, myth, and social consciousness among the Kayapó of central Brazil. In Jonathan D. Hill (ed.), *Rethinking history and myth: Indigenous South American perspectives on the past*, 195–213. Chicago: University of Illinois Press.

Turner, Terence. 1989. The Kayapo: Out of the forest. *Disappearing World*, 3–7. New York: Granada Television.

Turner, Victor. 1969. *The drums of affliction: A study of religious process among the Ndembu of Zambia.* Oxford: Clarendon Press.

Turner, Victor. 1982[1969]. *The ritual process, structure and anti-structure.* Ithaca: Cornell University Press.

Urban, Greg. 1988. Ritual wailing in Amerindian Brazil. *American Anthropologist* 90:385–400.

Verswijver, Gustaaf. 1982. 'Las femmes peintes', une cérémonie d'imposition de noms chez los Kayapó-Mẽkrìnotã da Brásil central. *Bulletin de la Sociête Suisse dos Americanistes* 46:41–59.

Verswijver, Gustaaf. 1985. Considerations on Mekragnoti warfare. Ph.D. dissertation, Rijks Universiteit Gent. 1984–1985.

Vidal, Lux. 1976. *Morte e vida de uma sociedade indígena Brasileira.* São Paulo: Editora Hucitec.

Vidal, Lux and Regina A. Polo Müller. 1986. Pintura e adornos corporais. In Berta G. Ribeiro (coordenação), *Arte India, Suma 3.* Darcy Ribeiro (gen. ed.). 119–148. Petropolis: Vozes.

Watkins, Mark Hanna. 1963[1943]. The West African "bush" school. In George D. Spindler (ed.), *Education and culture,* 426–443. New York: Holt, Rinehart and Winston.

Wax, Rosalie and Murray Wax. 1962. The magical world view. *Journal for the Scientific Study of Religion* 1:179–188.

Werner, Dennis. 1980. The making of a Mekranoti chief: The psychological and social determinants of leadership in a native South American society. Ph.D. dissertation. City University of New York.

Werner, Dennis. 1981a. Are some people more equal than others? Status inequality among the Mekranoti Indians of central Brazil. *Journal of Anthropological Research* 37(4):360–373.

Werner, Dennis. 1981b. Gerontocracy among the Mekranoti of central Brazil. *Anthropological Quarterly* 54(1):15–27.

Werner, Dennis. 1983. Why do the Mekranoti trek? In R. Hymes and W. Vicker (eds.), *Adaptive responses of native South Americans,* 225–238. New York: Academic Press.

Werner, Dennis. 1984. *Amazon journey: An anthropologist's year among Brazil's Mekranoti Indians.* New York: Simon and Schuster.

Wertsch, James. 1985. *Culture, communication and cognition: A Vygotskian perspective.* Cambridge: Cambridge University Press.

Wilbert, Johannes. 1984. *Folk literature of the Gê Indians,* 2. Los Angeles: University of California Press.

Wolcott, Harry F. 1990. Propriospect and the acquisition of culture. Authors files: ms[pre-publication draft].

SIL International
Publications in Language Use
and Education

1. **Reading is for Knowing,** by Patricia M. Davis, 2004.
3. *Namel Manmeri* **'The In-Between People': Language and Culture Maintenance and Mother-Tongue Education in the Highlands of Papua New Guinea,** by Dennis L. Malone, forthcoming in 2004.
4. **Language Contact and Composite Structures in New Ireland,** by Rebecca Sue Jenkins, forthcoming in 2004.

Publications in Sociolinguistics

8. **Borrowing Versus Code-Switching in West Tarangan (Indonesia),** by Richard J. Nivens, 2002.
7. **The Dynamics of Sango Language Spread,** by Mark E. Karan, 2001.
6. **K'iche': A Study in the Sociology of Language,** by M. Paul Lweis, 2001.
5. **The Same but Different: Language Use and Attitudes in Four Communities of Burkina Faso,** by Stuart Showalter, 2000.
4. **Ashéninka Stories of Change,** by Ronald James Anderson, 2000.
3. **Assessing Ethnolinguistic Vitality: Theory and Practice,** M. Paul Lewis and Gloria Kindell, eds., 1999.
2. **The Early Days of Sociolinguistics: Memories and Reflections,** Christina Bratt Paulston and G. Richard Tucker, eds., 1997.
1. **North Sulawesi Language Survey,** Scott Merrifield and Martinus Selsa, 1996.

For further information or a full listing of SIL publications contact:

International Academic Bookstore
SIL International
7500 W. Camp Wisdom Road
Dallas, TX 75236-5699

Voice: 972-708-7404
Fax: 972-708-7363
Email: academic_books@sil.org
Internet: http://www.ethnologue.com